29.95

International
Business Information
on the Web

International Business Information on the Web

Searcher Magazine's Guide to Sites and Strategies for Global Business Research

Sheri R. Lanza

Edited and with a Foreword by Barbara Quint

CyberAge Books

Information Today, Inc.
Medford, New Jersey

International Business Information on the Web:
Searcher *Magazine's Guide to Sites and Strategies*
for Global Business Research

Copyright © 2001 by Sheri R. Lanza.

Library of Congress Cataloging-in-Publication Data

Lanza, Sheri R., 1955-
    International business information on the web : Searcher magazine's guide to sites and strategies for global business research / Sheri R. Lanza ; edited and with a foreword by Barbara Quint.
        p. cm.
    Includes index.
    ISBN 0-910965-46-3 (pbk.)
    1. Business information services--Computer network resources--Directories. 2. Web sites--Directories. I. Quint, Barbara Gilder. II. Searcher (Medford, N.J.) III. Title.

    HF54.56.L364 2001
    025.06'65--dc21

                                                              2001028735

The publisher wishes to thank Carmen Suarez and the Canning House Library, Hispanic and Luso Brazilian Council (U.K.), for their gracious assistance.

Printed and bound in the United States of America.

Publisher: Thomas H. Hogan, Sr.
Editor-in-Chief: John B. Bryans
Managing Editor: Deborah R. Poulson
Production Manager: M. Heide Dengler
Copy Editor: Dorothy Pike
Copy Editor/*Searcher* Magazine: Lauree Padgett
Cover Design: Jacqueline Walter
Book Design: Kara Mia Jalkowski
Indexer: Laurie Andriot

DEDICATION

To my family, Ken, Kelsey, and Jessica;
thank you for your love, support, and
ability to survive without dinner
while I was buried, writing this book.
I love you all and couldn't have done it
without you.

And to my parents, Jackie and Eugene Ross,
who hopefully will now have
a better idea of what I do for a living.

TABLE OF CONTENTS

FIGURES

FOREWORD

No more felicitous good fortune could have occurred to this editor than to start the series of *Searcher* Magazine books with one written by Sheri Lanza. In over fifteen years of editing experience, I have worked with many, many wonderful authors and colleagues, but for sheer professionalism, I would have to award the purple to Ms. Lanza. Whatever wish or desire trickled across this editor's mind, she not only accommodated, but usually anticipated!

This *International Business Information on the Web* book began as a series of articles for *Searcher* magazine called "Around the World in 80 Sites." It concentrates on "open" or "public" Web sites that any user can reach, identifying authoritative sources or, at least, those with their biases showing. In many ways, the book serves as an educational tool, too. Since she could not cover every country in the space or time allotted, Ms. Lanza chose countries in each region not only for their inherent interest and importance, but also to demonstrate the different levels of information available and how to find it when dealing with diverse economies and governmental forms.

How little we knew when we started that journey around the Global Village and entitled the articles "Around the World in 80 Sites." Eighty? What a paltry sum! This book contains over a thousand Web sites stretching across dozens and dozens of countries all over the globe—many, many more than appeared in the original articles. It also corrects the URLs for many of those cited in the articles, although that, as all searchers know, remains a never-ending battle. Nonetheless, when readers know the site name and have descriptions of content, they should be able to chase down any URLs that may have changed since this book's publication.

No creatures on earth are more rapacious, greedy, and ungrateful than editors. I would love to see Ms. Lanza expand this into another volume or two and then into an edited encyclopedia of global business information sources, covering every country on earth and both free and pay sources. Her protestations of a desire to get a life, reconnect with family, earn a living, etc. fall on deaf ears.

The book you clasp in your hands is just the first in a series of books designed to enrich and expand upon material originally published in *Searcher* Magazine. Most of the books in the series should follow the model of this one. They will confirm, enlarge, and complete research begun to produce articles for the magazine. This should save desperate readers from scrambling around their offices looking for the one missing issue with the precise article in the series that they need right now. The books will also give authors the time and the leisure to lift that last rock and find just one more source before the final re-testing begins.

If any readers have suggestions for books in this series or article topics for *Searcher,* send them (e-mail bquint@mindspring.com). Together we can make a new world for searchers everywhere!

Barbara Quint
Editor
Searcher Magazine
May 2001

ACKNOWLEDGMENTS

When I think of all of the people I want to thank for their help and support, the list seems endless. I should probably start with my wonderful editor, Barbara Quint. I called Barbara one day about two years ago, even though we had never met. I had an idea for an article about international business information for her magazine, *Searcher*. Getting caught up in Barbara's enthusiasm, by the time our conversation was over, I had agreed to write a seven-part series of articles for her. A couple of days later, reality set in and I panicked at the thought of the seven articles. Then I reassured myself that writing these articles was a good thing and dove right in.

Several months later, after the first two articles had appeared in *Searcher*, I had a chance meeting with John Bryans, Editor-in-Chief of the Book Publishing Division at Information Today. We spoke about my articles, and the first seeds of the idea for this book were planted; eight months later, the contract was signed. Again, reality and panic set in and I had to reassure myself that writing this book was a good thing. So, my first two big thank yous go to Barbara and John; if it hadn't been for your encouragement and reassurance, I never would have written this book.

I'd like to thank my daughters: Kelsey, who at age 12 did her first Internet searching to help me with portions of this book, and Jessica, who showed remarkable patience for an 11-year-old when I had to tell her on numerous occasions that I was too busy writing this book to drive her here and there. There's also my husband Ken. Without his unfailing support, I could never have written this book, as I would have been paralyzed with fear.

A big thanks goes to my colleague and very close friend, Susan Weiler. Susan kept me on the straight and narrow by e-mailing me every week or so and asking "How's the book coming along?"

Finally, in order to keep this short, I'd like to give a blanket thank you to all of my friends, family, clients, and colleagues who kept hearing "Don't call me until after August 1," which was the deadline for this manuscript. Thanks to all of you for your patience and understanding. You may call me now.

INTRODUCTION

International business research. "What are the ten largest companies in Egypt?" "I want to know all of the countries in the world that make ball bearings. And rank them by size." "I'm thinking of opening a factory overseas. Countries under consideration include Turkey, Venezuela, and Pakistan. What information can I find about the economies of these countries, their labor laws, the education of the population, and their export policies?" "My company makes widgets and we'd like to expand by exporting the widgets. Which countries are currently the largest importers of widgets?" "I'm considering a partnership with a company in Argentina, and I need more information on the firm."

Business searchers receive requests similar to these all the time. And when the search extends beyond the boundaries of the business searcher's country, he or she must cope with the globalization of the requesters' questions. Despite the Disney mantra, "It's a small world after all," the world is still rather big with more than 200 countries. When looking for global business information, there's a lot of information out there and many places to look. Where do you start? Who has the best (or most) international information? Can you expect current information? How old is too old when the information concerns a small or remote country? Should you stick with traditional commercial online sources like Dialog, Factiva (Dow Jones Interactive/Reuters Business Briefing), Lexis-Nexis, etc.—the ones professional searchers often use? Should you go "all-Web"? Or should you start with phone calls?

These questions and more plague the international business-person and the international business searcher. This book will try to provide you with a ready-reference resource for Internet sites to use for your international research. For that reason, I only mention the traditional online services in passing and concentrate on the open Web. Think of it as an extremely long list of annotated bookmarks. (Note: The complete list of URLs in this book may be found in Appendix A and is available online at http://www.infotoday.com/ibidirectory.htm.)

International business information means different things to different people. It might refer to finding financial information on a company in another country or to finding an overseas buyer for a client's product or, conversely, to finding a supplier of something that your client wants to buy. Maybe you need a market research study or an industry analysis from a country other than your own. Often, country economic information will suffice to get you started. All of this (and more) helps to define what is meant by international business information.

Let's start at the broadest level, then tackle the world inch by inch. One caveat: Please be aware that this book has a bit of a U.S. bias; since that's where I'm located, it's the way I approach my research. However, that does not mean the information contained in this book is irrelevant to those living in other countries. Provided one has access to the Internet, virtually all of the sources (with a few exceptions) should be available to all readers. There is nothing to prevent someone in Spain from using these resources to research Zimbabwe, if he or she so desires. By having this book within arm's reach, a searcher's comfort level when looking for international business information should rise dramatically.

To begin, I present some of the Web sites that provide global information, and continue by focusing on each region of the world separately. The richness of each type of resource varies from region to region. Within each chapter, I discuss the types of resources roughly in the order of access most useful when conducting an initial investigation into that particular geographic area.

I also include sources for individual countries. Countries included in this book were chosen for a variety of reasons. Some countries, such as the United Kingdom, Germany, Brazil, Argentina, Egypt, Israel, Russia, Mexico, and Japan, were selected as being likely candidates for those looking for country-level international business information. Others, such as Bahrain, Guatemala, the Czech Republic, Azerbaijan, and Belgium, were chosen when the amount of information available for countries of this size was an unexpected, though greatly appreciated, surprise. And yet other countries were included because something about the country or the information piqued my interest and will hopefully pique yours, too.

My editor and I discussed including all countries in the world in this book but eventually realized the book would never be finished if we took that approach. By the time I could get through every country, the information in the first portion of the book would have been hopelessly outdated. How many iterations of each country would I have to go through before I could say, "Stop! Enough already! Publish the book!" Besides, if we included every country, it would most likely result in a book the reader wouldn't even be able to lift. So, with an eye to the future, a decision was made to cover as many countries as seemed reasonable. Future editions of this book will include additional countries.

One last detail before our trip about around the world begins. As many places throughout the book mention whether or not a site is searchable using Boolean logic, it would be a good idea to explain what that means. Boolean logic is a form of algebraic logic named after the nineteenth-century English mathematician George Boole. The three basic logical operators of Boolean logic are "or," "and," and "not." The use of these three operators permits an algebraic manipulation of logical statements and shows how a complicated statement may be rephrased in a simpler form without changing its meaning. All right, so how does algebra relate to international business research? Let's go through a simple example.

Say you and I wanted to look for information on textile exports from Guatemala. Assuming the search function we use supports Boolean searching, a very basic search statement could be "Guatemala and textiles and exports." This would retrieve all items that include the words "Guatemala," "textiles," and "exports." After we finish with the textile search, we might decide we want to know about other Guatemalan exports. Since we've already looked at textile exports, we would want to be certain that our results exclude that same information. A sample search statement could be "Guatemala and exports not textiles." In this case, the results would include all items that include the words "Guatemala" and "exports" but none that contain the word "textiles."

Using Boolean logic helps tremendously in a search strategy. A search function that supports Boolean is far more powerful than one that doesn't. It allows you to zero in on relevant information and to weed out some of the extraneous matter.

Let our travels begin!

CHAPTER 1

INTERNATIONAL
BUSINESS RESEARCH

What's the big deal? Why is conducting international business research any different from what you already do for domestic (U.S.) business research? Can't you just use your usual sources? Surely there must be international counterparts to the Internet resources you already use. But there is a difference, otherwise this book wouldn't exist. So, let's explore some of the differences between international and domestic business research. (Note: For the purposes of this book, the term "domestic business research" refers to research conducted from a U.S.-based perspective; i.e., research on companies, industries, etc. within the U.S.)

There are many resources we take for granted when looking for business information in the U.S. Public companies must produce annual and quarterly reports and file numerous forms with the Securities and Exchange Commission (SEC) that then become accessible to the general public. These various forms and reports are standardized with the same basic information elements available from company to company. Business researchers can easily find a U.S. public company's balance sheet, profit and loss statement, names of company directors and officers, and much more. There are even several options for accessing this information:

- **EDGAR—The Electronic Data Gathering, Analysis, and Retrieval System**
  http://www.sec.gov/edgarhp.htm
  This is the official site of the SEC. Some documents filed with the SEC still do not appear here, but it is the official online source for this information.

- **FreeEDGAR**
  http://www.FreeEDGAR.com

- **LIVEDGAR**
  http://www.gsionline.com
  Requires a subscription; not free.

- **Report Gallery**
  http://www.reportgallery.com

- **The Public Register's Annual Report Service**
  http://www.annualreportservice.com

Looking for similar information from other countries is not so straightforward. Often the information is simply not available. When looking for Canadian company information, thankfully, you can use SEDAR—System for Electronic Document Analysis and Retrieval [http://www.sedar.com], the Canadian equivalent to EDGAR. But, for most countries, you won't be as lucky, and the reason for this will vary by country. Some countries might not have similar reporting requirements for public companies. Others have some requirements but may not make the information available to the public or it is extremely expensive to obtain. In some cases, the information could be available but only in the local language and currency, which makes things more complicated.

Domestically, we have access to investment analyst reports, their analyses of a company's performance and how the company compares to its competition or its industry. In addition, countless free or low-cost sources for industry information can be readily obtained, some of which are listed here:

- **Hoover's Online**
  http://www.hoovers.com

- **U.S. Industry & Trade Outlook 2000**
  http://www.ita.doc.gov/td/industry/otea/outlook/index.html

- **U.S. Census Bureau—American FactFinder—
  Industry Quick Reports**
  http://factfinder.census.gov/java_prod/dads.ui.iqr. IndProfPage

- **U.S. Census Bureau—Current Industrial Reports**
  http://www.census.gov/ftp/pub/cir/www

- **U.S. Census Bureau—Statistical Abstract of the United States**
  http://www.census.gov/statab/www

Finding equivalent sources for industry information in other countries is quite a challenge.

Press releases are another useful source for business information. In the U.S., we are inundated with press releases: announcements of new companies, new products, new management hires, management promotions, alliances, mergers, joint ventures, etc. In the rest of the world, press releases may be few and far between (or even nonexistent) as well as difficult to access.

Industry and trade associations are good resources for further industry information, and in the U.S. there is no shortage of them. Often these organizations post their data on their Web sites, link to outside data, or make data available for purchase from the site. Not only do industry and trade associations have a Web presence, there are even directory-type sites that allow you to search for these associations. Industry and trade associations exist in other countries, but generally not as many as in the U.S. And it is less likely that the online content is as rich as what may be found domestically.

Local and financial newspapers and trade press publications for the U.S. abound on the Internet: city newspapers, financial newspapers and magazines, local business publications, and much more. Some sites provide the entire content of their print publications online; some provide selected articles; many offer searchable archives. Many international publications also make their articles available via the Internet, but you may find several obstacles to overcome when attempting to access them. Often, fewer articles are available online. Archives, if they exist, might not be searchable.

Then there's that language barrier to overcome. In my experience, many countries will have an English-language newspaper geared to expatriates living in the country. However, these newspapers generally do not publish daily; most are weekly and some even monthly. The amount of business information in them is often weak. They will more likely cover local events with cursory treatment of serious business information.

Three other reasons that make business information easier to find in the U.S. are listed here:

- The abundance of packaged industry and market research reports focusing on the U.S. outnumber by far those focusing on other parts of the world.

- Many industries in the U.S. are regulated. As such, a regulating agency for an industry will provide a collection of useful information.

- A plethora of U.S. government sites, such as those mentioned previously, will carry useful business data.

Lastly, it is easier for us to judge a source's reliability when dealing with domestic business research. For example, when we find information on a consulting firm's Web site, we often know immediately whether or not the firm is credible due to name recognition. How many of us can quickly recognize and assess the names of foreign consulting firms? Again, we are generally comfortable with the data sourced from a U.S. or state government Web site. However, if you aren't intimately familiar with a country, its government, its reporting requirements, and its data collection methods, it is difficult to gauge the reliability of the information found there.

Now, if I haven't scared you off yet, and I hope I haven't, the following chapters will help you learn how to deal with the challenges of conducting international business research. There are no magical answers, no guarantees that you will find everything you search for, no promises that you will overcome all of the obstacles mentioned here. But with this book by your side, you will certainly be well equipped to tackle the international challenges that come your way.

CHAPTER 2

THE WORLD

As we start our journey, let's look at some basic sources useful to have on hand throughout. At times, broad-brush, overview information can suffice in deciding whether or not to pursue a project or venture. This chapter will help you find such information.

Country Facts and Figures— Courtesy of the U.S. Government

Not surprisingly, the U.S. government is a treasure-trove of international information. For a variety of reasons, you can be sure that one or more federal agencies somewhere have every country in the world under study. While this sometimes means a lot of duplication, checking a few key sources can paint a pretty useful picture of any country.

When trying to get a "feel" for a country, first try the World Factbook [http://www.odci.gov/cia/publications/factbook/index.html], an annual from the Central Intelligence Agency. Covering more than 260 countries from Afghanistan to Zimbabwe, each entry includes a map, statistics on the population and the size of the country, descriptions of natural resources, and overviews of the country's government, economy, exports, and imports. The World Factbook is considered such a mainstay for international information that you will undoubtedly come across excerpts from it at many other sites.

You should definitely supplement World Factbook information with the U.S. State Department Background Notes [http://www.state.gov/www/background_notes]. When you click on the desired region of the world, a list of the countries within that region having available reports appears along with the date of the most recent report. Notations indicate which countries the Background Notes do not cover. While the Background Notes overlap with the World Factbook, they offer additional information on U.S. relations with the country, history, and travel advisories. After searching these two sites, you should have a good overall picture of the country in question. Occasionally, the search will end here. Maybe you will find that the country doesn't like Americans, that its economy is in a tailspin, or that its government harbors terrorists.

Jump Right In

Tradeport [http://www.tradeport.org] is a good jumping off point for international business information. An initiative of BAYTRADE (Bay Area Economic Forum) and LA TRADE (Los Angeles Area Chamber of Commerce), it offers a one-stop shop for comprehensive trade information, trade leads, market research reports, and more. Tradeport receives assistance from the U.S. Department of Commerce Economic Development Administration, the U.S. Commercial Service (described below), the California Trade and Commerce Agency, as well as others. Much of the information at the site comes from the STAT-USA database (discussed later in this chapter). The most useful international information, the Market Research area, contains reports by industry and by country. The Industry Library covers the following industries:

- Agriculture and Processed Foods

- Bioscience/Biomedical Technologies and Instruments

- Computer and Related Electronics

- Environmental Technologies

- Multimedia and Information Technologies

- Telecommunications

Material in the Country Library sorts as follows (see Figure 2.1):

- Country Overview

- Industry Sector Analysis Reports

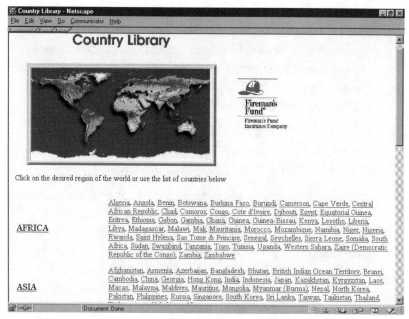

Figure 2.1   Portion of Tradeport Country Library

- Key Contacts

- Market Research Reports

- Other Sites

- Sources of Financing

- Trade Information

- Travel and Culture

The *Financial Times* site, FT.com [http://news.ft.com] is full of international news, country surveys, industry briefs, and more. The *Financial Times* has been called *The Wall Street Journal* of the United Kingdom. In truth, this site offers so much, you may find it confusing to navigate through it all. These are some of the highlights:

- News & Analysis—This area covers Market News, Business News, World News, Company News, Special Reports (key issues of the day), and Surveys. The Financial Times publishes more than 200 surveys a year; some are Country Briefs and others are Industry Briefs.

- Country Surveys—These cover topics such as Top Stories, Political Overview, Regional Focus, Economy, Fact File (the Constitution, Economic Statistics, and some general statistics), Diplomacy, and Industry. Countries in the Americas, Asia/Pacific, Europe, the Middle East, and the U.K. and Ireland are included. Country Surveys are generally updated every year or two.

- Industry Briefs—Very current reports cover topics such as Latin American Finance, Global Investment Banking, African Mining, and India: Information Technology.

- Premium Research—This section contains Analyst Estimates, an order form for Annual Reports (for purchase online and delivery by mail), and Company Financials. Company Financials entries look like directory entries and generally include contact information, company URL, number of employees, senior management names, industry, product lines, business description, and company financial data (revenue, income, assets, liabilities, profit margin percentages, etc.).

- Market Prices—World Market Closing Prices for most exchanges around the world, Currencies, IPOs, Economic Indicators, and more are found here.

- Industry View—This section presents current news articles on the following industries:

• Aerospace	• Manufacturing
• Autos	• Media & Entertainment
• Chemicals	• Medical
• Consumer	• Natural Resources
• Energy	• Services
• Financial	• Telecoms
• Information Technology	• Transportation

- Global Archive—Searches of the headlines and/or text of articles from the *Financial Times*, as well as more than 3,000 publications, are offered. There are options for date limitations (up to three years back) and sorting by date or relevance. The system also lets you save searches for re-execution at a future time.

Comparing Countries

You want to open a factory somewhere in Latin America. As far as you know, all of the countries in Latin America are pretty much the same. Most of the countries are Spanish-speaking, except for Brazil and a few of the smaller countries, so how much difference could there be?

The World Bank has put together some great statistics called Competitiveness Indicators [http://wbln0018.worldbank.org/psd/compete.nsf] to help assess economic performance and the environment for competitive business development. Here you can obtain a quick snapshot of the business environment for a country, compare the situation for a country with the averages for the region and the income group to which the country belongs, and rank the relative standing of a country for a specific indicator of interest. The database can be searched in two ways: by country or by indicator. Choosing indicator, we see five categories:

- Financial Dynamism
- Human & Intellectual Capital
- Infrastructure & Investment Climate
- Macro & Market Dynamism
- Overall Performance

Clicking down into the Infrastructure & Investment Climate link, we see three subcategories: Information and Communication Network, Physical Infrastructure, and Socio-Political Stability. Each of these is segmented even further. For example, Information and Communications Network divides into nine subsections:

- Average Price per Call
- Daily Newspaper Circulation
- Fax Machines
- Internet Hosts
- Personal Computers
- Phone Faults
- Phone Lines

- Televisions

- Waiting Time for Phone Lines

If the success of your product plans depends upon the reliability and effective reach of local phone service, you might want to know which Latin American country has the most phone lines per thousand people (see Figure 2.2). Scrolling down the list (containing 130 countries ranked from highest to lowest), we see that Argentina, at number 42, is the first Latin American country to appear. The next several on the list are Chile (#47), Costa Rica (#48), Colombia (#54), Venezuela (#56), Mexico (#60), and Brazil (#61).

```
Netscape                                                          _ | 8 | X
File  Edit  View  Go  Communicator  Help
```

Phone lines per 1000 people
Number of telephone exchange mainlines per 1000 persons. A telephone mainline connects the subscriber's equipment to the switched network and has a dedicated port in the telephone exchange. Note that for most countries, main line also include public payphones.
Source: 1998 World Development Indicators (WDI), available on line from the World Bank Socio-economic Time Series Access and Retrieval System (STARS).
Unit: number of mainlines per 1000 population
Coverage: 1996, 1997.
Ranking: Highest to Lowest. Available for 130 countries.

Ranking	Country	Indicator
30	LATVIA	298
31	CZECH REPUBLIC	273
32	LITHUANIA	268
33	HUNGARY	261
34	SLOVAK REPUBLIC	232
35	KUWAIT	232
36	TURKEY	224
37	URUGUAY	209
38	BELARUS	208
39	MALAYSIA	183
40	UKRAINE	181
41	RUSSIAN FEDERATION	175
42	ARGENTINA	174

```
Document: Done
```

**Figure 2.2   World Bank Competitiveness Indicators—
Phone Lines**

When considering overseas operations, you should also peruse Ernst & Young International Doing Business In ... [http://www.doingbusinessin.com]. Here you can choose from more than 140 countries and get a quick overview of the investment climate, taxation, forms of business organization, and business and accounting practices for each country. Pricewaterhouse Coopers has International Briefings [http://www.pwcglobal.com/extweb/frmclp11.nsf/ViewAgentByCurrMonth?OpenAgent] that contain articles on business, economic, and political developments by region and country.

Data Downlink's .XLS

What if you want to partner with an overseas applications software company? You've already done some background work on a few countries and now want to focus on India. What's the next step in your search to find candidate companies? You might try turning to Data Downlink's .XLS [http://www.xls.com]. Searching the service does not cost, but retrieving what you find does. We searched for the applications software industry in India using the Advanced Search page, and got a list of eight companies. Checking out the first one, BFL Software Ltd., we found company and financial information available in Business & Industry News, Extel Data from Primark, and I/B/E/S Earnings Estimates (see Figure 2.3). We also found a list of the company's industries by SIC. Following through, we got price quotes on the different kinds of information—eight stories from Business and Industry (@ $3.50/story), a variety of financial data reports from Extel (ranging from $16 to $56 each), and three reports from I/B/E/S ($8 to $50). So, by doing one simple search and spending as little as $50 or as high as a few hundred dollars, you've started

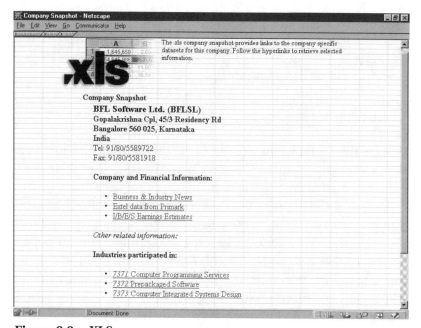

Figure 2.3   .XLS

to put together a nice topline picture of BFL Software, which you can supplement with information from other sources.

U.S. International Trade Administration

Moving on to an underutilized gem, the Department of Commerce's International Trade Administration (ITA) site [http://www.ita.doc.gov] is a "must-see" site, jam-packed with information and research. Trust me. It really deserves a very close look. If you don't know much about the ITA, take a moment and click on the link About ITA. Also, check the Site Map to get a brief overview of what the site offers.

Big Emerging Markets—BEMs, a resource page, is especially useful. It covers the following countries that are considered to be, as the name of the section implies, Big Emerging Markets:

• Argentina	• Poland
• Brazil	• Singapore
• Brunei Darussalam	• South Africa
• China	• South Korea
• India	• Taiwan
• Indonesia	• Thailand
• Malaysia	• Turkey
• Mexico	• Vietnam
• Philippines	

Each BEM country listing includes four categories of information: Overview, Exporting, Statistics, and Links (government and public sector).

Back on the main page, the Countries and Regions link leads to a listing, by region, of various ITA pages with information on individual countries and regions. Choosing Trade Information Center's Regional Pages, one finds boxes for each region of the world. As an example, under Middle East and North Africa, click on View All Documents by Country, and then select Egypt. You will now have a listing of all documents relating to Egypt, along with the date of publication (see Figure 2.4). In some cases the site will carry the full report; in other cases it will post contact information for obtaining the report.

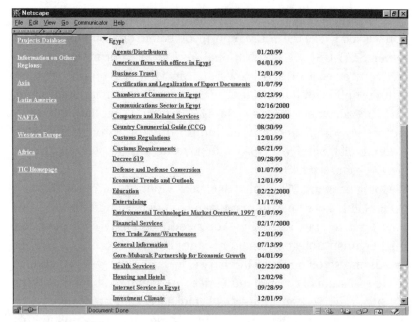

Figure 2.4   ITA

In the document list for Egypt, one of the available reports is the Country Commercial Guide. The Guides are prepared annually at most U.S. embassies around the world and give an overview of the country's commercial environment with an eye toward the business needs of U.S. firms. Generally, each country report has the following sections:

• Executive Summary

• Economic Trends and Outlook

• Political Environment

• Marketing U.S. Products and Services

• Leading Sectors for U.S. Exports and Investments

• Trade Regulations and Standards

• Investment Climate

• Trade and Project Financing

• Business Travel

• Appendices

At one time, only the Executive Summary was available online. If you wished to see the entire report, you had to order it directly from either STAT-USA or the National Technical Information Service (NTIS) at a cost of $20. Now you can view the reports in their entirety online for free. (Note: The Country Commercial Guides may also be accessed directly via ITA's Trade Compliance Center [http://www.mac.doc.gov/tcc/index.html] or through the U.S. Commercial Service's USATrade.gov site [http://www.usatrade.gov/Website/ccg.nsf].)

Going back to ITA's home page, take a look at the Industries and Sectors link. Let's say you manufacture cutlery sold in the U.S., but now want to start exporting. You need to identify countries that might constitute good market candidates. Click on Consumer Goods and scroll down to Industry Coverage. Here you can choose to view a listing of covered industries sorted either alphabetically or by SIC Code. Several industries listed have dedicated pages with pertinent reports. After you find the listing for cutlery, follow this link to reach Trade Tables 1992–1999 in the middle of the page. Clicking on Exports: Cutlery brings up a nicely formatted table entitled Top 25 U.S. Export Destinations for Cutlery. From the chart we can see that the United Kingdom, Canada, and Mexico are the best bets. If you combine the U.K. with the other Western European countries on the list (France, Germany, Netherlands, and Belgium), then Western Europe seems to have great potential.

One more government site worth visiting is STAT-USA Internet [http://www.stat-usa.gov]. For $175/year or $75/quarter, you get unlimited Internet access to a broad range of market research reports and other studies. (The much more expensive CD-ROM version costs $59/month or $575/year. The superior Internet product updates several times a day, making it not only more cost effective, but more timely.) Among available offerings, you will find market research studies and Industry Sector Analysis (ISA) reports prepared by the overseas offices of the Commercial Service. The full text of the previously mentioned Country Commercial Guides are also included in the STAT-USA subscription.

The STAT-USA sections of primary interest to us are GLOBUS & NTDB. GLOBUS (Global Business Opportunities) offers the following:

- Daily trade leads from the Trade Opportunities Program (TOPS) and the Department of Agriculture

- Daily procurement activity from the Defense Logistics Agency, the United Nations, and the Commerce Business Daily

NTDB (National Trade Data Bank) provides access to these resources:

- Best Market Reports

- Country Commercial Guides

- Market Research Reports

- U.S. Import and Export Statistics

- More than 75 other various reports and programs

Until recently, with the exception of the Country Commercial Guides, none of the above-mentioned NTDB reports were available for individual purchase without a subscription. However, unrestricted, free access to NTDB was (and still is) available at all Federal Depository Libraries. (The Federal Depository Library Program provides government publications to designated public and academic libraries throughout the U.S. Most collections are customized for local community needs and interests. Locations of local and regional Depository Libraries are available at http://www.gpo.gov/su_docs/locators/find libs/index.html.)

Scroll down to Market and Country Research, the most important GLOBUS & NTDB section for international business research, and you will find eight categories:

- Best Market Reports—alphabetical by title

- Country Commercial Guides—by country—PDF and Word formats

- Foreign Agricultural Market Reports (AGWorld) (Current & Historical)

- Industry Sector Analysis Reports (Current)—by date and country

- International Marketing Insight (IMI) Reports—sorted by country, industry, and report date

- Market Research Reports (IMI & ISA Historical)

- Multilateral Development Bank (MDB) (Current & Historical) —by date

- Pacific Island Reports—economic reports from the Bank of Hawaii

Other sections relating to international business research include:

- CIA International Trade Statistics

- Commercial Service International Contacts

- Current Exchange Rates

- Merchandise Trade Statistics

In December 1998, a new STAT-USA service, Newsstand, was launched, offering access to the most popular and useful files (including the Country Commercial Guides and most market research reports) on a transaction basis. By registering and providing credit card information to Newsstand, you can purchase single documents via the Internet at prices ranging from $1 to $20. The system allows for micropayments and bills you once at the end of the month for your usage. Newsstand was designed in response to customers' needs. If NTDB receives enough requests for other NTDB documents, it will add them to the list of already available reports.

The U.S. Commercial Service, part of the U.S. Department of Commerce, is charged with promoting and protecting U.S. business interests around the world. The Commercial Service is committed to increasing the number of U.S. firms, especially small to medium-sized firms, that benefit from international trade. This worldwide network includes offices in more than 100 U.S. cities and at more than 80 U.S. embassies overseas.

Via the U.S. Commercial Service's home page [http://www. usatrade.gov/website], one can link to a directory of all of the overseas Commercial Service offices, as well as to many of those offices' Web sites. These offices provide additional information difficult to find elsewhere. Going back to your plans to export cutlery, let's say you decide to export to Germany. You have found the names of a few companies in Germany that might want to import your cutlery, but you haven't had any success in finding financial information on some of those companies. For $100 per company, the Commercial Service office in Germany will prepare an International Company profile for you. This investigative report will include key contact information, bank and trade references, financial data, sales volume, reputation, and market outlook. Additional information may include subsidiary-parent relationships, recent news items about the firm, the firm's U.S. customers, operational problems, activities of prominent owners, and branch locations. The commercial specialists who conduct your research will also provide their recommendation as to whether you should enter into a business relationship with the subject firm, and, if so, on what basis. And at all times, they will maintain your client's confidentiality.

Many other useful products and services are available through ITA's Trade Information Center (TIC) in Washington, DC. The International Trade Specialists are very well informed, eager to help, and anxious to spread the word about what they have to offer. When you're not sure where to turn, call first at 800/USA-TRADE (800/872-8723). TIC may have already done the research that you seek.

Now Where to Go? Try Dun & Bradstreet

Back to our software partnership project. You've pulled together the information from .XLS on BFL Software and some other companies, but you still need further financial information. At this point in the preliminary planning stages, you don't want to spend too much money. So try using Dun & Bradstreet's (D&B) GlobalSeek product; it only requires registration (free) to use. Member registration and log-in [https://www.dnb.com/product/retail/menu.htm] are easy; you do not even need to supply a credit card number to register. Once you've registered, options appear for three different types of reports, including GlobalSeek (the other two reports are U.S. information only). For $5, you can order a GlobalSeek report that will provide basic company information, including topline financial information, SICs, number of employees, and parent company information. No credit information appears in a GlobalSeek report (see Figure 2.5).

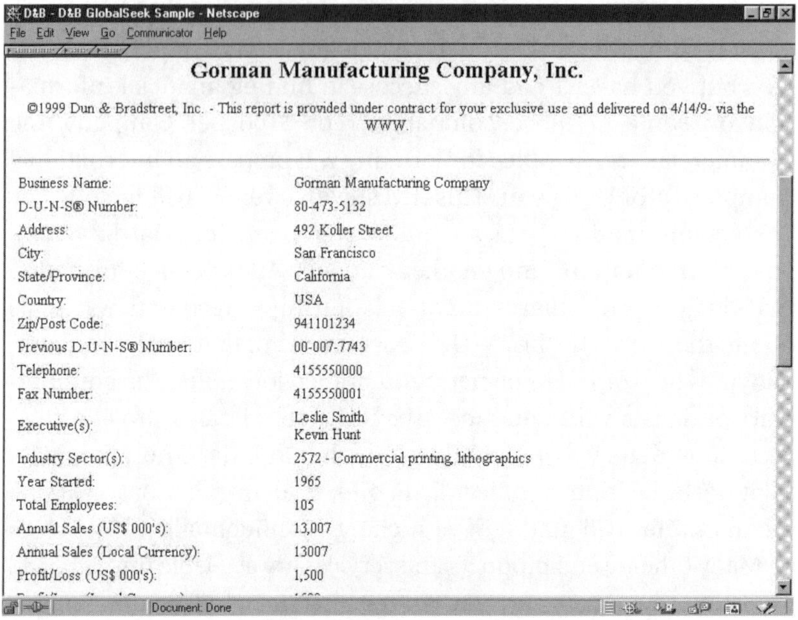
D&B - D&B GlobalSeek Sample - Netscape

File Edit View Go Communicator Help

Gorman Manufacturing Company, Inc.

©1999 Dun & Bradstreet, Inc. - This report is provided under contract for your exclusive use and delivered on 4/14/9- via the WWW.

Business Name:	Gorman Manufacturing Company
D-U-N-S® Number:	80-473-5132
Address:	492 Koller Street
City:	San Francisco
State/Province:	California
Country:	USA
Zip/Post Code:	941101234
Previous D-U-N-S® Number:	00-007-7743
Telephone:	4155550000
Fax Number:	4155550001
Executive(s):	Leslie Smith Kevin Hunt
Industry Sector(s):	2572 - Commercial printing, lithographics
Year Started:	1965
Total Employees:	105
Annual Sales (US$ 000's):	13,007
Annual Sales (Local Currency):	13007
Profit/Loss (US$ 000's):	1,500

Document: Done

Figure 2.5 Portion of Sample D&B GlobalSeek Report

If you've searched various D&B files online and can't find information on the company in question, try calling the D&B Customer Resource Center (800/234-3867); the staff is very experienced in helping you to find what you need. Maybe you or your client misspelled a company or city name due to language nuances. If indeed a record does not exist for the company, you can order a D&B investigation. A marketing record will cost between $5 and $10, a credit record, more. (Pricing varies for different parts of the world.) Depending upon the region in which the company is located, you should have the results of the investigation within three to fifteen days.

D&B also offers direct access to its comprehensive WorldBase database. While portions of WorldBase are available on other online services, D&B indicates that at present, the only way to access all report elements for all 52 million records is via D&B's own system. Using WorldBase, you can search the Global Marketing database, the Global Corporate Linkages database, and the previously mentioned GlobalSeek. While you could pay an annual subscription, you can also choose the transaction-based pricing plan, which carries about a $30/month fee. Charges vary depending upon the type of record, but most fall within the 30¢ to $3 range.

Economic and Financial Information

Much can be learned about a country or a foreign company from financial data such as banking and stock market information. While individual regional chapters in this book will cover stock market and banking sites in detail, some of these sites not only list stock market and banking data, but also link to general worldwide information. These include:

- **BankInfo.com**
  http://www.bankinfo.com/intereye/international.html
  This site provides weekly and historical exchange rate data, topical articles.

- **The Bank for International Settlements**
  http://www.bis.org/cbanks.htm
  Here you find links to the majority of the Central Banks around the world; updated frequently. (A Central Bank is a country's primary monetary authority, such as the Federal Reserve Bank in the U.S. Central Banks usually have responsibility for issuing currency, administering monetary policy, holding member banks' deposits, and facilitating the nation's banking industry. They are, in a sense, the banks for other banks.)

- **BankSITE Global Directory**
  http://www.banksite.com/cmapitl.htm
  Choose a region of the world for a listing of banks and links to their sites.

- **Euromoney.com**
  http://www.euromoney.com/index.html
  Registration is required, but is free.

- **IndustryWeek's Ranking of the World's Top 50 Banks**
  http://www.industryweek.com/iwinprint/data/chart2-4.html

- **IndustryWeek's Ranking of the World's Top Securities Dealers**
  http://www.industryweek.com/iwinprint/data/ chart2-7.html

- **Institute of Finance and Banking at the University of Göttingen—Market Places and Quotations**
  http://www.gwdg.de/~ifbg/stock1.htm

- **Institute of Finance and Banking at the University of Göttingen—Banks of the World**
  http://www.gwdg.de/~ifbg/bank_2.html

- **Ohio State University—Virtual Finance Library**
  http://fisher.osu.edu/fin/overview.html
  Check World Markets (links by region) and Investment Banks (mostly U.S. but foreign ones also noted).

- **The Internationalist—Stock Markets of the World**
  http://www.internationalist.com/business/Stocks.html

- **Worldclass Stocks by Country**
  http://web.idirect.com/~tiger/stockcou.htm

For a good overall financial directory-type site, try Qualisteam Banking and Finance [http://www.qualisteam.com]. With information available in English, French, and Italian (the company is based in Paris), its slogan is "The Easy Access to Essentials" and it really is, if you're interested in international banking and finance. My only dissatisfaction with the site is that it is very slow going from page to page within the site. The main page includes the following categories:

- Banks in the World—This area contains links to over 3,000 banks around the world broken out by region. Number of countries covered for each region are: Asia (21), Europe (39), Latin America (31), Africa (10), and Pacific (Australia and New Zealand).

- Financial Markets—In addition to the U.S., this section contains links to the various financial markets around the world including stock exchanges, bonds, mutual funds, options/futures, and commodities.

- Yellow Pages Online Banks Database—This is a searchable database of nearly 2,000 banks around the world having a presence on the Internet.

If you want to find economic data quickly, try The Dismal Scientist [http://www.dismal.com]. Here you will find GDP (Gross Domestic Product) and employment situation statistics prepared by economists for the following countries:

- Argentina
- Germany
- Australia
- Hong Kong
- Brazil
- India (GDP only)
- Canada
- Japan
- China (GDP only)
- Mexico
- France
- United Kingdom

For employment situation information, a table compares the most recent four months of data; for GDP, it covers the last four quarters. For each country, the site notes the source for the data and the frequency of its release, along with a description, summary, and analysis of the figures. You can also register to be notified electronically when Dismal Scientist updates the information.

The OECD (Organisation for Economic Cooperation and Development) [http://www.oecd.org] is an international organization, in existence since 1961, with 29 member countries (see Figure 2.6). Its predecessor agency, the Organisation for European Economic Cooperation, was formed at the end of World War II.

The OECD's mandate is to strengthen the economies in its member countries, increase free trade, and contribute to development in industrialized and developing countries. While much of the information from the OECD is only available in a print version, there are some interesting economic statistics on its Web site [http://www. oecd.org/std/fas.htm] (see Figure 2.7) including the following types of data:

- Annual Comparison of Levels of GDP Per Capita—based on both exchange rates and on purchasing power parities (PPPs)
- Composite Leading Indicators—a composite indicator based on other indicators of economic activity (qualitative opinions on production or employment, housing permits, financial or

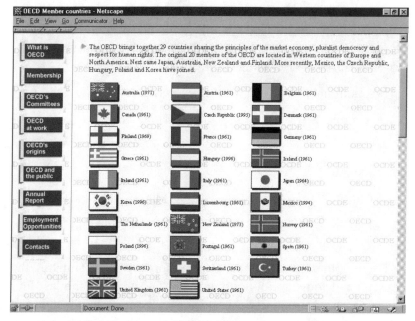

Figure 2.6   OECD Member Countries

monetary series, etc.), which signals cyclical movements in industrial production from six to nine months in advance

• Consumer Price Indices

• Gross Domestic Product—in US$billions, based on exchange rates

• Latest Short-Term Indicators—GDP, leading indicators, consumer price indices, current balance, unemployment rates, interest rates

• Quarterly Growth Rates in GDP at Constant Prices—percentage changes from previous period, seasonally adjusted, at quarterly rates

• Purchasing Power Parities (PPPs) for all OECD Countries

• Purchasing Power Parity Based Comparative Price Levels

• Standardized Unemployment Rates

Now, while much of this information might seem like gibberish to the noneconomist, the statistics given and the comparisons shown can prove very helpful and illuminating to a company interested in

GDP per capita based on exchange rates and on PPP - Netscape

File Edit View Go Communicator Help

GDP per capita, 1998
at current prices, in US dollars

PIB par tête, 1998
aux prix courants, en dollars des États-Unis

OECD Member Countries	based on current exchange rates	based on current purchasing power parities	Pays Membres de l'OCDE
Canada	19610	24882	Canada
Mexico	4338	7848	Mexico
United States	32328	32328	United States
Australia	19877	24047	Australia
Japan (1)	29908	23874	Japan (1)
Korea	6908	14476	Korea
New Zealand (1)	13925	17560	New Zealand (1)
Austria	26168	23725	Austria
Belgium	24541	23571	Belgium
Czech Republic	5479	13011	Czech Republic
Denmark	32878	25689	Denmark
Finland	24938	21751	Finland
France (2)	24034	21150	France (2)
Germany	26217	22998	Germany
Greece	11561	14143	Greece
Hungary	4645	10288	Hungary
Iceland (1)	30193	26071	Iceland (1)
Ireland	22921	23160	Ireland
Italy	20579	21346	Italy

Document: Done

Figure 2.7   Sample OECD Statistics

doing business in another country. When considering two countries, all other factors being equal, the comparative strength of the two economies might decide the issue.

Worldwide Directory Sites

When you don't know where to start searching or after you've exhausted all the usual sources, turn to lists and directories prepared by others. Some organization, often a library or a university, probably has prepared a list of Internet sites on your topic. Here are some that target international business information.

Statistical Data Locators [http://www.ntu.edu.sg/library/stat/statdata.htm] is a service of the Nanyang Technological University Library in Singapore. The page is broken into the following regions:

• Africa (South Africa)

• Asia (Singapore, Brunei, China, Hong Kong, India, Indonesia, Japan, Korea, Malaysia, Mongolia, Myanmar, Philippines, Sri Lanka, Taiwan, Thailand)

- Europe (Denmark, Finland, France, Ireland, Netherlands, Norway, Slovenia, Sweden, United Kingdom)

- International

- Latin America (Argentina, Bolivia, Brazil, Chile, Colombia, Mexico, Paraguay, Peru, Venezuela)

- North America (U.S. and Canada)

- Oceania (Australia, New Zealand)

- Others (Egypt, Israel, Russia, Singapore, Turkey)

Each region has numerous links for locating statistical data by country, such as economic indicators, population profiles, country risk reports, and banking. Each time I have visited the site, it has updated within the last month, so the links are very current. With such frequent updating, it might be worth your while to check the site even if your country of interest is not on the above list. They could have added it.

The site also links to a Financial Data Locators page that contains links to many Singapore-related financial sites, as well as international financial sites in the following categories:

- Banking, Finance, Money

- Corporate Governance

- Currency, Exchange Rates

- Gov. Finance, Bonds

- Financial Online News and Newspapers

- Stock Exchanges and Securities Markets

- Bibliography on International Statistics Sources

- Investor's Listing

- Banks on the Web

- Finance Journals

- Interest Rates

- Financial Software

- International Trade

The University of Strathclyde's Department of Information Science in Glasgow, Scotland, has a series of useful international business directory sites. While some overlap, you should still check each one. Updating for the various pages in this series of sites does not appear to be uniform. Some update very currently, while others have had no updates for close to a year. Business Information Sources on the Internet: Directories Worldwide and Other Countries [http://www.dis.strath.ac.uk/business/directories.html] basically lists international business directories. It begins with global sources and then breaks out on a regional and country basis. It includes both fee-based and free sites. Business Information Sources on the Internet: Company Profiles and Financial Information [http://www.dis.strath.ac.uk/business/financials. html], as the name suggests, is a directory of sites and services on the Internet specializing in international company profiles and financial information. The Business Information Sources on the Internet series includes these sites:

- Commercial Market Research Companies
  http://www.dis.strath.ac.uk/business/marketres.html

- Country Information
  http://www.dis.strath.ac.uk/business/countries.html
  Country- and region-specific, as well as worldwide

- Statistical, Economic, and Market Information
  http://www.dis.strath.ac.uk/business/market.html

- Trade Directories
  http://www.dis.strath.ac.uk/business/trade.html
  Currently includes the categories Banking, Computing, Chemicals, Consultants and Information Brokers, Engineering, Fashion, Food, Hotels, Libraries, Manufacturing (U.S. & Canada), Media, Oil and Gas, Pipelines, Polymers & Rubber, Promotional Merchandise, Telecommunications, Training, Welding, and Wood and Paper

The Andersonian Library at the University of Strathclyde runs the BUBL 5:15 site [http://bubl.ac.uk/link/five/wor.html]. BUBL, established in 1990, originally stood for BUlletin Board for Libraries. Today they call it the BUBL Information Service, or BUBL for short. The goal of the site is to provide at least five relevant resources for every subject included and a maximum of fifteen resources for most subjects, which explains the 5:15. However, as they do not strictly adhere to the fifteen maximum, you may find up to thirty-five items for some subjects. From the drop-down menu, you can select a country. Alongside the name of each site, they provide a description of the type of information found at the site. They claim to check all links once a month. By going to the BUBL Updates page [http:// bubl.ac.uk/link/updates/current.html] you can check what they have added to BUBL within the last couple of weeks.

BUBL also has a Countries and Continents page [http://bubl.ac. uk/link/countries.html] that appears to list almost every country in the world. Selecting a country will retrieve a list of links similar to those found by searching the 5:15 page. For some reason, slightly different results are returned from the two searches, so if you haven't found what you need, be sure to search both pages. A portion of the results of a search on Egypt appears in Figure 2.8.

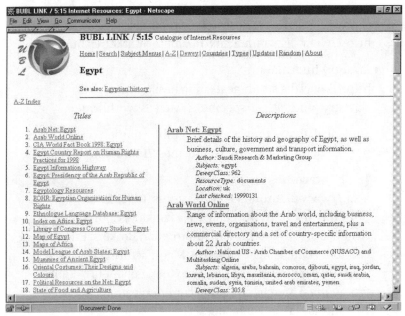

Figure 2.8   BUBL Country Search

Michigan State University's Center for International Business Education and Research (MSU-CIBER) has an index called International Business Resources on the WWW [http://ciber.bus. msu.edu/busres.htm]. You can use this site in two ways—either through the internal search engine or by scrolling down the page and choosing a category from the Index, such as Regional or Country Specific Information (Africa). This will then bring you to a list of sites that contains African business information. The Index contains about twenty categories including these:

- Government Resources

- International Trade Information

- News/Periodicals—International

- Regional or Country Specific Information: General, Africa, Asia and Oceania, Europe, Central and South America, and North America

- Statistical Data and Information Resources

Here are a few more directory sites worth taking a look at:

- **Everything International**
http://faculty.philau.edu/russowl/russow.html
Maintained by a faculty member at Philadelphia University, this site covers Country & Regional Data, International Organizations, Product Classification Systems, Company & Industry Data, Market Entry (Export) Assistance, and more. The site states that they check all the links approximately once every ten days.

- **Global Reach—Global Business Center**
http://www.glreach.com/gbc/index.php3
This site carries lots of information in languages other than English. For starters, the site itself can be viewed in nine languages. The contents of the site are organized by languages and regions: Chinese, German, English, Spanish, Finnish, French, Greek, Italian, Japanese, Korean, Dutch, Portuguese, Scandinavia, Pacific Rim, Central/Eastern Europe, and Africa/Middle East. Each of these sections includes, among others, a business category containing links to English and non-English sites.

- **Marketing and International Business Links**
http://wtfaulty.wtamu.edu/~sanwar.bus/otherlinks.htm
This is another site maintained by a faculty member, this time from West Texas A&M University. Keep scrolling down

the page; it's long, but don't get frustrated. Topics covered include International Business, Marketing, and Trade Journals; Barter & Countertrade; Country Rankings & Regional Studies; Doing Business Guides & Surveys; Multinational Corporations—Rankings & Surveys; and much more.

• **VIBES—Virtual International Business & Economic Sources**
http://libweb.uncc.edu/ref-bus/vibehome.htm
From the University of North Carolina, Charlotte, this site divides into three sections: Comprehensive (the whole world), Regional (one continent or region), and National (one country). All sites listed are in English and free. The Table of Contents gives you a good idea as to the topics covered (see Figure 2.9).

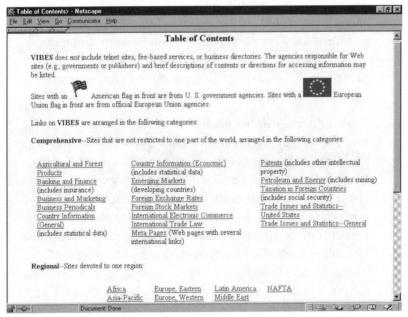

Figure 2.9 VIBES Table of Contents

- **Nanyang Technological University Library**
  http://www.ntu.edu.sg/library/biz/inttrade.htm
  While the listings on this site focus on either Singapore or the
  Asia/Pacific Region, it also links to international trade fairs,
  multilateral development organizations, international trade
  statistics, global commerce and trade sites, and more.

- **Rutgers University Libraries (RUL) Resources for
  International Business**
  http://www.libraries.rutgers.edu/rul/rr_gateway/research_
  guides/busi/intbus.shtml
  This directory is divided into seven categories: Background
  Materials, Regions, Countries, Statistics, News, Useful
  Resources, and Infoservers. Two other pages at the RUL site
  cover Banks and Financial Services [http://www.libraries.rut
  gers.edu/rul/rr_gateway/research_guides/busi/banks.shtml]
  and Company Research [http://www.libraries.rutgers.edu
  /rul/rr_gateway/research_guides/busi/company.shtml]. While
  the links on these two pages aren't exclusively international, if
  you keep scrolling down, you'll find the relevant sites.

- **Global Business Web**
  http://www.globalbusinessweb.com
  Here you will find global and regional business links, along
  with links to regional business news.

- **Pepperdine University Libraries International Business Web
  Sites**
  http://rigel.pepperdine.edu/resources/Guides/Bibintl.htm
  Short descriptions are provided for the various links for sites
  divided into the following categories: Countries, International
  Organizations, Trade, Companies, Finance, Currency,
  Business Reference Helpers, and Other Links.

- **Worldclass Supersite**
  http://web.idirect.com/~tiger/supersit.htm
  More than 1,000 sites from nearly 100 countries appear here. The
  most relevant categories are Reference, News, Money, and Trade.

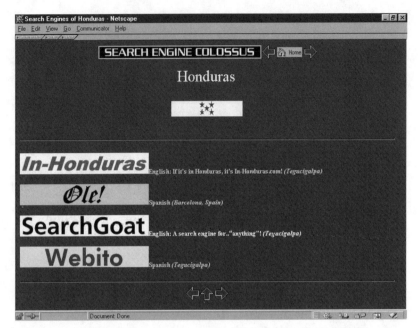

Figure 2.10   Search Engine Colossus Entries for Honduras

Search Engines

When searching the Web for international business information, try using one or more international search engines. Arnold IT [http://www.arnoldit.com/lists/intlsearch.asp] has compiled a very extensive list of the search engines available. It covers countries from Angola to Yugoslavia, as well as the regions of Africa, Asia, Europe, and the Middle East. While most of the search engines are not designed to retrieve business information in particular, and some might not be searchable in English, this is still a valuable road to take when you're stumped. Here are some other directories of international search engines:

- **Search Engine Colossus**
  http://www.searchenginecolossus.com
  This source contains listings for approximately 100 countries, each showing the name of the search engine and the language used for searching it (see Figure 2.10).

- **Search Engines Worldwide**
  http://www.twics.com/~takakuwa/search/search.html

Five regions, 130 countries, and links to almost 1,000 international search engines can be found here; no indication as to language.

Foreign Embassies

When you look for information on an overseas company or a market study and nothing turns up, it can be very frustrating. Here are a few more avenues to travel.

Often, the embassy of a country will have international business and trade information at its Web site. It might have specific economic information or it might have a list, with links, of major companies in the country. Try The Embassy Web [http://www.embpage. org], a searchable database with over 50,000 addresses, phone numbers, and e-mail addresses of diplomatic posts worldwide. Here you will find most diplomatic offices (embassies, consulates, etc.) across the world. For example, if you select Japan, you will receive a list of links to the various foreign embassies and consulates located within Japan. The Embassy Web also has a section, called International Sites, that links to many diplomacy, international affairs, trade, and policy sites. It also offers international news. The site undergoes some updating on a daily basis. It will soon offer weekly reviews and snapshots of some of the best sites on its list.

Check The Electronic Embassy [http://www.embassy.org], which provides information on all the foreign embassies in Washington, DC. When you choose a country, at the very least you will get contact information for that embassy; sometimes you will also get a link for the embassy's Web site. If an e-mail address is provided, you may find it tempting to send off a quick e-mail inquiry asking for information. In my experience, most of those messages go unanswered. Not so long ago, while working on a project, I sent messages to about half a dozen different embassies asking for very simple contact information and received not one reply. When I followed up with phone calls, an official at one embassy informed me that no one reads the incoming e-mail messages for the address listed at the Web site.

Either The Embassy Web or The Electronic Embassy provided the URLs for the following countries' embassy Web sites in the U.S.:

- **Algeria**
  http://www.algeria-un.org/nspage.html

- **Antigua & Barbuda**
  http://www.undp.org/missions/antigua_barbuda

- **Argentina**
  http://www.embassyofargentina-usa.org

- **Armenia**
  http://www.armeniaemb.org

- **Australia**
  http://www.austemb.org

- **Austria**
  http://www.austria.org

- **Azerbaijan**
  http://www.azembassy.com

- **Bahrain**
  http://www.bahrainembassy.org

- **Bangladesh**
  http://www.un.int/bangladesh

- **Belarus**
  http://www.undp.org/missions/belarus/index.html

- **Belgium**
  http://www.belgium-emb.org/Atlas/atlas.asp?lng=EN

- **Bosnia and Herzegovina**
  http://www.bosnianembassy.org

- **Brazil**
  http://www.brasilemb.org

- **Bulgaria**
  http://www.bulgaria-embassy.org

- **Burkina Faso**
  http://www.burkinaembassy-usa.org

- **Cambodia**
  http://www.embassy.org/cambodia

- **Chad**
  http://www.chadembassy.org

- **China, Peoples Republic of**
  http://www.china-embassy.org

- **China, Republic of**
  http://www.taipei.org

- **Colombia**
  http://www.colombiaemb.org

- **Costa Rica**
  http://www.costarica.com/embassy

- **Croatia**
  http://www.croatiaemb.org

- **Czech Republic**
  http://www.czech.cz/washington

- **Denmark**
  http://www.denmarkemb.org

- **Dominican Republic**
  http://www.domrep.org

- **Ecuador**
  http://www.ecuador.org

- **Estonia**
  http://www.estemb.org

- **Finland**
  http://www.finland.org/index.html

- **France**
  http://www.info-france-usa.org

- **Georgia**
  http://www.georgiaemb.org

- **Germany**
  http://www.germany-info.org/f_index.html

- **Ghana**
  http://www.undp.org/missions/ghana

- **Greece**
  http://www.greekembassy.org

- **Guatemala**
  http://www.guatemala-embassy.org

- **Haiti**
  http://www.haiti.org

- **Hungary**
  http://www.hungaryemb.org

- **Iceland**
  http://www.iceland.org/index.html

- **India**
  http://www.indianembassy.org

- **Indonesia**
  http://www.kbri.org

- **Iran**
  http://www.daftar.org/default_eng.htm

- **Ireland**
  http://www.irelandemb.org

- **Israel**
  http://www.israelemb.org

- **Italy**
  http://www.italyemb.org

- **Jamaica**
  http://www.emjam-usa.org

- **Japan**
  http://www.embjapan.org

- **Jordan**
  http://www.jordanembassyus.org

- **Kenya**
  http://www.kenyaembassy.com

- **Korea**
  http://www.mofat.go.kr/en_usa.htm

- **Kuwait**
  http://www.undp.org/missions/kuwait

- **Laos**
  http://www.laoembassy.com

- **Latvia**
  http://www.latvia-usa.org

- **Lebanon**
  http://www.lebanonembassy.org

- **Liberia**
  http://www.liberiaemb.org/

- **Lithuania**
  http://www.ltembassyus.org

- **Madagascar**
  http://www.embassy.org/madagascar

- **Malaysia**
  http://www.undp.org/missions/malaysia

- **Mali**
  http://www.maliembassy-usa.org

- **Marshall Islands**
  http://www.rmiembassyus.org/usemb.html

- **Mauritius**
  http://www.idsonline.com/usa/embasydc.html

- **Mexico**
  http://www.embassyofmexico.org/english/main2. htm

- **Micronesia**
  http://www.fsmgov.org/fsmun

- **Moldova**
  http://www.rol.org/moldova

- **Mongolia**
  http://members.aol.com/monemb

- **Nepal**
  http://www.undp.org/missions/nepal

- **Netherlands**
  http://www.netherlands-embassy.org/f_netscape.html

- **New Zealand**
  http://www.nzemb.org

- **Norway**
  http://www.norway.org/index.html

- **Pakistan**
  http://www.pakistan-embassy.com

- **Papua New Guinea**
  http://www.pngembassy.org

- **Peru**
  http://www.peruemb.org/intro.html

- **Philippines**
  http://www.embassyonline.com

- **Poland**
  http://www.polishworld.com/polemb

- **Portugal**
  http://www.portugalemb.org

- **Romania**
  http://www.roembus.org

- **Russian Federation**
  http://www.russianembassy.org

- **St. Kitts and Nevis**
  http://www.stkittsnevis.org

- **Saudi Arabia**
  http://www.saudiembassy.net

- **Singapore**
  http://www.gov.sg/mfa/washington

- **Slovak Republic**
  http://www.slovakemb.com

- **Slovenia**
  http://www.embassy.org/slovenia

- **South Africa**
  http://usaembassy.southafrica.net

- **Spain**
  http://www.spainemb.org/ingles/indexing.htm

- **Sudan**
  http://www.sudanembassyus.org

- **Sweden**
  http://www.swedenemb.org

- **Switzerland**
  http://www.swissemb.org

- **Thailand**
  http://www.thaiembdc.org

- **Turkey**
  http://www.turkey.org/start.html

- **Turkmenistan**
  http://www.turkmenistanembassy.org

- **Uganda**
  http://www.ugandaweb.com/ugaembassy

- **Ukraine**
  http://www.ukremb.com

- **United Kingdom**
  http://www.britain-info.org

- **Uruguay**
  http://www.embassy.org/uruguay

- **Uzbekistan**
  http://www.uzbekistan.org

- **Venezuela**
  http://www.embavenez-us.org

- **Vietnam**
  http://www.vietnamembassy-usa.org

- **Yemen**
  http://www.yemenembassy.org

On occasion, a local government office might have the data needed. Purdue University Libraries offers THOR—The Online Resource [http://thorplus.lib.purdue.edu/vlibrary/reading/govdocs/foreign.html]. THOR contains links to various branches of foreign governments starting with Albania (Office of the President) and going through Zimbabwe.

Chambers of Commerce and Industry

Chambers of commerce or industry can be useful resources for international business information. Chambers can take many forms. They are generally organizations whose members comprise individuals and/or companies with a common business interest. There are chambers for cities, states, countries, industries, and more. Sometimes chambers are private with specific membership criteria; others are open to anyone with an interest in the chamber's "theme." As with embassies, overseas chambers may have one or more lists of local businesses, often with links to their Web sites. Sometimes the chambers have market research reports, industry studies, or other publications available for sale at the Web site. The U.S. Chamber of Commerce has an international division [http:// www.uschamber.org/intl/index.html] that offers a variety of programs and services. One of the most useful portions of this site is the section concerning the American Chambers of Commerce Abroad (AmChams) [http://www.uschamber.org/intl/amcham.htm], international affiliates of the U.S. Chamber of Commerce. AmChams are associations of business executives interested in U.S. foreign trade and investment. This site offers a list of all of the AmChams worldwide, many of them with links to their Web sites. If your country of interest does not have a Web site link, I would suggest calling the International Division of the U.S. Chamber of Commerce (202/463-5460) and asking for contact information. (Note: Individual country AmCham links will appear in the regional chapters.)

The World Chambers Network [http://www.worldchambers.com] (WCN) is an online network that links more than 10,000 chambers of commerce and industry worldwide. It is managed by three organizations: International Bureau of Chamber of Commerce (IBCC)/ International Chamber of Commerce (ICC), The Paris Chamber of Commerce and Industry (CCIP), and The Global Management Center of the Trade Information Network of the UN/G77 Chambers of Commerce (GMC/TIN). WCN maintains an index of chambers of commerce and industry searchable by region, country, city, state, or name. For example, searching on Venezuela in South America returns ten chambers sorted by city (see Figure 2.11).

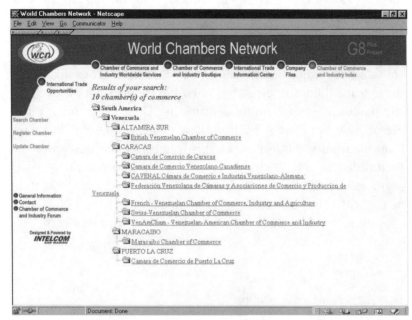

Figure 2.11   World Chambers Network Search Results

Lists, Lists, and More Lists

People love making lists. We make to-do lists, shopping lists, Christmas card lists. And someone is always doing a Best of ... List or a Top (fill in the appropriate number) List. International Business is no exception. The lists are out there; you just need to find them. Forbes has The 2000 Forbes International 800 [http://www.forbes. com/international800]. You can search the list by company name, industry, country, or rank. Close to forty industries are represented including Aerospace & Military Technology, Banking, Business & Public Services, Energy Sources, Forest Products & Paper, Telecommunications, and Utilities— Electrical & Gas. When you find a company of interest, you get a short directory listing with contact information, number of employees, revenue, assets, profitability information, the company's ranking on the list, and a link to the company's Web site.

The Forbes list updates annually with the lists for the previous two years also available. You can also search for the 100 Largest Foreign Investments in the U.S., the Top 100 International Bargains, the Top 100 U.S.-Traded Foreign Stocks, and the 100 Largest U.S. Multinationals.

Not to be outdone, Fortune has The 2000 Fortune Global 500 [http://www.fortune.com/fortune/global500/index.html], which contains very similar information to the Forbes list. The rankings on the two lists differ somewhat as the Forbes list does not include U.S. companies. Therefore, on the Fortune list, General Motors is number one; on the Forbes list, it is DaimlerChrysler Group. Since we want international information, this is not a serious omission. The Fortune list has a FAQ page that provides definitions to many of the terms used. A few more industries appear on the Fortune list than on the Forbes list, as well as industry median statistics.

Fortune provides links to retrieve the top performers in the following categories:

- Biggest employers

- Biggest increases in profits

- Biggest increases in revenue

- Highest profits

- Highest returns on assets

- Highest returns on revenue

Figures 2.12 and 2.13 show the entry for DaimlerChrysler from Forbes and Fortune, respectively.

And, in case Forbes and Fortune don't answer your questions regarding top international companies, you can always turn to The BusinessWeek Global 1000 [http://www.businessweek.com/2000/00_28/b3689009.htm]. Here you will find companies sorted by rank, country, and alphabetically, along with the Top 200 Emerging Market Companies. The nice thing about the BusinessWeek tables is that you can view them in either HTML or PDF format (see Figure 2.14).

IndustryWeek [http://www.industryweek.com] compiles numerous Top ... Lists. As the site is a bit difficult to navigate, I've included the URLs for most of the international ones here:

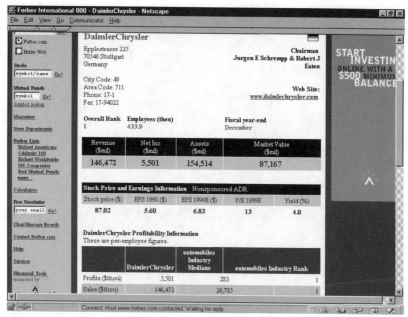

Figure 2.12   Forbes International 800 Listing

- **100 Largest IT Companies**
  http://www.industryweek.com/iwinprint/data/chart4-7B.html

- **Industry Financial Performance Benchmarks**
  http://www.industryweek.com/iwinprint/data/chart3-2.html

- **International Freight and Passenger Transport by Country**
  http://www.industryweek.com/iwinprint/data/chart4-13.html

- **International Electricity Costs**
  http://www.industryweek.com/iwinprint/data/chart4-5.html

- **Largest Advertising Agencies by Billings**
  http://www.industryweek.com/iwinprint/data/chart2-3.html

- **Largest Executive Search Firms**
  http://www.industryweek.com/iwinprint/data/chart2-2.html

- **Largest International Law Firms**
  http://www.industryweek.com/iwinprint/data/chart2-5.html

- **Stock Markets of the World by Market Capitalization**
  http://www.industryweek.com/iwinprint/data/chart2-1.html

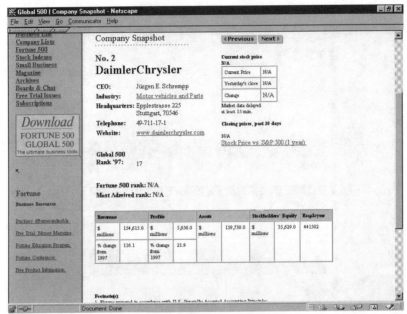

Figure 2.13 Fortune Global 500 Listing

The Top 200 Emerging-Market Companies

RANK 1999	RANK 1998		COUNTRY	MARKET VALUE U.S. $ MIL.	PRICE PER SHARE U.S. $	%CHANGE FROM 1998 (U.S. $)	%CHANGE FROM 1998 (LOCAL)	PRICE/ BOOK VALUE RATIO	P/E RATIO	YIELD %	SALES U.S. $ MIL.	PROFITS U.S. $ MIL.	ASSETS U.S. $ MIL.	RETURN ON EQUITY %	INDUSTRY CODE
1	4	TELEFONOS DE MEXICO (TELMEX)	Mexico	33305	4	67	84	3.1	18	1.8	8063	1690	13180a	16.9	55
2	3	CHINA TELECOM (HONG KONG)	China	25294	2	21	21	3.9	30	0.0	3182	833	NA	12.8	55
3	1	GAZPROM	Russia	24502	10	-26	-26	1.3	61	0.1	5530a	405a	NA	2.1d	12
4	7	TAIWAN SEMICONDUCTOR MFG.	Taiwan	21627	4	45	40	8.8	57	0.0	1535	469	NA	15.6	35
5	32	KOREA ELECTRIC POWER (KEPCO)	Korea	19752	31	214	165	1.3	21	1.6	11870*	929*	41623*	6.1	12
6	11	ANGLO AMERICAN	South Africa	18487	45	-5	14	1.6	13	2.0	NA	808	8266	12.4	71
7	12	YPF	Argentina	15146	43	38	38	2.1	28	2.1	5501	580	13148	7.4	11
8	NR	KOREA TELECOM	Korea	14731	51	NA	NA	3.0	68	0.7	7396*	218*	NA	4.4	55
9	9	CATHAY LIFE INSURANCE	Taiwan	14157	3	11	7	6.6	31	1.4	NA	NA	NA	21.3	63
10	6	PETROBRAS	Brazil	13317	146	-24	13	1.3	20	2.4	10473	807	23313	6.4	11
11	46	SAMSUNG ELECTRONICS	Korea	12050	70	96	65	1.9	40	0.7	16929*	264*	19442a*	4.6	41
12	21	HINDUSTAN LEVER	India	11764	54	40	44	36.3	52	1.0	2213*	195*	823a*	69.7d	44
13	5	ELETROBRAS	Brazil	11142	21	-34	-2	0.3	6	1.2	5033	1159	51257	4.9	12
14	8	HELLENIC TELECOMMUNICATIONS ORGANIZATION	Greece	10926	22	-18	-16	3.8	16	1.6	3039	687	NA	23.8d	55
15	59	NATIONAL BANK OF GREECE	Greece	10879	70	103	108	6.1	102	1.5	NA	78a	NA	6.0	61
16	37	ASUSTEK COMPUTER	Taiwan	9723	12	61	55	10.2	25	0.8	1076	354	NA	40.3	35
17	26	UNITED MICROELECTRONICS	Taiwan	9548	2	32	27	4.2	71	0.0	563*	135*	NA	5.9	35
18	NR	QUANTA COMPUTER	Taiwan	8922	21	NA	NA	17.1	32	0.2	1586	282	NA	54.1	33
19	28	TELEKOM MALAYSIA	Malaysia	8722	3	27	48	3.4	41	0.8	1781	215	5415a	8.5d	55
20	23	GRUPO MODELO	Mexico	8511	3	13	24	2.7	32	1.2	2125	242	NA	8.5	43
21	NR	TELEKOMUNIKACJA POLSKA (TPSA)	Poland	8503	6	NA	NA	3.7	32	0.0	2544	264	NA	11.6	55
22	18	DE BEERS CONSOLIDATED MINES	South Africa	8291	22	3	24	2.2	20	4.1	NA	407	4012a	10.8	26
23	27	CIFRA	Mexico	8044	2	20	32	2.9	27	0.0	5304	287	3661	10.8	54
24	83	POHANG IRON & STEEL (POSCO)	Korea	7767	81	134	97	1.2	8	1.3	9388*	946*	16540a*	14.8d	25
25	NR	KRUNG THAI BANK	Thailand	7552	1	304	271	3.4	-5	0.0	NA	-1660*	28721*	NEG	61
26	10	TELECOMUNICACOES DE SAO PAULO (TELESP)	Brazil	7397	123	-42	-13	1.1	12	5.5	2381*	630*	8246a*	9.6	55
27	164	SK TELECOM	Korea	7369	1117	281	221	6.1	58	0.1	2988*	128*	3459a*	10.5d	55
28	16	VALE DO RIO DOCE	Brazil	7048	18	-13	31	1.3	12	6.1	NA	599	9914a	10.7	25
29	20	TELEFONICA DE ARGENTINA	Argentina	6959	3	-1	-1	2.1	14	4.3	3435	511	6549	15.2	55
30	29	CHINA DEVELOPMENT INDUSTRIAL BANK	Taiwan	6790	2	-1	-4	3.3	24	0.0	NA	222a*	NA	13.9	62
31	66	ALPHA CREDIT BANK	Greece	6724	68	42	46	7.0	26	1.9	NA	246	NA	27.1d	61
32	35	GRUPO TELEVISA	Mexico	6432	21	6	17	4.4	-492	0.0	1734	79	4338	NEG	51
33	25	LUKOIL HOLDING	Russia	6378	9	-11	-11	4.0	230	0.1	2170a	73a	NA	1.7	11
34	NR	PANAFON HELLENIC TELECOM	Greece	6377	25	NA	NA	28.8	48	NA	660	133	NA	59.9	55

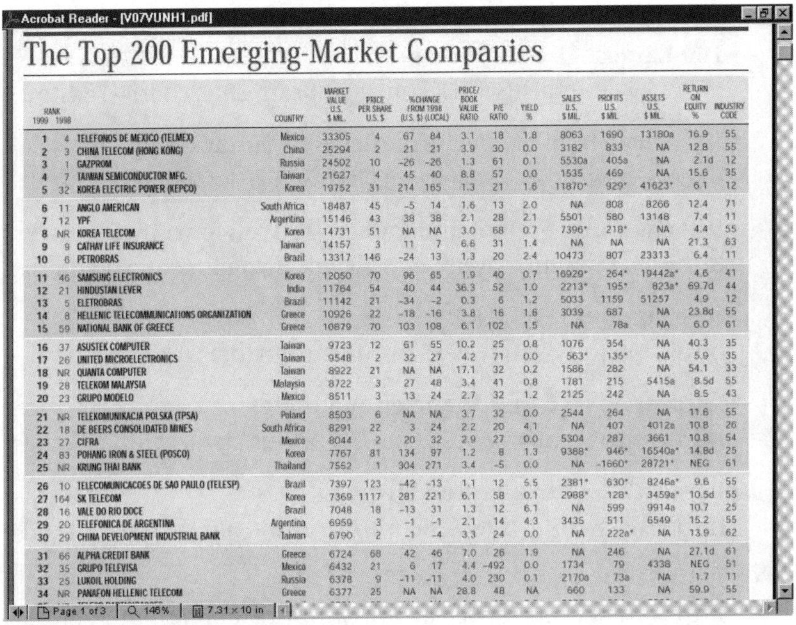

Figure 2.14 BusinessWeek Top 200 Emerging Market Companies

- **Top 25 International Accounting Networks**
  http://www.industryweek.com/iwinprint/data/chart2-6.html

- **Top 1000 Global Manufacturers**
  http://www.industryweek.com/iwinprint/data/chart3-1.html

- **Top Consulting Firms**
  http://www.industryweek.com/iwinprint/data/chart6-2.html

- **World's Best Hotels**
  http://www.industryweek.com/iwinprint/data/chart4-9.html

- **World's Best-Managed Companies**
  http://www.industryweek.com/iwinprint/data/chart3-4.html

- **World's Largest Steel Producers**
  http://www.industryweek.com/iwinprint/data/chart4-3.html

- **World's Top 50 Transnational Corporations**
  http://www.industryweek.com/iwinprint/data/chart8.html

- **World's Top Airlines**
  http://www.industryweek.com/iwinprint/data/chart4-8.html

- **World Trade Centers**
  http://www.industryweek.com/iwiprint/data/chart5-4.html

The Old Stand-Bys—Commercial Services

Many professional searchers start any search for international business information with one or more of the traditional online services: Dialog, DataStar, Factiva, Lexis-Nexis. (Note: Each of these services has its own pricing structure with various plans available including flat-fee and pay-as-you-go options. Be sure to contact the companies for this information.) Professional searchers usually know how to search specific familiar vendors effectively, but even professionals have to avoid getting into a rut and returning to the same old databases over and over again without checking to see what else is out there—especially at a better price—on the Web. Most of the traditional services have opened access to general users via credit card payments.

The Dialog Corporation [http://www.dialog.com] has put a few things up on its Web site that you may find extremely helpful when searching for international business information on their services.

Start with Dialog's Subject Content page [http://www.dialog. com/info/content/subject] and scroll down to the Business and Finance section. Two links appear: Company Intelligence Smart Tool Sheets and Products & Markets Smart Tool Sheets. Click on Company Intelligence and you will go to a page with a drop-down menu that starts with Company Profiles. Some of the other options include Company Financial Data and Company News. Select Company Profiles and Go to Table. Here you will find a table of all Dialog and DataStar databases that contain company profile information. The table lists each database by name, where it is available (Dialog or DataStar), the number of companies covered, the geographic area covered, the type of data available (directory, full-text, etc.) and the information available in the database (see Figure 2.15). A quick scroll through the table and you can easily pick out which databases could help you with an international search. Similar tables follow the other options on the drop-down menu.

Going back to the Subject Content page and following the Products & Markets link, the categories available include Market Information (broken out by Market Research Studies, Market Share Data, and Demographic Data), Multi-Industry Sources, and Product Information. Again, by going through the relevant table, you can select which databases to search for international market information.

Factiva [http://www.factiva.com], the new joint Dow Jones/ Reuters organization running Dow Jones Interactive (DJI) and Reuters Business Briefing (RBB), has made a concerted effort to increase its non-U.S. content, the kind of material the international business searcher finds particularly useful. According to Clare Hart, President and Chief Executive Officer, out of the approximately 6,000 publications on DJI, more than one-third come from non-U.S. sources and about fifteen percent are non-English. DJI has steadily increased the number of editors working with international content, particularly in the area of emerging markets. In 1999, worldwide Associated Press content was added to the Publications Library, including current and archive material. About the same time, Dow Jones began offering an interface to the previously mentioned Dun & Bradstreet WorldBase database. The connection is seamless and Factiva users search it using the familiar DJI search screens.

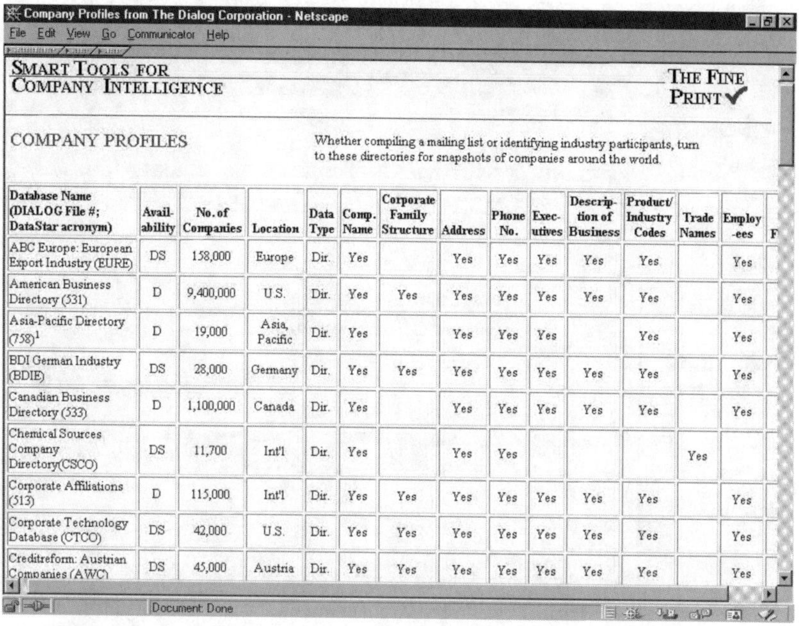

Database Name (DIALOG File #; DataStar acronym)	Avail-ability	No. of Companies	Location	Data Type	Comp. Name	Corporate Family Structure	Address	Phone No.	Exec-utives	Descrip-tion of Business	Product/ Industry Codes	Trade Names	Employ-ees	F
ABC Europe: European Export Industry (EURE)	DS	158,000	Europe	Dir.	Yes		Yes	Yes	Yes	Yes	Yes		Yes	
American Business Directory (531)	D	9,400,000	U.S.	Dir.	Yes	Yes	Yes	Yes	Yes	Yes	Yes		Yes	
Asia-Pacific Directory (758)[1]	D	19,000	Asia, Pacific	Dir.	Yes		Yes	Yes	Yes		Yes		Yes	
BDI German Industry (BDIE)	DS	28,000	Germany	Dir.	Yes	Yes	Yes	Yes	Yes	Yes	Yes		Yes	
Canadian Business Directory (533)	D	1,100,000	Canada	Dir.	Yes		Yes	Yes	Yes	Yes	Yes		Yes	
Chemical Sources Company Directory(CSCO)	DS	11,700	Int'l	Dir.	Yes		Yes	Yes				Yes		
Corporate Affiliations (513)	D	115,000	Int'l	Dir.	Yes	Yes	Yes	Yes	Yes	Yes	Yes		Yes	
Corporate Technology Database (CTCO)	DS	42,000	U.S.	Dir.	Yes	Yes	Yes	Yes	Yes	Yes	Yes		Yes	
Creditreform: Austrian Companies (AWC)	DS	45,000	Austria	Dir.	Yes	Yes	Yes	Yes	Yes	Yes	Yes		Yes	

Figure 2.15   Dialog Corporation Company Profiles Table

The Dow Jones Web Center greatly expands international business research capabilities. Currently, they provide links to approximately 250 non-U.S. Web sites. Of those, close to half are non-English sites. One can search in nine languages: English, Dutch, French, German, Italian, Norwegian, Portuguese, Spanish, and Swedish. For those who only have an English keyboard, DJI even offers a pop-up keyboard with the necessary non-English characters.

If you'd like to search for useful Web sites, click on the Web Site Reviews tab on the left. You can choose how you would like the results arranged—by title, total score, etc. I did a simple search on "international business" and asked for the results to be ranked by total score. My search resulted in reviews of 11 sites, including IBM and two sites from the U.S. State Department (see Figure 2.16).

The Reuters Business Briefing interface is offered in eleven languages with content appearing in more than twenty languages. An additional plus for RBB is the inclusion of news photos, not generally found in other online sources.

World Reporter is a database developed jointly by Dow Jones, The Dialog Corporation, and Financial Times Information. It consists of more than 600 worldwide publications, including newspapers,

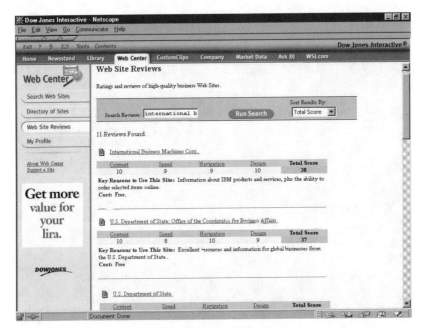

Figure 2.16   Dow Jones Interactive Web Center

business magazines, newswires, etc. Only news directly related to business appears in World Reporter, so you will not find extraneous information such as local sports, entertainment, etc. Political news appears only if it has a direct bearing on the business environment. Using DJI, the individual publications that comprise World Reporter appear separately in the Publications Library; you do not search the database separately as you would on Dialog (File 20).

Lexis-Nexis [http://lexis-nexis.com/lncc] has a number of libraries useful for locating international business information. The major libraries include Company (COMPNY), Market Research Reports (MKTRES), and World (WORLD). They also break the collection down into regional country collections. These libraries contain numerous files with international company financial information, international market research information, and international news. To review the individual libraries and their contents easily and for free, go to the Lexis-Nexis Source Locator [http://lexis-nexis.com/lncc/sources].

Where Do We Go From Here?

We have outlined general sources for international business information, but usually your needs will be much more specific, focusing on a particular region or country. To that end, you will need to complement the global information with more targeted regional or country information. So keep reading. We're about to tackle the rest of the world, region by region. It'll be a long trip and, of course, some areas will be harder to navigate than others. But, the same could be said about the early explorers trying to map the world. We'll be on a similar journey, only ours will be virtual.

CHAPTER 3

WESTERN EUROPE

Western Europe is tremendously diverse geographically, cultur-
ally, linguistically, and ethnically. It should come as no surprise
then that its sources of business information are equally diverse.
At times one must work through difficulties to find the precise
information sought, and, if found, the information may only
appear in a foreign language. If you don't understand the language, your problems have only begun.

On the other hand, the stricter reporting requirements imposed
by many European governments can make business research easier too. Facts and figures generally considered proprietary by U.S.
privately held companies often must be reported in European
countries as a matter of public record. Whether or not a privately
held U.S. company operating in Europe would be held to the same
reporting requirements would vary country by country and likely
depend upon the organization of the European operations (subsidiary, branch, etc.). Unfortunately, given the sheer number of
countries that comprise Western Europe, we cannot cover all of
them in-depth; to do so would be a book unto itself. Let's start by
looking at general business sources for the region. Then we'll
tackle some of the individual countries in greater detail: Belgium,
Denmark, France, Germany, Italy, the Netherlands, Portugal,
Spain, Sweden, and the United Kingdom.

The European Union (EU) comprises fifteen countries: Austria,
Belgium, Denmark, Finland, France, Germany, Greece, Ireland,
Italy, Luxembourg, the Netherlands, Portugal, Spain, Sweden, and

the United Kingdom. The Delegation of the European Commission to the United States hosts a site called the European Union in the U.S. [http://www.eurunion.org] designed to inform Americans about what's going on in the European Union. A publication at the site titled *The European Union: A Guide for Americans* offers a useful introduction to a basic understanding of the EU (see Figure 3.1). (Note: A print version, including graphics not found in the Web version, may be ordered at no charge directly from the EU.)

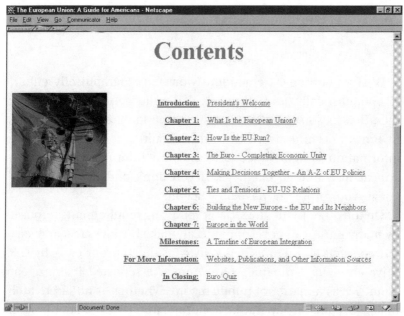

Figure 3.1   Table of Contents—The EU Guide for Americans

The Delegation itself does not get involved in business development and offers no services in that area. It has, however, compiled a very useful list, The European Union Business Resources [http://www.eurunion.org/infores/index.htm]. Several topics are covered here:

- Business Directories, Links, Databases, and More Covering the EU—European business directories (print and electronic), databases, and other sources

- Chambers of Commerce of the EU Members in the U.S.— contact details and links to the sites

- European Trade Associations

- Grants and Loans Available from the EU

- Investment Opportunities in Europe—a list of European trade, investment, and commercial offices in the U.S., often located within the country's embassy

- U.S. Government Services for Exporters

- U.S. Private Sector Organizations

The Business Directory section also links to The European Commission's One Stop Internet Shop for Businesses. This page answers many questions about doing business with EU countries, as well as a mechanism for obtaining personalized advice.

Search Engines and Directories

EuroFerret [http://www.euroferret.com/old_version.html] is an interesting European search engine. Established in 1996, it claims to have indexed more than 35 million documents. In addition to English, you can search EuroFerret in the following languages:

- Czech
- Danish
- Dutch
- Finnish
- French
- German
- Icelandic

- Italian
- Norwegian
- Polish
- Portuguese
- Spanish
- Swedish

EuroFerret does not use Boolean searching. For more precision, you may limit your search by country. Weather symbols indicate the relevance of a document to your query. After you see your search results, the system suggests how to refine the search.

Since I was hungry when I tested this site and, therefore, thinking about chocolate, I decided to see what EuroFerret might find on the subject. Entering "chocolate industry" as my search term, limiting the search to Belgium (supposedly one of the best sources for chocolate), and "match all terms," I got 16 hits, each with a bright yellow sun, which I assumed meant EuroFerret considered them all highly relevant. The first one came from the Belgian Foreign Trade Board (BFTB) site (see more on this under the Belgium subhead later in this chapter). Since I already knew about the BFTB site and liked it, I took this as a sign that EuroFerret was indeed a proficient search engine.

The latest variation on EuroFerret is WebTop.com [http: //www.webtop.com/search/topferret?PAGE=search&LOOK=eur oferret]. It belongs to the Web Solutions Division of Bright Station (formerly The Dialog Corporation). Try as I might, I had little success trying to use WebTop.com; e-mails to the company requesting additional information went unanswered. Eventually, I reverted back to the previous EuroFerret version that remains available.

Europages, the European Business Directory [http://www.euro pages.com] works something like a value-added European business Yellow Pages, with more than 500,000 listings, thirty countries, and searchable in English, German, Spanish, French, Italian, and Dutch. The first page allows searching the directory by product, service, or company name or selecting one of the twenty-five major sectors. I decided to see what happened when I chose Chemicals and Pharmaceuticals as the sector to search. This brought up a page with an extensive listing of subsectors (see Figure 3.2). Choosing "Other Search Options" at the bottom of the page gave me the additional choices of Selection by Company Data and Geographical Selection. Search results for either could be sorted by amount of information, alphabetical order, or alphabetical order by country. I could now scroll down the page and choose a subsector. I thought Herbs for Medicines and Cosmetics sounded interesting. By continuing to scroll, I could narrow my search by choosing Type of Activity (manufacturer, distributor, etc.), Workforce Size, Turnover (sales), and Country. For more specific searching, one can choose which region(s) within a country to search.

Having made my choices, Europages returned my results with only one company meeting all of my criteria. The company's entry included basic contact information and a brief description of the company's products, as well as a link to the company Web site.

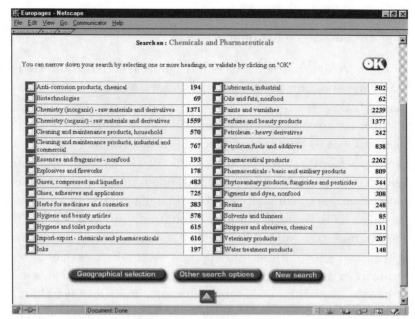

Figure 3.2   A Subsector List—Europages

Going back to the Europages home page, you can search for Company Catalogs in a similar fashion, although you cannot narrow the search quite as much. One drawback to this section: Even if you search in English, the catalog could very well appear in another language. (I tried using Globalink's Web Translator software on a few of the catalogs. Sometimes it worked, sometimes it didn't. It depends upon whether the text on the page is truly text or really graphics. See Conclusion for more information on translation software.)

The best feature of the Europages Web site is the Business Links section. A Practical Guide presents an overview of the European market divided into eight sections:

- Communicate with the World

- Converting to the Euro

- Exporting to and from Europe

- Jobs with a Future

- Macroeconomics Overview

- Setting Up a Company

- The Computer's Revolution

- The Euro and Your Company

These sections have great facts and figures in narrative and tabular format under the subheadings of Did You Know?, Useful Links, and Statistics.

A discussion of European business directories would not be complete without at least a brief mention of the Thomas Register of European Manufacturers (TREM) [http://www.tremnet.com]. You must register to use the site, but registration is free. The TREM database covers approximately 180,000 manufacturers and service providers in seventeen European countries. You can search in English (both U.S. and U.K. versions), German, French, Spanish, Italian, and Dutch. The simply designed site offers searching by product/service or company name. You may also include keywords, although the site does not support Boolean searching. Unfortunately, it has no drop-down list to define products and services, so sometimes you must use trial and error to identify the appropriate terminology for the industry in question.

Search results come back with Product Headings from which to choose. Choose the relevant heading(s) and you receive a list of companies sorted by country. Click on the company to view contact information including an e-mail address. You will also learn whether the company's catalog is available for perusal online. If the catalog is not available, then the TREM site is admittedly a bit slim in the information provided. But, it still could prove useful in the early stages of a project when you have to locate companies within a particular industry.

The TREM site has a couple of other interesting features. It lets you create your own Contact List. Each company listing has an option to add that company to your Contact List. As you find companies of interest, you may add them to your list and then review and print the compiled list. The list, which can store up to ten companies, will be kept even after you log out of the site, unless you delete the companies.

You may also review your search history for the current session and rerun your searches or link directly to the listings for the companies from your search results.

About.com has a section at its site called European Search Engines & Directories [http://websearch.about.com/internet/

websearch/msub12-m13.htm]. While not all of the sites listed specialize in business information in particular, it's certainly worth the
time to take a look at them. You never know where one site will lead
you. In addition to a section on General European Search Engines &
Directories, it covers the following individual countries:

• Belgium	• Italy
• Denmark	• Malta
• France	• Romania
• Germany	• Spain
• Holland	• Sweden
• Hungary	• Switzerland
• Iceland	• United Kingdom

(Note: Some of these countries will also appear in the chapter on
Central and Eastern Europe.)

Here are other European search engines and directories to try:

- **AltaVista United Kingdom**
  http://uk.altavista.com

- **Belgian Search and Navigation Matrix**
  http://mailserv.cc.kuleuven.ac.be/belgiansearch.html

- **DENet**
  http://info.denet.dk
  DENet is a directory of Danish sites.

- **EuroSeek**—European Directory
  http://webdir.euroseek.com/?ilang=en&catid=260
  You'll find that this site is not the easiest to use. Click on the
  name of a country, then Business and Economy. Results usually include local companies and associations with links and
  brief descriptions.

- **Sear.ch**
  http://search.bluewindow.ch/search?pg=home&lang=en
  This Swiss directory is searchable in English, German, French,
  and Italian.

- **Search Europe**
  http://www.searcheurope.com

- **The Web Collection**
  http://www.hugmot.is/ssafn/english
  This site is a directory of Icelandic resources.

- **UK Plus**
  http://www.ukplus.co.uk/ukplus/SilverStream/Pages/
  pgUKPlusHome.html
  Here you'll find a directory for the U.K.

- **VIBES—Virtual International Business & Economic
  Sources—Western Europe**
  http://libweb.uncc.edu/ref-bus/reg.htm#eurw
  This site from the University of North Carolina, Charlotte,
  includes Banking & Finance, Business & Marketing, Trade
  Issues & Statistics, Stock Market, and more. It also contains a
  list of European countries with links to companies and other
  country sources.

- **Voila**
  http://www.voila.com/Network
  Voila is a search engine covering the Netherlands, Belgium,
  United Kingdom, Spain, Portugal, Denmark, France, Italy, and
  Germany. It is searchable in English, Danish, Dutch, French,
  Italian, Portuguese, and Spanish.

Yellow Pages

In a similar vein to directories, an online yellow pages directory is
always a good business reference. The British Telecommunications
Yell Business site [http://www.yellowpagesbusiness.co.uk] works
well for the U.K., particularly since the business area is separate
from the leisure area. It is, however, quite a bit different from the traditional yellow pages sites.

Yell Business is divided into three sections: International Trading,
U.K. Business Services, and Direct Marketing. Most portions of the
site require free registration. You may search for companies using
various criteria and receive a count of the number of companies
that match the criteria. The data itself, however, is not free. The cost
displays in British pounds; after viewing it, you can purchase the

information immediately online and download the data. You may also search for credit reports on U.K. companies, which are available for a fee.

Other Western European online yellow pages sites are listed here:

- **Austria**
  http://www.gelbeseiten.at

- **Belgium**
  http://www.infobel.com/belgium/yp/search/default.asp

- **Denmark**
  http://www.degulesider.dk (not in English)

  http://www.yellowpages.dk (English)

- **France**
  http://wf.pagesjaunes.fr/pj.cgi?lang=en

- **Germany**
  http://www.teleauskunft.de/NSAPI/Anfrage?AKTION=
  zeSuchseiteGelbeSeiten&SPRACHE=EN&SESSIONID=
  0380b1902938aa7a210007a40b&VERZEICHNIS=3&BUAB=
  BUNDESWEIT&H_NUTZUNGSBEDINGUNGEN=TRUE

- **Ireland**
  http://www.goldenpages.ie

- **Italy**
  http://multilingua.seat.it/cgi-bin/webdriver?MIval=mdrindex
  &lingua=INGL

- **Luxembourg**
  http://www.directory.lu/ap/default.asp?lang=3

- **Netherlands**
  http://www.detelefoongids.nl (not in English)

- **Norway**
  http://www.gulesider.no/index.jsp?spraak=3

- **Portugal**
  http://www.paginasamarelas.pt/home_e.html

- **Spain (not in English)**
  http://www.paginas-amarillas.es/buscador/home_f.html

- **Sweden**
  http://www.foretagstele.se/home-en.html

- **Switzerland**
  http://www.directories.ch/index-en.html

Stock Exchanges

When looking for financial information, a country's stock market often proves a good source. While some stock market sites might only carry stock quotes, others might include news and analysis of companies and/or industries. The following sites cover Western European stock markets with a presence on the Internet:

- **Austria—Vienna Stock Exchange**
  http://www.wbag.at/index_english.html

- **Belgium—Brussels Exchange**
  http://www.stockexchange.be

- **Denmark—Copenhagen Stock Exchange**
  http://www.xcse.dk/uk/index.asp

- **Europe—Pan European Exchange**
  http://www.easdaq.be/easdaq.htm

- **Finland—Helsinki Stock Exchange**
  http://www.hex.fi/eng/index.html

- **France—Paris Stock Exchange**
  http://www.bourse-de-paris.fr

- **Germany**

  Frankfurt Stock Exchange
  http://www.exchange.de/INTERNET/EXCHANGE/index_e.htm
  Baden-Württembergische Wertpapierbörse zu Stuttgart
  http://www.boerse-stuttgart.de
  Bayerische Börse—Munich Stock Exchange
  http://www.bayerischeboerse.de/start.html

- **Italy**

   Italian Stock Exchange
   http://www.borsaitalia.it/29/129.html
   Milan Stock Exchange—Stock Quotes
   http://robot1.texnet.it/finanza

- **Luxembourg—Luxembourg Stock Exchange**
   http://www.bourse.lu/english/index.shtml

- **Netherlands—Amsterdam Exchanges**
   http://www.aex.nl/aex.asp?taal=en

- **Norway—Oslo Stock Exchange**
   http://www.ose.no/english

- **Portugal—Lisbon Stock Exchange**
   http://www.bvl.pt

- **Spain**

   Barcelona Stock Exchange
   http://www.borsabcn.es
   Bolsa de Madrid
   http://www.bolsamadrid.es/homei.htm

- **Sweden—Stockholm Stock Exchange**
   http://www.omgroup.com/transaction

- **Switzerland—Swiss Exchange**
   http://www.swx.com/top/index_en.html

- **United Kingdom—London Stock Exchange**
   http://www.londonstockexchange.com

Chambers of Commerce and Industry

As mentioned in the second chapter, Chambers of Commerce can be very useful sources of business information. (See Chapter 2—The World for more information on chambers.) Founded in 1958, Eurochambres, Association of European Chambers of Commerce and Industry [http://www.eurochambres.be] currently has more than 1,300 member chambers in more than thirty countries. Approximately 14 million businesses are represented by Eurochambre members. A Members Address List has members broken out by European Union,

Central and Eastern Europe, Mediterranean, and European Free Trade
Association. In all, it lists thirty-two chambers, most with an e-mail
address. Eurochambres also has numerous publications and lists
available, some at no charge, on topics ranging from economic surveys
to electronic commerce.

Numerous American Chambers of Commerce (AmChams) are
located in Western Europe:

- **American Chamber of Commerce in Austria**
  http://www.amcham.or.at

- **American Chamber of Commerce in Belgium**
  http://www.amcham.be

- **American Chamber of Commerce in Denmark**
  http://www.amcham.dk

- **American Chamber of Commerce in France**
  http://www.amchamfrance.org

- **American Chamber of Commerce in Germany**
  http://www.amcham.de

- **American Chamber of Commerce in Italy**
  http://www.amcham.it

- **American Chamber of Commerce in Luxembourg**
  http://www.amcham.lu

- **American Chamber of Commerce in the Netherlands**
  http://home.planet.nl/~amchamnl

- **U.S. Chamber of Commerce in Norway**
  http://www.am-cham.com

- **American Chamber of Commerce in Sweden**
  http://www.amchamswe.se

- **Swiss-American Chamber of Commerce**
  http://www.amcham.ch

Remember that cutlery export business we wanted to start? Using
the International Trade Association (ITA) Web site, we determined
that Western Europe was a large importer and that Germany in particular imported a great deal of cutlery. After mulling over this information, we have a new idea and need more information. In addition

to exporting our company's cutlery to Germany, we'd like to look at Germany's own cutlery manufacturers. Maybe we should partner with or acquire someone who already has a factory in Germany and increase their production capabilities. Where should we look for detailed company information?

A good start is Amadeus by Bureau van Dijk [http://www.bvdsuite.com]. Suzanne Clare, Bureau van Dijk's vice president of U.S. Marketing, described this Belgian company, which has operated for more than twenty-five years as a publisher of international company financial information. Bureau van Dijk has numerous products available in CD-ROM, DVD-ROM, and for use via the Internet or a company intranet, generally on a subscription basis. Most of the products are specific to Europe, although one product focuses on Japan. Amadeus (Analyze Major Databases from European Sources) includes information on more than 3.5 million private and public companies in thirty-one countries and updates every month. The data is organized into a standardized format to mitigate the problems of dealing with the different currencies and reporting methods of multiple countries. Bureau van Dijk receives data from almost thirty source companies throughout Europe. The information originates from the official records of various regulatory agencies.

Bureau van Dijk has another product, Fame—Financial Analysis Made Easy (available from the same site), which is very similar to Amadeus but only covers companies in the U.K. The financial information available on a given company is in much greater detail, since they don't need to standardize data across countries as in the "lowest common denominator" data collection in Amadeus. More than 440,000 public and private companies are included in the Fame database. The look and feel of searching Fame is much the same as Amadeus. Once you've climbed the learning curve on one, you can easily use the other.

While Amadeus and Fame do require subscriptions, two free features are available at the Bureau van Dijk site. On the main page of the site, there is a link for Top 20 European Companies. Clicking on any of the companies listed will get you a full financial report on that company, including location, sales, industry codes, balance sheet, and income statement (generally five years' worth of data), graphs comparing various company financial ratios to its peer group, ownership and management information, and a listing of subsidiaries.

The second free feature is also accessed from the main page: Free Directory. It offers various options for locating companies:

- Company Activity

- Company Name

- Company Size—three options: Very Large/Large, Medium Large/Medium/Medium Small, and Small/Very Small

- Country—specify individual country or all countries

The search results will include the company name(s), industry, and size (using the above-mentioned size criteria). The types of reports available for each company will also display; however, you must subscribe to the service to access the reports. If you need the names of companies meeting specific criteria, this is an easy and free way to do so.

I found Bureau van Dijk's customer support excellent. Phone training was extremely useful and answered all my questions easily. Customer service is strong.

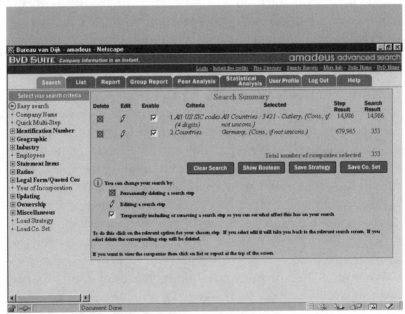

Figure 3.3   Bureau van Dijk Search Summary

Getting back to our cutlery example, we started by searching for cutlery manufacturers. Amadeus offers numerous options when searching by industry, including U.S. SIC (Standard Industrial Classification), NAICS (North American Industrial Classification

System), and numerous other country-specific industry codes. Using the Advanced Search function and drilling down to SIC 3421—Cutlery, I found 14,986 companies listed in the database. Referring to Figure 3.3, we see that by limiting to companies in Germany, we narrow the field down to 353. (In addition to limiting by country, Amadeus offers the options of limiting by city or region within a country.) There are options for saving and/or editing the strategy. (Note: I ran this same search a little over a year earlier. At that time, only 105 companies appeared under SIC 3421 and only sixteen of those in Germany. This shows how quickly the Amadeus database has been growing.)

Choosing the List option from the top of the page provides a list of the first 20 companies in descending order by revenue. The last year for which financial information appeared and the number of employees also display (see Figure 3.4).

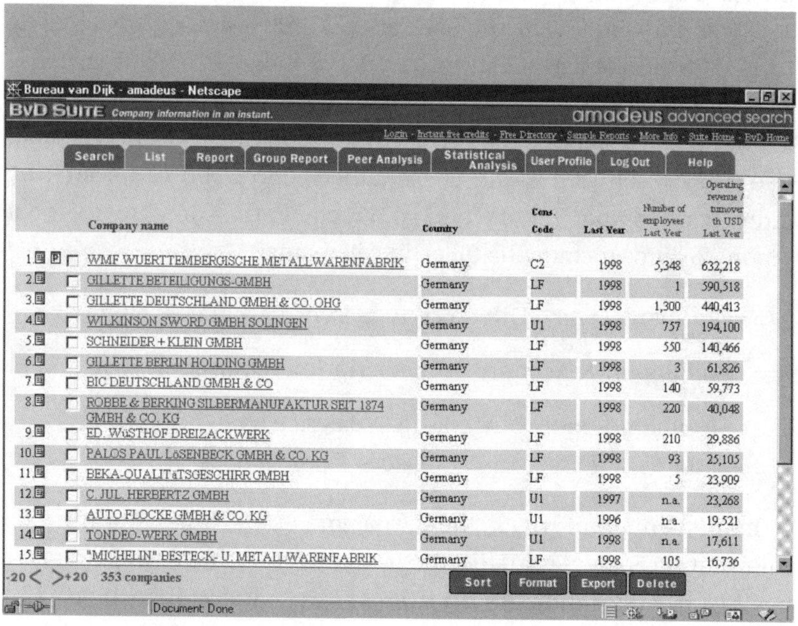

Figure 3.4   Bureau van Dijk Search Results

To see a detailed financial report on any company on the list, highlight the company and click on the Report option. Various graphs, charts, and analyses can be created from the report. Graphical representations of company Profit and Loss Statements also appear. Results can also be exported in various formats including Excel, Word

(.rtf), and ASCII text. By selecting different companies on the list and compiling reports and analyses, we have plenty of information for our cutlery exporting project.

United Kingdom

The United Kingdom is a good place to start. The common language makes it easier to get around the various information sources. Often some of the information that a client seeks may appear in an annual report. Company Annual Reports On Line (CAROL) has a separate section entitled Reports UK [http://www.carol.co.uk] where you can search for the annual report of a company located in the United Kingdom. Search options include searching alphabetically by a company's name or by type of industry, with close to forty industries represented. Once you select the company, the system provides the company's annual report.

If you don't find what you seek at the CAROL site, try the recently revised Corporate Reports [http://www.corpreports.co.uk] (see Figure 3.5). Currently, Summary Reports are free (although you must register at the site); Full Reports require a subscription. You must download a free plug-in software, Djvu, to view the reports. You can search by industry or company name and go directly to the company's annual report. Records include the following elements:

- Company Data—Directory-type information (see Figure 3.5)

- Full Report & Accounts—Subscription required

- Summary Report & Accounts—Balance Sheet, Chairman's Statement, Directors & Advisers, Profit & Loss

Implemented in 1996, the Department of Trade & Industry's Information Society Initiative Programme for Business (ISI) is a partnership between industry and the U.K. government to help U.K. businesses compete in the information-based global economy. ISI obviously realizes the value of trade associations as good sources for business information, since it sponsors the Trade Association Network Challenge (TANC) [http://www.brainstorm.co.uk/TANC/Welcome.html], which produces a long (and searchable) list of U.K. trade associations. Unfortunately, many companies list only their snailmail address in the contact information, but those with a Web site link directly. Another page at the site [http://www.brainstorm. co.uk/TANC/Bookmarks/Welcome.html] separately lists trade associations with a Web site, along with links to government and NGO (nongovernmental organization) sites, business sites, business directories, trade opportunities, and more. These sites mostly focus on business in the U.K., although some have a more general European or international scope.

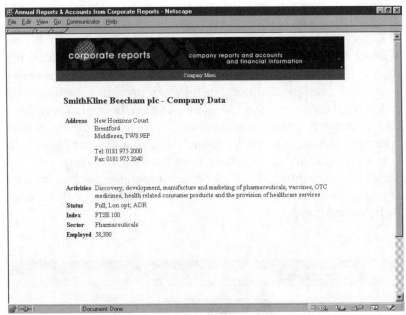

Figure 3.5   Company Data from Corporate Reports

Company Directories

When compiling a list of companies or looking for directory-type information, several free places deserve a quick check before heading to the traditional fee-based systems. Start with Companies House [http://www.companies-house.gov.uk], an agency of the British government responsible for the registration of companies in the U.K. and the dissemination of company information. More than 1.5 million companies list with Companies House. While you can use the site to obtain detailed information on the process of registering a company in the U.K., the site also has a section that provides Free Company Information [http://www.companies-house.gov.uk/frame.cgi?OPT=free]. Here you can search by name to determine whether or not an individual has been disqualified from serving as a company director. The Company Name and Address Index lets you search by company name and obtain information regarding the company's address, date of incorporation, type of company, nature of business, mortgage, previous name(s), branches, and overseas operations. Remember, however, that the search sections in this site only operate on weekdays from 8 A.M. to 8 P.M. (GMT). Forget about using it on weekends and plan to work your time zone schedule around Greenwich Meridian Time.

For more directory information, try AppleGate Directories [http://www.apgate.com]. The company publishes six directories for the U.K. and Ireland: Agribusiness, Electronics, Engineering, Oil & Gas, Plastics & Rubber, and Recruitment Services. You can search the directories by company name, product, town, postal code, or senior personnel. Listings are brief, but they can provide a good starting point in a search, since they do include at least the company address and a contact name. Some entries will also include an e-mail address, Web site, and cursory financial information (see Figure 3.6). One word of caution: AppleGate does not research companies for inclusion in the directories. Companies voluntarily ask for inclusion in one or the other of the directories, so the directories on this site are by no means comprehensive.

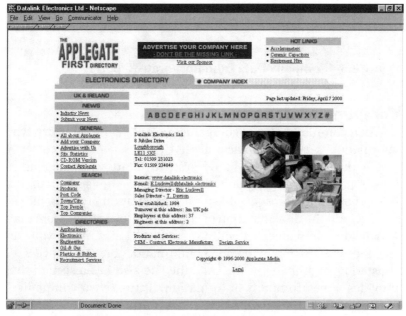

Figure 3.6   Sample Entry from the AppleGate Directory

The Enterprise Zone [http://www.enterprisezone.org.uk] targets small and medium enterprises (SMEs). While it provides a great deal of information about starting a company in the U.K., the site also has a Business Directory. Here you can search by company name, product or service, town, county, or postal code. Searching on the pharmaceutical industry returned over fifty companies. The search results screen shows the company name, town, and specialty. Some companies also have links to e-mail and Web sites (see Figure 3.7). The specialty section allows you to link to more traditional directory-type listings. One word of caution, when using this site, don't assume that the first companies on the list are the biggest or the most well-known. For a fee, companies can have their names listed at the top of the list.

British Trade International [http://www.brittrade.com], a government organization, is a joint effort of the Foreign and Commonwealth Office and the Department of Trade and Industry to support British trade and investment. The most interesting portion is the industry overviews with profiles on almost 50 industries, including Aerospace, Biotechnology, Construction, Environmental, Pharmaceuticals, and Telecoms. Some of the topics covered in the profiles are as follows:

- Links to sector exhibitions and seminars

- Priority markets for trade promotion for the next three to five years (countries segregated by high priority and priority)

- Sector overview

- Sector trade associations

- Subsectors covered

Directory information for British Trade International comes from TradeUK [http://www.tradeuk.com]. In the International Buyers section, you choose your own country in order to get to the search screen. You may then search for British suppliers by company name, product, sector, or service.

Searchengine.com [http://uk.searchengine.com/english] offers searching in multiple categories; most of them consumer-oriented. However, a category for Business allows you to search by numerous business categories and industries (see Figure 3.8). Once you choose a category, the system will display subcategories. For example, if you choose Engineering, you will see Civil Engineering and Mechanical Engineering as subcategories. After selecting either of them, you will get a list of companies displayed that includes links to the companies' Web sites.

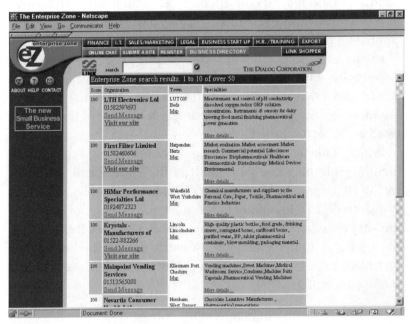

Figure 3.7   Search Results—The Enterprise Zone

As our final directory site, we recommend Yahoo! Finance—UK & Ireland [http://uk.biz.yahoo.com/p/ukie/a]. Here, as with most other directories, you can search by company name or industry. When searching by industry, you can also sort companies by market capitalization. Searching on Food Producers & Processors, we see that Unilever clearly leads the pack, followed by Cadbury Schweppes PLC (see Figure 3.9). Going to the profile for Unilever, we get a nice overview of the company, including activities, head office, and topline financial information (see Figure 3.10).

The Customs House has collected customs duties for England since the eighth century. At some point The Customs House was renamed The HM Customs and Excise Information Service [http://www.hmce.gov.uk] and now has a government Web site that helps to explain various business taxes and regulations, including VAT, excise, and customs. For information not available directly online, the site provides a local contact for obtaining further details.

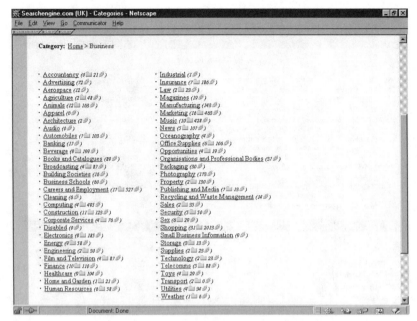

Figure 3.8 **Business Categories for SearchEngine.com**

Food producers & processors		Market Capitalisation Listing - Alphabetical Listing		
Company	Recent Share Price (£)	Market Cap (Mill.£)	Last AR	
			Profit Margin %	ROCE %
Unilever	411.00	31,512.00	11.20	31.50
Cadbury Schweppes PLC	413.00	8,341.00	16.30	41.80
Associated British Foods PLC	376.00	2,979.00	7.50	14.10
United Biscuits (Holdings) PLC	263.00	1,244.00	7.30	22.20
Tate & Lyle PLC	228.00	1,043.00	5.30	10.50
Unigate PLC	300.00	688.00	6.10	20.20
Northern Foods PLC	107.00	629.00	8.50	21.60
Geest PLC	501.00	369.00	5.20	25.00
Brake Bros PLC	638.00	333.00	4.00	21.10
Booker PLC	128.00	316.00	0.90	8.90
Express Dairies PLC	87.50	261.00	8.30	39.60
Hazlewood Foods PLC	82.50	191.00	6.00	17.60
Dairy Crest Group PLC	137.00	155.00	6.10	23.40
Matthews (Bernard) PLC	112.00	139.00	8.20	18.90
Perkins Foods PLC	93.50	117.00	7.80	23.40
Devro PLC	58.00	93.10	12.00	17.80
PIC International Group PLC	31.50	92.30	-2.50	4.30
W T Foods PLC	47.50	72.30	11.50	25.80

Figure 3.9 **Food Producers & Processors by Market Cap—Yahoo!
Finance**

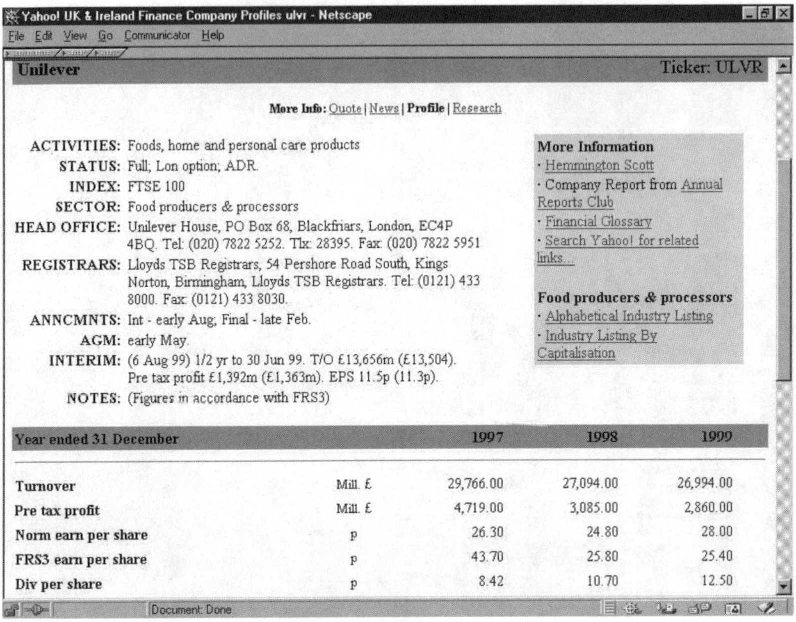

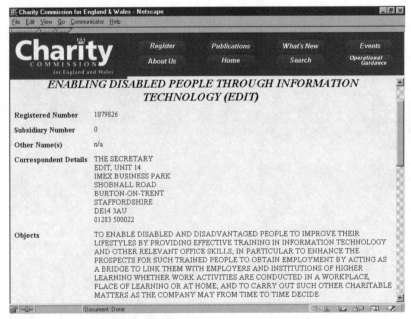

Figure 3.10   Partial Company Listing—Yahoo! Finance

Figure 3.11   Partial Entry—Charity Commission for England & Wales

The Charity Commission for England and Wales maintains a database of over 180,000 charities in those two countries [http://www.charity-commission.gov.uk]. To find a charity, you can search by name, keywords, area, or registered number. Entries include other names for the charity, contact information, objectives, and any subsidiaries (see Figure 3.11).

France

Looking for information about doing business in France? If you look nowhere else, check out Invest in France Agency—North America (IFA-NA) [http://www.investinfrancena.org]. DATAR (Délégation à l'Aménagemment du Térritoire et à l'Action Régionale), the French government agency responsible for foreign investment, established IFA in 1969 to assist North American companies doing business in France. This site overflows with information—and all of it free!

The section "Doing Business in France" covers areas such as legal structures, taxation, employment regulations, financial assistance, environmental protection, international trade, and industrial and intellectual property rights. This represents key information for anyone trying to decide whether or not to begin operations in France. Pair this with what's found in the Why France? section (economic statistics, including market size, inflation, and gross domestic product, as well as information on transportation and infrastructure, the telecommunications network, productivity and labor costs, and corporate and personal income taxes), and you might be ready to make a decision.

The Key Industries and Operations section carries small market research reports on the automotive, biotechnology, computer hardware and peripherals, semiconductors, software and multimedia, and telecommunications industries. The reports contain a great deal of useful information, much of it in chart, graphical, or picture format (see Figure 3.12). They also offer short overviews of four types of operations: Call Centers, Headquarters, Logistics, and Research & Development. Announcements and descriptions of existing facilities available for purchase or lease appear in this section, often accompanied by photos of the facility.

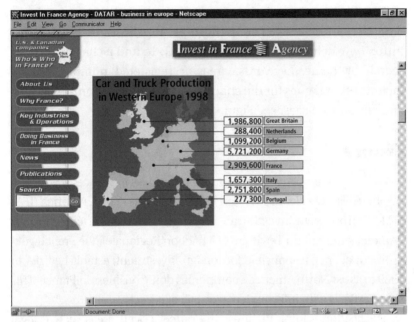

Figure 3.12   Map from Market Research Study—Invest in France

The Publications section has more detailed reports available in PDF format. Topics covered include the auto supply industry, biopharmaceuticals, call centers, human resources, and information technology.

News covers a variety of topics and contains the monthly publication News@Invest in France. Investment Reports list new corporate activities in France by industry and company.

A final interesting portion to the site is Who's Who in France. This contains The 200 Largest French Subsidiaries of North American Corporations as of December 1999, case studies of twelve American companies with successful operations in France, and quotes from American executives involved in operations in France.

The site's search function, which I had found agonizingly slow a year before, has improved greatly. Results appear about as quickly as one would expect and include relevancy rankings, title, abstract, and a direct link to the article.

If what you need doesn't appear at the site, try calling one of the seven IFA-NA offices in North America. You can find contact information at the site. Given the comprehensive coverage and beautiful layout of the IFA site, one can anticipate a pleasant and productive experience from communicating with one of the offices directly.

Belgium

From France, let's hop on over to nearby Belgium. The Belgian Foreign Trade Board (BFTB) [http://www.obcebdbh.be/en/obce/index.html] provides a site loaded with information and statistics. After reviewing this site, you might wonder how you (and your clients) have overlooked all that little Belgium has to offer. Contrary to the name, the site actually combines information on Belgium and Luxembourg, or the Belgium-Luxembourg Economic Union (BLEU). Some interesting statistics can be found here:

- BLEU is the world's eleventh biggest exporter and tenth biggest importer
- BLEU is the world's leading exporter of raw and cut diamonds
- BLEU is the world's second biggest exporter of chocolate and chocolate products

If diamonds are a girl's best friend, then between the diamonds and the chocolate, Belgium must be a girl's favorite country.

At the BFTB site, you will find reports and statistics on BLEU foreign trade; lists of Trade Federations and Associations, Chambers of Commerce, Airports, Port Associations, and a Traders Association (most with links directly to the Web sites); and a calendar of International Trade Fairs in which the BFTB will participate throughout the year. An Exporters' Directory carries approximately 11,000 listings searchable by company name or product/service. BFTB also creates and hosts Web sites for small and medium-sized enterprises (SMEs). You can search these sites either alphabetically by company name or by industry sector.

Belgian Economic Assets has brief statistical overviews of the following fourteen industries:

- Agriculture
- Banking
- Chemicals
- Construction
- Diamonds & Jewelry
- Electrical Engineering/ Electronics
- Food & Drinks
- Furniture
- Glass
- Mechanical Engineering
- Metal & Plastic Products
- Non-ferrous Metals
- Textiles, Clothing, & Leather Products
- Transportation Equipment

Going to The BFTB Publications for the Foreign Business World page [http://www.obcebdbh.be/en/Services/biec.html], you will find a brief discussion of the quarterly review *Belgium Economic & Commercial Information*. Scrolling down the page, you see links for about twenty previous and future issues, each one a detailed industry analysis for areas such as Belgian leather, food processing, telecommunications, and plastics.

If all else fails and you cannot find what you need online, you can use the list of Belgian Chambers of Commerce abroad, including two in the United States, to initiate contacts for additional information.

One complaint: While loaded with wonderful information (and all for free!), the BFTB site loads that information extremely slowly. Going from page to page within the site is painful. Before you tackle this site, be certain you have some paperwork on hand to keep you busy while the pages load.

The Federation of Belgian Companies (VBO/FEB) [http://www.vbo-feb.be/ukindex.htm] is another useful site. The VBO/FEB is an employers organization representing more than 30,000 Belgian companies. Unfortunately, a good portion of the material in this site is only available in French or Dutch, but you can still find some useful information on Belgium in English.

The Members section covers three different categories of members, each with its own listing. Most listings include a description of the member's activities, as well as contact information and links to Web sites. Many of the entries are associations, always helpful contacts when conducting research. The Other Sites section includes several additional essential sites for anyone interested in business in Belgium.

Spain

Finding business information about Spain on the Web was more difficult than I anticipated; there was little available in English. While I expected that the majority of sites would be in Spanish, I never dreamt that I would also encounter Castellano, Catalan, Basque, and even Galician. (I must confess, I was intrigued by the mention of Galician, as I had never heard of it. So, like any good researcher, I set out to learn more. Galicia is an area in northwestern Spain composed of the provinces Lugo, La Coruña, Pontevedra, and Orense. Galician is a Romance language belonging to the Iberian romance family of languages. Looking at some language examples, it appears to be a combination of Spanish and Portuguese.)

Since I'm partial to chambers of commerce, let's begin our journey through Spain with the Spain–U.S. Chamber of Commerce [http://www.spainuscc.org/index.html]. Based in New York, the Chamber was founded in 1959 and, as expected, is focused on fostering trade and investment between the two countries. While the site doesn't contain too much value-added material, it does offer some suggestions.

The most useful portion of the site might well be the links to the Web sites of most of the Chamber's corporate members; in both the U.S. and Spain, several products are offered on a fee-for-service basis, such as:

- Macroeconomic statistical data

- Commercial and/or industrial statistical data

- Tariffs and customs fee information

- Directories of Spanish manufacturers

- Listings of importers and exporters in Spain

- Customized market research studies

Spain: The Business Link is a quarterly business journal published by the Chamber with an emphasis on bilateral trade issues. The previous two issues are available at the site; while the issues aren't searchable, the tables of contents are listed along with links to the stories.

Two potentially interesting publications are offered for sale: Spanish Subsidiaries of U.S. Corporations and U.S. Subsidiaries of Spanish Corporations. A sample page of each is displayed at the site.

The Chamber has compiled a list of useful links covering topics such as the Spanish financial markets, banks, media, trade and business directories, government sites, and more. Few, if any, of these sites have an English option.

Typically Spanish [http://www.typicallyspanish.com/] is a good site for news from Spain, with searchable archives dating back to January 2000. The site is updated daily and has a synopsis of that day's news. And, for those of you interested in gambling, the winning lottery numbers are also posted.

Links to Spanish newspapers, magazines, and television and radio stations are supplied via the Media page. While there is a Business section, I did not find it particularly useful. The content at Typically Spanish is offered in eight other languages: Spanish, French, German, Italian, Dutch, Polish, Russian, and Swedish.

Invest in Spain [http://www.investinspain.org] is organized by the Spanish Ministry of Economy. Choose About Spain from the main page and click on The Economy. Here there is information on structural reforms, basic economic indicators, market size, and foreign trade statistics. Spain's main trading partners are the European Union countries; interestingly, the U.S. only accounts for approximately 5% of both Spanish imports and exports. However, looking at the FDI Statistics section (Foreign Direct Investment), we see that the U.S. is responsible for over 25% of the foreign direct investment in Spain.

Following the Industry link, you will find overviews of six industry sectors:

- Automotive
- Chemical
- Electronics
- Food
- High Tech
- Telecommunications

The site also contains a discussion of Spain's infrastructure, including roads, railways, ports, airports, and national technology parks. The FAQ section answers questions about Spain's labor market regulations and includes a link to an English version of the Labor Guide, prepared by the Ministry of Labor and Social Affairs.

There are two categories in the Links area: Regional Agencies and Guide to Business. Regional Agencies displays a map of Spain divided into the various Autonomous Communities (regions) of the country with links to the local government sites for each. The Guide to Business has been prepared by ICEX (Instituto Español de Comercio Exterior). These areas, among others, are covered:

- The Spanish Financial System

- Company and Commercial Law

- Investment Grants and Incentives in Spain

- Labor and Social Security Regulations

As mentioned previously, there really isn't a great deal of Spanish business information on the Internet in English; this may change with time. If you're really stuck and the above sites don't answer your questions, try some of the search engines and directories listed in Chapter 5—Latin America and the Caribbean. Occasionally these sources include Spain, even though it's obviously not located in Latin America. Depending upon what you need and if you have even a rudimentary knowledge of Spanish (or French or Italian), you might also try some of the sites offered by the Spanish government. Sometimes you can look at a chart or graph and discern the headings, which makes the numerical content easy to interpret. Start with the site of the Instituto Nacional de Estadística (National Statistics Institute) [http://www.ine.es/]. As the Spanish government's agency for collecting and disseminating statistics, it offers a great deal of statistical information on economics, industry, agriculture, demographics, and more.

Portugal

When I was in junior high, my social studies class studied Europe. Each student had to write a report on his or her assigned country and do a presentation in front of the class. I had the misfortune of being assigned Portugal, which was considered a relatively insignificant country. My trip to the local library turned up nothing, aside from the requisite write-ups in the various encyclopedias. I remember cajoling my parents into taking me to the big library downtown, where I finally found a few measly books on Portugal. Needless to say, my grade on that project was not one of my highest, due to the lack of information. If only today's Internet had existed then, my whole future might have turned out differently.

For example, I could have tried Welcome to Portugal [http://www.portugal.org], developed by Investment, Trade and Tourism of Portugal (ICEP), a government agency that operates under the Ministry of Economy. The Information section offers basic background information about Portugal (history, geography, population, GDP, airports) as well as socioeconomic indicators. It also describes brochures covering about a dozen industries that export from Portugal including wine, home textiles, apparel, auto components, cork, and natural stone and tile. The actual brochures may be ordered at no charge.

The Buying section breaks into three parts:

• Trade Shows—dates, locations, industries

• Associations and Financial Institutions—primarily contact information for banks

• Contacts and Addresses—contact information for industry associations and chambers of commerce

Much of the useful information for the business researcher appears in the Investing section including details of major investment projects. Each project lists the company, country, dollar amount of the investment, and more (see Figure 3.13). Investing also contains more economic data and a few detailed (considering they're free) industry market studies: auto sector, electric and electronics, and the service industry. There are descriptions for a Guide for Investors and Business Portugal, a monthly newsletter on the country's business climate; both are available for ordering. The Investment Links section covers government sites of importance to the foreign investor.

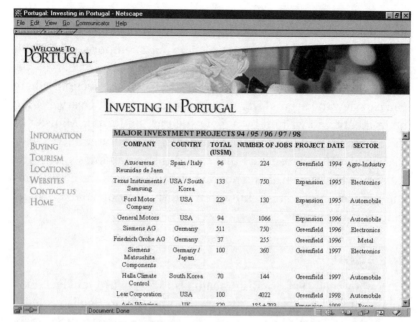

**Figure 3.13   Partial List of Investment Projects—Investing in
            Portugal**

At one time, this site had a search function, but it didn't work well.
That probably explains the current lack of any search capabilities.
Still, given all of the information available at Welcome to Portugal, I
would certainly use the site and keep checking to see if the search
function reappears.

One last note: For nonworkaholics, the site also provides a comprehensive section on tourism.

If you don't find everything you need at Welcome to Portugal,
check out PortugalOffer [http://www.portugaloffer.com], put
together by the Portuguese company Financetar and managed by its
Chairman and CEO, António Neto da Silva, a Portuguese entrepreneur, who is the former Deputy Chairman of the Portuguese Export
Promotion Board and former Secretary of State for External Trade
and Foreign Investment. The number of companies listed at the site
is purposely limited to offer only the "créme de la créme" (presumably in the opinion of Mr. da Silva). As with many of the other business sites discussed, you can search the site by company name,
region, industry, number of employees, and annual sales.

The first page of the site offers links to summaries of some of the
current top Portuguese business news articles. They also offer an

archive that goes back approximately two-and-a-half months. The Portugal Overview link leads to an extensive business overview of Portugal, including information on exports, imports, and GDP. Clicking on either Agriculture & Fisheries, Industry, or Services & Trade will take you to the main page for each of those sections where you can view the Sector Overview for that area. Sector Overviews are quite meaty and written by people such as the former Minister of the Economy and the former Minister of Agriculture. Each sector also divides into subsectors that in turn list companies within the subsector. Here you will find not only descriptions of the companies and contact information, but often information on market share, exports, and revenue.

Sweden

Do they really eat Swedish meatballs in Sweden? Frankly, I don't know, but finding Swedish business information in English is quite a trick. As one would expect, most of what exists appears in Swedish. Since my trusty translation software doesn't handle Swedish, that makes things a bit difficult.

BolagsFakta [http://www.bolagsfakta.se/bolagsfakta/index_eng_start.html] has provided annual reports and other financial information about quoted Swedish companies since 1995. The site is a bit confusing to navigate at first but, with practice, becomes easier to use.

Start out by choosing an industry sector. These sectors are represented:

- Automotive
- Building & Construction
- Business
- Chemical
- Consultory Services
- Education & Employment
- Energy
- Environment & Recycling
- Fairs & Exhibitions
- Finance
- Forestry
- Healthcare & Medical
- Iron & Steel
- Software
- Textile & Clothing
- Travel & Tourism

Some categories provide links to industry articles and an alphabetical list of companies. Company names link to directory-style information that includes a good description of the company and its products. Other categories contain links to industry associations.

The site offers the opportunity to subscribe to more than thirty e-mail newsletters on a variety of topics, some a bit more specialized than you might expect, such as Early Adopters, E-commerce, Web Profits, and Web TV.

When last checked, the site appeared to have undergone a massive overhaul and some of the best information no longer appeared. But I hope that the overhaul will continue and the missing information will reappear in some form or another.

Italy

Finding Italian business information on the Internet in English is almost impossible. While on my quest for information in English, I decided to cheat a little and found the site for the Italian Trade Commission in Canada (ITC) [http://www.italcomm.com/e/index.html]. Here, of course, I had my choice of three languages: English, French, or Italian. I decided to play it safe and choose English. Even here, however, not all links led to English. Let's look at those that did.

The first stop at the ITC site should be the Economic News section, which is full of charts and graphs dealing with Italy's economic outlook. Some of the more useful topics that are covered relate to imports, exports, and trade balance. Next, let's check the Select Opportunities section, which appears as a pop-up window. Eight industry sectors are represented here along with some of the companies in each sector. You can either scroll down the list to view the entries for all of the companies or you can choose the name of a company and go directly to its entry that contains contact information, industry sector, e-mail and Internet links, and a short description of the company's business.

With the Links section, it's hit or miss as to whether the listed sites will appear in English. For example, I was pretty confident that the site Business and Investment in Italy would be in English, but it wasn't. Surprisingly, the National Institute of Statistics (ISTAT) [http://www.istat.it/homeing.html] provides an English option. This is extremely helpful, as ISTAT compiles some very useful information. (Note: Even with the English option, some of the sections of the ISTAT site are still only available in Italian.)

One of ISTAT's reports is *Italy in Figures*, a PDF document covering Italian demographics, economic statistics, and imports and exports by sector in good detail. The report has little text; most of the information is presented in tables, charts, graphs, and maps. The News section has new statistical releases such as industrial turnover, retail trade index, and foreign trade.

Back in the Links section of the ITC, another site turned out to offer English options:

- **Italian Ministry of Foreign Affairs**
  http://www.esteri.it/eng/index.htm

The ITC has several publications online available for download in PDF format. Topics include High Technology (several documents), Bottling Technology, and Food Processing. To order other publications, follow the instructions for obtaining a list. Lastly, ITC maintains a directory of industry trade shows held in Italy.

Germany

Speaking of countries for which I don't speak the language, let's give Germany a try. I figured with Italy I had it a bit easier because I spoke Spanish, a language somewhat similar to Italian. Anything in German would definitely fall outside my reach. Luckily, the first German site I tried was in English and quite useful too.

Founded in 1870, Commerzbank [http://www.commerzbank.com] is one of the top three private-sector banks in Frankfort. In the left column on its main page, choose Economic Data and Forecasts. Several documents containing information on the German Economy appear in this section:

- Cost of Living Index—compares all of Germany to Eastern and Western Germany

- Economy Monthly—selected monthly economic indicators

- Forecast—historical economic indicators and a one-year forecast

- Producing Sector Expected Output—historical and projected output by industry

- Sector Update—an industrial overview with specifics on a few key industries

A great deal of international information is also available here including:

- Commodity Prices—an international overview

- Interest Rate Forecasts for Industrialized Nations

- Interest Rates and Currencies for Germany and Europe

- Viewpoint—articles on German and European economic issues

The Federal Commissioner for Foreign Investment in Germany [http://www.foreign-direct-investment.de] has a site relatively short on substance, but long on useful links. Before getting to the links, let's discuss what the site itself offers.

Click on Germany at a Glance and you will see several categories. Economy gives an up-to-date view of the economy and Economic Sectors discusses the structure of German industry and competition. After reading those two sections, I'd suggest skipping ahead to the Additional Information area and perusing the links listed.

These links had information in English:

- **Confederation of German Employers' Associations**
  http://www.bda-online.de/www/bdaonline.nsf/EnglishFrameSet

- **Federal Statistical Office—Germany**
  http://www.statistik-bund.de/e_home.htm

- **Hamburg Institute for Economic Research**
  http://www.hwwa.de/hwwa_engl.html

- **Institute for Economic Research**
  http://www.ifo.de/orcl/dbssi/main_e.htm

- **Invest in Germany**
  http://www.invest-in-germany.de/Engl/index1.htm

For directory information on German companies, try the Seibt Directories [http://industrie.seibt.com/e_index.htm]. Five different directories are available for searching:

- Environmental Technology

- Industry

- Medical Technology—surgical instruments, medical devices, pharmaceutical technologies, dental goods, pharmaceutical equipment, rehabilitation devices, hospital equipment

- Packaging Industry

- Surface Technology

As with many other directories, companies pay for inclusion. So use caution with your search results and don't expect them to be all-inclusive for any particular industry, product, or service.

One more directory for German companies is the Hoppenstedt Company Database [http://www.Firmendatenbank.de/endex.html]. You can search the database by company name, town, postal code, state, industry, sales, number of employees, or products, with drop-down menus available to help with postal codes and industry titles. If you don't have a subscription to the database, you can only access the contact information. With a paid subscription, you also receive names, titles, and functions of key personnel, industry, products, import/export activities, annual sales, number of employees, legal status, year founded, banking addresses, equity capitalizations, subsidiaries and branch offices, shareholdings in affiliated companies, land ownership, vehicle fleets, EDP-equipment, special product lines, and detailed financial data (in the case of banks).

If you think you would find this database useful on a regular database, you can try it out for two weeks free.

Denmark

I tend to get excited when I find great sites (in English, preferably) from very small countries. It's kind of a Samson versus Goliath type of thing; the little guy trying to make his voice heard. Well, I must admit that Denmark is really out there hustling with some great business information.

Start with Invest in Denmark [http://www.investindk.com], a government investment promotion organization. The site has four main sections:

- Company Profiles

- Facts and Figures

- Invest in Denmark

- News and Info

Invest in Denmark should be the first stop on your tour. Here you find that Denmark promotes four major sectors and why. One is wireless communications, for which they offer a lengthy report. The report includes a discussion of the business climate in Denmark and profiles of companies and suppliers. The profiles cover several topics:

- Background and Core Competencies

- Business Strategy

- Company Policy

- Contact Information

- Number of Employees

- Partnering Interests

- Products

- Turnover

A similar report covers power electronics, defined as the use of microprocessors for the control and/or conversion of electrical power.

Another strong industry sector is distribution and call centers. The full text of the publication, *Hub Denmark*, appears on the site and includes information on Denmark's capabilities in these areas, comments from major international companies regarding their Danish operations, and a list of foreign companies with distribution or call centers in Denmark.

The final sector addressed is medical, referred to as Medico. It too carries overview information and statements from foreign companies with Danish operations.

The News and Info section has current and past copies of the *Newsletter*. Each *Newsletter* contains current news on important industry sectors as well as the latest news from foreign companies established in Denmark.

Facts and Figures covers many aspects of business in Denmark. These are some of the areas touched upon:

- Business Costs—property market, leaseholds, electricity, and telecommunications costs

- Distribution and Logistics—infrastructure, distribution system by road, air, and sea

- Education and Labor Qualifications

- Establishing a Business in Denmark

- Facts About Denmark—economic statistics, overview of the economy

- Foreign Direct Investments

- Incentives

- Labor Costs and Productivity

- Living in Denmark

- Taxation

- The Danish Labor Market

The Company Profiles section is a bit of a misnomer. Although more than thirty companies have entries here, the section doesn't really offer full profiles. Instead, each has an overall description of the company and its Danish operations, followed by remarks responding to the question "Why Denmark?"

If you want statistics on the electronics industry, the Danish Electronics Industry Association [http://www.ei.dk/default.asp] is the place to go. It has over five years of data compiled and the following tables:

- Ten Largest Markets for Danish Electronics (see Figure 3.14)

- Danish Electronics by Industry Group

- Total Danish Electronics Imports and Exports—professional electronics, consumer electronics, and components

- Total Sales in the Danish Electronics Industry

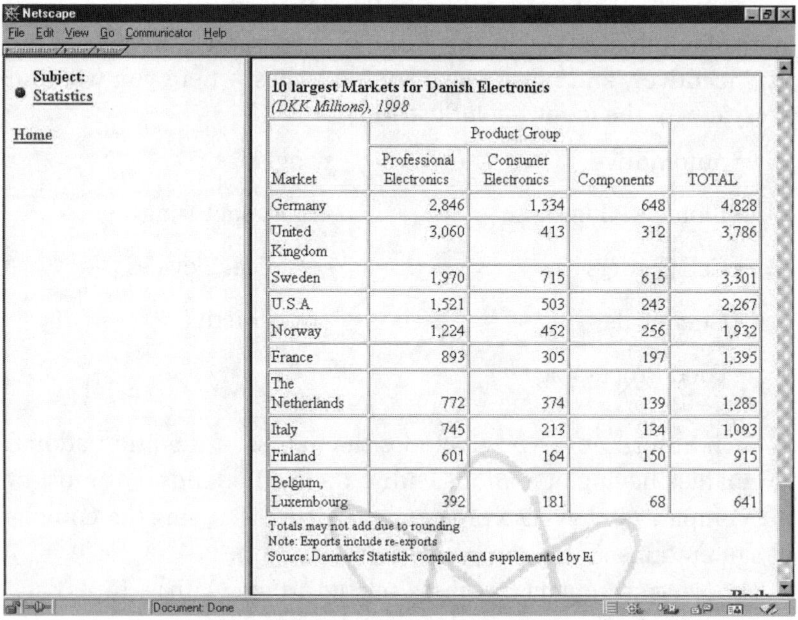

10 largest Markets for Danish Electronics
(DKK Millions), 1998

Market	Product Group: Professional Electronics	Consumer Electronics	Components	TOTAL
Germany	2,846	1,334	648	4,828
United Kingdom	3,060	413	312	3,786
Sweden	1,970	715	615	3,301
U.S.A.	1,521	503	243	2,267
Norway	1,224	452	256	1,932
France	893	305	197	1,395
The Netherlands	772	374	139	1,285
Italy	745	213	134	1,093
Finland	601	164	150	915
Belgium, Luxembourg	392	181	68	641

Totals may not add due to rounding
Note: Exports include re-exports
Source: Danmarks Statistik. compiled and supplemented by Ei

Figure 3.14 Ten Largest Markets for Danish Electronics—Danish Electronics Industry Association

It also provides a directory of companies belonging to the association. Directory entries include contact information, a link to the company's Web site, top personnel, e-mail links, and a brief description of the company's activities. You can also search for companies via an alphabetical product list. Additional information at the site appears only in German.

Members of the Danish IT Industry Association [http://www.itb.dk] include manufacturers, importers, distributors, retailers, OEMs, and software houses with products ranging from office equipment to sophisticated computer and telecommunications systems. All members are listed alphabetically in the association's database. Information includes contact information and a paragraph describing the company and its activities. The site does have a search function searchable in Danish or English, with appropriate little flags at the bottom of the page. However, everything else on the search screen is in Danish and, as hard as I tried, I could not figure out how to search in English.

The Netherlands

The Netherlands Foreign Investment Agency (NFIA) [http://www.nfia.com] makes a very compelling argument for investing in the Netherlands. Start with About the Netherlands and you will learn about the workforce, the economy, geography, transportation, tax incentives, and more. Next, try Industries, where you will find overviews of the following industries:

- Automotive
- Biotechnology
- Call Centers
- Chemicals
- Food Processing
- Logistics
- Manufacturing
- Medical Devices
- New Media

Each industry overview includes the names of the international companies having operations within the Netherlands. For most of the companies, they also provide an article discussing the company's operations in the Company Profiles section.

The News section has business-related articles with archives back to June 1997. The NFIA publishes *Netherlands Investment News* three times a year and provides the full text at the site. Articles in *Netherlands Investment News* generally include a profile of one of the country's regions, a report on the investment climate, news about the foreign companies in the country, special industry reports, and more.

Regional Wrap-Up

As you can see, sources for Western European business information are, quite literally, all over the map. I would venture a guess that many of us will fail to explore many excellent sites due to language barriers. For example, according to Guido Moradei, an information professional in Italy, few Italian producers have taken the opportunity to share information online using international hosts or directly via modem dial-up access. In cases where you have problems with language or access, you might consider developing a contact within the country and considering a subcontracting arrangement.

CHAPTER 4

CENTRAL AND EASTERN EUROPE

Central and Eastern Europe—has an exotic ring to it, doesn't it? Many of us know so little about that part of the world, and the rapid changes over the last decade have made it hard to keep current. Seems like every time we turn around, a new country springs up. The upside of all the change is that a whole new area for business and trade has opened up. Previously inaccessible markets have become hotbeds of competition. Open a newspaper or a magazine, turn on the television news, and you're bound to come across stories about this area.

Don't be fooled, though. In spite of all the change and all the news, it's not easy to find reliable business information for this region. It takes a lot of digging and creativity. The languages alone are enough to make your head swim. When you add all of the wars, fighting, and general discontent into the equation, it's amazing that there is so much interest in doing business here. Companies entering (or continuing) in business in Central and Eastern Europe need to be extremely aware of the potential dangers to personnel and property. All of this attests to the extreme necessity of assessing the regional situation on a continuing basis. To help you on your way, the countries of Azerbaijan, the Czech Republic, Estonia, Greece, Poland, Russia, Latvia, and Lithuania are covered individually in this chapter.

Search Engines and Directories

For a good jumping off point, try Orientation [http://www.orientation.com], from Orientation Global Network, Inc., an Internet portal with regional services for Central and Eastern Europe, as well as Africa, the Middle East, Asia, Oceania, and Latin America/Caribbean. Started in Hong Kong in 1998, the company is now based in New York, though still maintaining Hong Kong offices. The Orientation Global Network currently has approximately twenty products: six are regional and more than twenty are country. They license regional products to local partners in each country. For example, Orientation Czech Republic is a joint effort of Orientation and the local partner, a company called Yellow Duck. Partners tend to be leading ISPs or content providers in each country.

The main page for Central and Eastern Europe [http://eeu.orientation.com] offers a variety of options for searching, including a focus by country or topic. More than twenty countries are represented with topics running the gamut from Art & Literature to Travel & Exploration. For our purposes, the most useful topic would likely be Business & Trade, although, depending upon the search, I would not rule out Health & Science or Internet & Computers.

Choosing Business & Trade, we see several subtopics displayed:

- Associations & Organizations

- Business Opportunities

- Classifieds

- Companies & Industries

- Cybermalls & Shops

- Directories

- Doing Business In ...

- Economy

- Finance

- Marketing

- Media/Publications

- Shows & Events

- Transport

Click on any of the subtopics and you will see a list of the sites Orientation has indexed on that topic. Each item includes a brief description, the name of the country covered, and the language of the site. Descriptions tend to be quite frank, and, if a site is not useful, Orientation will quickly note that fact. For example, they commented on one site, the Czech Top 100, "Absolutely useless listing of names of 100 Czech companies. No criteria are given and there are no links" (see Figure 4.1).

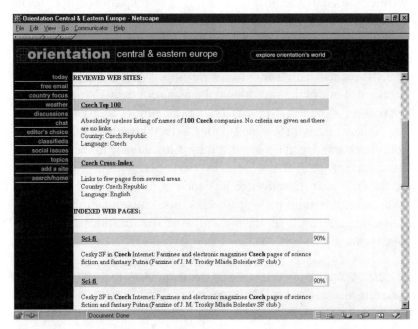

Figure 4.1 Web Site Reviews—Orientation—Central & Eastern Europe

Similarly, if you choose a country from the main page, the system will return a list of subtopics for that country, as well as news headlines, a weather report, and an exchange rate converter. Several countries in this region have their own Orientation sites:

- Albania
- Bulgaria
- Czech Republic
- Hungary
- Moldova
- Romania
- Russia

The site provides other useful information as well. The Today section offers the top news stories of the region, including business and sports coverage. You can also listen to news in eleven different languages, read the top stories of the day from each country, and browse Orientation's newspaper, magazine, radio, and television Web site collections. Social Issues provides some interesting tools for nonprofits including Find a Consultant, Nonprofit Guides, and Nonprofit Conferences.

The Central and Eastern European Business Directory [http://www.ceebd.co.uk/ceebd/business.htm] can help find companies in a particular industry. However, please keep in mind that companies list in this directory on a voluntary basis, so it is by no means a comprehensive listing.

Two sections of this site could prove especially useful. If you want an overview of one of the countries in the region, click on Countries in the left portion of the screen to see a list of twenty-four countries. Choosing any of them takes you to a copy of the CIA World Factbook entry for that country. Granted, you could get this by going directly to the CIA World Factbook site [http://www.odci.gov/cia/publications/factbook/index.html], but if you're already here, it's handy.

Back on the main page again, this time choose Directory. Scroll down the page and you have a choice of sixteen Industry Sections (see Figure 4.2).

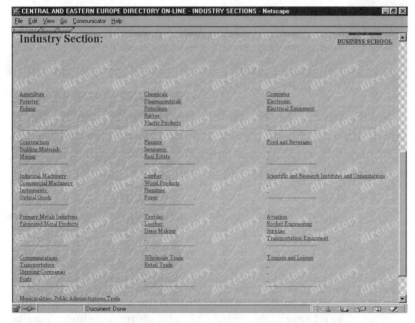

**Figure 4.2   Central & Eastern European Directory Online—
Industry Sections**

I decided to choose Textiles, Leather and Dress Making (#11) and received a list of twenty companies along with a short description of each company. Ivanovo Worsted Mill (production of a wide range of ready-made fabrics of wool blend and yarns) looked promising, so I checked out its entry. I must admit, for a free directory with voluntary listings, the information provided is impressive. In addition to the usual contact information, it carried the e-mail address and the names of the president and managing director. Here's more of what I learned:

- Year founded—1963

- Type of ownership—joint stock company

- Number of employees—3,000

- Annual production—up to 6 million running meters

- Fabrics produced—wool fibers in combination with polyester fibers

- Raw materials used—merino wool fiber, polyester fiber

- Price of ready-made fabric—US$4 to US$8 per running meter

- Awards won by the company—1994 Golden Globe (obviously not the one awarded in the entertainment industry)

- Market share in the region—16%

Not bad for free. Granted, the accuracy of the data could be questioned due to the manner of its collection, but in a part of the world where business information is hard to come by, this is definitely a good start.

Other relevant country and regional search engines and directories contain useful information:

- **CARNet—Croatian Academic and Research Network Directory**
  http://www.hr/wwwhr

- **DIR.bg—The Bulgarian Directory**
  http://www.dirbg.com
  An option for English is at the top of the page. Business & Economics category has many subheadings.

- **East European Search Engine—Sherlock**
http://www.sherlock.cz
You can search all of Eastern Europe or just the Czech Republic or Slovakia.

- **Internet Resources in Kyrgyzstan**
http://www.kg

- **Kyrgyzstan On-line**
http://www.online.kg

- **LATNET—Welcome to Latvia**
http://www.latnet.lv

- **List of Home Pages in Lithuania**
http://neris.mii.lt/serveriai/bendra/servers.html

- **Moldova Internet Resources**
http://www.ournet.md

- **REENIC—Russian and East European Network Information Center**
http://reenic.utexas.edu/reenic.html
This directory is compiled by the Center for Russian, East European, and Eurasian Studies at the University of Texas at Austin.

- **REESWeb—Russian and East European Studies Internet Resources**
http://www.ucis.pitt.edu/reesweb/Econ/econind.html

- **RoBBy—The Hellenic Search Engine**
http://www.robby.gr
Categories such as Government, Science & Education, Organizations, and Computer & Internet are included.

- **Russia on the Net**
http://www.ru
This site is produced by the University of Pittsburgh Business, Economics, and Law Resources.

- **SEEBN.net—Southeastern Europe Business Network**
http://www.seebn.net/search.cfm
This business directory is searchable by company name, country (Albania, Bosnia, Bulgaria, Croatia, Kosovo, Macedonia, Montenegro, or Romania), product group, or product. The site is supported by the U.S. Agency for International Development.

- **VIBES—Virtual International Business & Economic Sources—Eastern Europe**
  http://libweb.uncc.edu/ref-bus/reg.htm#eure
  From the University of North Carolina, Charlotte, this site includes Banking & Finance, Business & Marketing, Business Periodicals, Country Economic Information, and Meta-Pages.

- **YuSearch.com (Yugoslavia)**
  http://www.yusearch.com/start.html

Also, remember to check the directories and search engines listed in the Western Europe chapter. Many of them include Central and Eastern Europe as well.

Yellow Pages

YelloWeb Hungary [http://www.yelloweb.hu/index.asp?lang=1] lets you search for businesses in Hungary. While not comprehensive and charging companies for a listing, it is in English and searchable by category. The more than twenty business categories listed range from Agriculture to Tourism and Catering. You can even drill down within a category to become more specific. For example, I started with Telecommunications and got five subcategories back (see Figure 4.3):

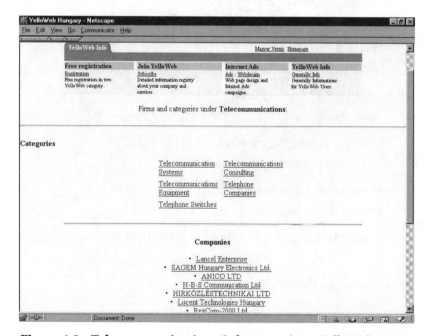

Figure 4.3   Telecommunications Subcategories—YelloWeb Hungary

Telecommunications Systems, Telecommunications Consulting, Telecommunications Equipment, Telephone Companies, and Telephone Switches. The entries contain simple contact information and links to the company's Web site, if available.

Other Internet Yellow Pages sites cover the region with some countries having more than one:

- **Business Belarus**
  http://www.telemedia.by

- **Croatian Telecommunications Telephone Directory**
  http://imenik.hinet.hr/imenik-asp/index.asp?lang=us

- **Czech Republic Golden Pages**
  http://www.zlatestranky.cz/enindex.html

- **Czech Yellow Pages**
  http://www.infobank.sk/cz/indexe.htm

- **Hellas Yellow Pages—Greece**
  http://www.hellasyellow.gr

- **Hungarian Internet Yellow Pages**
  http://www.yellowpages.hu/default.asp

- **Latvia Yellow Pages**
  http://www.telemedia.lv/en

- **Lithuanian Internet Yellow Pages**
  http://www.visalietuva.lt/starten.htm

- **Moldova Yellow Pages (a Yahoo!-style directory)**
  http://www.moldova.net/english

- **Moscow Business Telephone Guide**
  http://www.mbtg.net

- **Poland Yellow Pages (a Yahoo!-style directory)**
  http://www.yellowpages.pl

- **Romanian Yellow Pages**
  http://www.romanianyellowpages.com

- **Romanian Yellow Pages**
  http://www.yellowpages.ro

- **Romanian Yellow Pages Online**
  http://www.imago.ro

- **Slovakia Yellow Pages**
  http://www.yellowpages.sk

U.S. Government Resources

After all your searching in databases for business information on Central or Eastern Europe, perhaps you still haven't found too much useful or current information. Face it, with all the strife and turmoil going on in that part of the world for the last decade or so, collecting and compiling statistics and business information about the area may not have risen high on the list of things to do for the locals. Unless you're actually on the ground in the region and know your way around, it could prove pretty difficult to find what you need. Here's where the U.S. government can help a lot. When it comes to business resources for Russia, the New Independent States (NIS), and Central and Eastern Europe, the U.S. government overflows with information.

For your first stop, go to the Business Information Service for the Newly Independent States (BISNIS) [http://www.bisnis.doc.gov], a service of the U.S. Department of Commerce established in 1992. After looking at this site, all I can say is that the people in the U.S. embassies must be awfully busy trying to make things easier for U.S. companies to do business in the region. The site apparently undergoes frequent revisions.

The section Latest News updates every few days with reports from the various embassies in Eastern Europe. Most of the reports carry updates on financial and economic developments in the individual countries, although occasionally they provide more focused special reports. Upcoming tenders and events in the region are also described. Previously, this section was searchable and had archives going back about five years. Hopefully, as the site continues to evolve, this search function will return.

The main page for Country Reports divides into four parts covering the following areas:

- Caucusus—Georgia, Armenia, Azerbaijan

- Central Asia—Kazakhstan, Kyrgyzstan, Tajikistan, Turkmenistan, Uzbekistan

- Russian Federation

  - Central Region—Kaluga, Lipetsk, Moscow City & Oblast, Oryol, Ryazan, Tula, Tver, Vladimir, Voronezh, and Yaroslavl

  - Northwest Region—Arkhangelsk, Kaliningrad, Karelia, Murmansk, Novgorod, Pskov, Saint Petersburg/Leningrad Oblast, and Vologda

  - Volga Region—Chuvash Republic, Kirov, Mariy El, Mordovia Republic, Nizhny Novgorod, Saratov, Samara, Sotchi, Tatarstan, and Volgograd

  - Southern Region—Dagestan, Krasnodar, and Rostov

  - Urals—Republic of Bashkortostan, Chelyabinsk Oblast, Perm Oblast, Sverdlovsk Oblast, Tyumen Oblast, and Udmurtia

  - Siberia—Altai Krai, Republic of Buratya, Irkutsk, Krasnoyarsk, Novosibirsk, Omsk, and Tomsk

  - Far East Region—Amurskaya Oblast and Jewish Autonomous Region, Chita, Chukotka, Kamchatka, Khabarovsk, Magadan, Primorskiy Krai, Sakha/Yakutia (Yakutsk), and Sakhalin Oblast (Yuzhno-Sakhalinsk)

- Western NIS—Belarus, Moldova, Ukraine

Topics covered in the Country Reports vary from one country to another:

- Banking and Finance

- Business and Professional Services

- Country Commercial Guides (yet another source)

- Economic and Financial Developments

- Industry Reports

- Legal and Regulatory

- Links and Contacts

- Political Developments

- Taxes

- Tenders

An extensive selection of market survey reports appears in the Industry Reports section. Reports here date from 1997 to the present and cover the following industries:

- Banking and Finance

- Certification

- Computers, Software, and Electronics

- Consulting and Related Services

- Consumer Goods

- Construction and Real Estate

- Energy Sector

- Environmental Technologies

- Food Sector and Agribusiness

- Natural Resources

- Legal and Regulatory

- Medical Sector

- Miscellaneous and Defense

- Telecommunications

- Transportation and Distribution

A partial listing of market studies in Telecommunications may be seen in Figure 4.4.

The BISNIS Bulletin is published monthly in PDF format and contains reports on NIS market developments, trade agreements, business opportunities, financing information, and trade event calendars. The searchable versions of the current issue, as well as the archives back to 1997 are posted at the site. Other information available at the BISNIS site includes annual U.S. exports to the NIS by state (year by

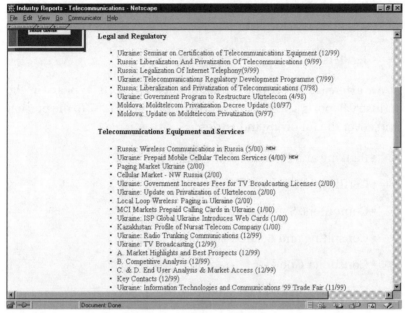

**Figure 4.4   Partial Listing of Telecommunications Reports—
BISNIS**

year back to 1995), trade leads, events, a quick reference guide to the major import charges and customs procedures in NIS countries, a general guide to sources of financing, currency exchange rate data (via Bloomberg.com), and, of course, useful links.

For a Central and Eastern Europe counterpart to BISNIS, try CEEBICnet—Central and Eastern Europe Business Information Center [http://www.mac.doc.gov/eebic/ceebic.html]. CEEBIC, established in 1990 and sponsored by the U.S. Department of Commerce, covers the following countries:

• Albania	• Hungary
• Bosnia and Herzegovina	• Latvia
• Bulgaria	• Lithuania
• Croatia	• Poland
• Czech Republic	• Romania
• Estonia	• Slovak Republic
• FR Yugoslavia	• Slovenia
• FYR Macedonia	

Coverage for each country includes several market research reports—even a country as small as Estonia has fifteen market research reports (see Figure 4.5). There is also a list of U.S. companies operating in each country. This could be useful on more than one front. You can identify already established competition or use the list to conduct your own market research by contacting some of the companies and discussing their experiences in the country.

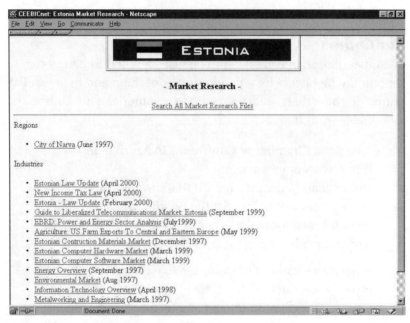

Figure 4.5   Partial Listing of Market Research Reports for Estonia—CEEBIC

Trade and investment leads are available for agribusiness/food processing, automotive, computer/electronics, consumer goods, energy/environment, housing/construction, manufacturing, medical, chemicals, metals/mining/raw materials, technology, transportation, retail, services, and miscellaneous. The list of leads includes the country name and the date posted. You can browse through an archive of previous leads.

Other topics offered by CEEBIC include sources of financing, U.S. Embassy reports, trade fair information, a taxes and tariffs chart, and key regional contacts.

Chambers of Commerce and Industry

This region consists of many small countries that may change identities. As in most parts of the world, there are numerous chamber of commerce Web sites, all offering different types of information. Some of the sites offer little more than a listing of members with contact information. But this can prove more valuable than you might initially think, helping you to identify companies currently doing business in the country.

AmChams

Rather than go into great depth on just a few of the chamber sites, let's hit the highlights for a good number of them and then just list some of the others, starting with the American Chambers of Commerce (AmChams):

- **American Chamber of Commerce in Azerbaijan**
  http://www.amchamaz.org
  Unfortunately, the pickings on this site are a bit slim. No list of members, but it does list the Board of Directors that includes each individual's company name and title. It also has a very brief Doing Business in Azerbaijan section.

- **American Chamber of Commerce in Bulgaria**
  http://www.amcham.bg
  Contact information for state institutions and agencies, embassies, banks, travel agencies, airlines, press, and the European Council of American Chambers of Commerce (ECACC) can be found here as well as current and past issues of *AmCham Bulgaria Magazine*, featuring analyses of current business issues, profiles of members, and business opportunities.

- **American Chamber of Commerce in the Czech Republic**
  http://www.amcham.cz
  This site features an alphabetical list of members, a brief assessment of current business climate, and descriptions of business opportunities.

- **American Chamber of Commerce Estonia**
  http://www.acce.ee
  This site has a list of members, including detailed contact

information and products, a newsletter archive featuring articles such as Franchising in Estonia, and useful links.

• **American Chamber of Commerce in Hungary**
http://www.amcham.hu
An alphabetical list of members (individuals and companies) shows contact information only. The full text of *Business Hungary* is available back to 1999.

• **American Chamber of Commerce in Latvia**
http://www.amchamlatvia.lv
Information on this site includes an alphabetical listing of members with contact information and industry designation, current and previous issues of the quarterly publication *American Investor*, and links to Latvian government and business sites.

• **American Chamber of Commerce in Lithuania**
http://www.acc.lt
This site provides a membership listing, contact information, industry, and Web site link, as well as a page of useful links.

• **American Chamber of Commerce in Poland**
http://www.amcham.com.pl
A list of more than 300 member companies is sorted by sector. Unfortunately, it doesn't always work properly. A complete directory is available for purchase. The current issue of the monthly publication *American Investor* can be accessed.

• **American Chamber of Commerce in Romania**
http://www.amcham.ro
General information about the Chamber is provided in addition to a list of members; with contact information, industry, and Web site (no link). Excerpts from Chamber newsletter, general business and tax overview provided by Deloitte & Touche Romania, legal aspects of doing business in Romania, and monthly tax bulletins from Arthur Andersen Romania are also available.

• **American Chamber of Commerce in Russia**
http://www.amcham.ru
The list of more than 480 member companies is presented

both alphabetically and by product/service, some with links to Web sites. Other information includes white papers (market and industry studies), past issues of *AmCham News* (each issue highlighting an industry), and a collection of Business Resources links.

• **American Chamber of Commerce in Ukraine**
http://www.amcham.kiev.ua
 Profile of the Chamber includes a list of the Board of Directors and their affiliated companies, plus a list of member companies. However, at my last visit, all information about the companies had moved to a Members Only section.

Other Chambers—Not AmChams

• **Athens Chamber of Commerce and Industry**
http://www.acci.gr
A member directory is searchable by industry but only contact information is provided. The alphabetical listing of member companies includes links to Web sites. The full-text of *Trade with Greece*, current and back issues is accessible.

• **Association of Balkan Chambers**
http://www.abcinfos.com
Member countries are Albania, Bulgaria, Cyprus, Greece, F.Y.R. Macedonia, Romania, Turkey, and F.R. Yugoslavia.

• **Chamber of Economy of Bosnia and Herzegovina**
http://www.komorabih.com/eindex.html
Searchable membership directory entries include a description of business activity, information on reconstruction and development projects, and commodities and services (both offered and needed). Bosnia and Herzegovina in Figures is an overview aimed at the foreign business community. The remainder of the site is still under construction, but looks promising.

• **Bulgarian Chamber of Commerce and Industry**
http://www.bcci.bg
Among the information on this site are a searchable list of member companies, current and historical exchange rate

information, a searchable system for posting business opportunities, links to Web sites of Bulgarian companies, contact information for regional Chambers of Commerce and Industry in Bulgaria, current and past issues of *Infobusiness Newsletter*, and a country profile.

- **Croatian Chamber of Economy**
http://www.hgk.hr
Searchable company database entries include standard contact information and business activity. Entries are a mix of English and Croatian.

- **Latvian Chamber of Commerce and Industry**
http://sun.lcc.org.lv
The alphabetical directory of member companies contains contact information and brief company descriptions. Full-text of *Importers Guide to Latvia—1999* is available.

- **Economic Chamber of Macedonia**
http://info.mchamber.org.mk
The list of member companies is organized by industry. Some companies have links to their Web sites; others have a description at the Chamber's site. A list of major products exported from Macedonia is also provided.

- **Chamber of Commerce and Industry of Romania and Bucharest**
http://www.ccir.ro
This site provides links to other Chambers of Commerce and Industry in Romania. There is also a list of investment projects by industry, a searchable database of business opportunities, virtual trade fairs and exhibitions, a good Useful Links page, and a searchable listing of Romanian companies via ROBIX (ROmanian Business Information eXpress). Contact and some additional information is available for free in a demo version. Opportunity to subscribe for more complete information is offered.

- **Russian American Chamber of Commerce**
http://www.rmi.net/racc
A good set of links by numerous categories highlights this site. It also includes several industry links and news excerpts.

• **Russian Federation Chamber of Commerce and Industry**
http://www.rbcnet.ru/eng_home.htm

• **Yugoslav Chamber of Commerce and Industry**
http://www.pkj.co.yu/YCCI.htm
This site presents an overview of the Yugoslav economy and
the country as a whole, as well as a list of Yugoslav banks and
insurance companies. Caution: This is a very slow loading site.

Banking, Finance, and Stock Exchanges

The European Bank for Reconstruction and Development
(EBRD) [http://www.ebrd.org] covers almost the entire alphabet of
countries in Central and Eastern Europe: Albania to Uzbekistan.
Established in 1991, the EBRD promotes private sector development in the region by investment and management of development
projects. For detailed information on the EBRD and its projects,
download the Annual Report available in PDF format.
Unfortunately, this site can be confusing at first use. It does not
make readily apparent which sections have what information. In the
lower-right corner, there is a link to the Site Map—use it! This is one
instance where it really helps to make this your first stop. Although
not as detailed as one might like, it does cut down on the learning
curve time. Additionally, the site has a rudimentary search function.

In order to find EBRD activities by country or sector, click on
Operations. From here you can find the sectors emphasized for each
country and the projects funded in the following broad sectors:

• Agribusiness

• Energy efficiency

• Equity funds

• Financial institutions

• Municipal and environmental infrastructure

• Natural resources

• Power and energy utilities

• Property, tourism, and shipping

• Telecommunications, informatics, and media

• Transport

This gives a good indication as to the needs in the various countries. For example, the transport sector listed commitments for five new railway projects, approval of a loan for the restructuring of the M1/M15 motorway project in Hungary, and a loan to the Albanian Government as part of an international effort to modernize the main east-west highway linking Albania with the former Yugoslavia and the rest of southeastern Europe.

The EBRD publishes a Country Investment Profile [http://www.ebrd.org/english/opera/Country/index.htm] for each country in the region. The profiles include sections on the economy, investment climate, financial sector, key contacts, legal and regulatory environment for foreign investors, and more. The profiles are now available online, in PDF format. You can also order hard copies of individual reports or a full set of all twenty-six reports.

If you have ongoing research needs in this region, you might want to purchase the *EBRD Directory of Business Information Sources*. This directory details more than 2,000 print, online, and CD-ROM sources for Central and Eastern European business information.

Created in July 1996, The Federal Commission for the Securities Market (FCSM) [http://www.fedcom.ru/ewelcome.html] is the successor agency to the Federal Commission on Securities and the Capital Market of the Russian Federation. This agency supervises the development of Russia's capital market and tries to ensure the protection of investors' rights. The site contains decrees, documents, resolutions, and regulations pertaining to securities and the capital market dating back to 1995. The FCSM also published a 1998 Annual Report. News items relating to the FCSM and new decisions post on the site in a very timely manner. Many of the documents at the site are available in either HTML or PDF format—a nice feature. One section provides links to other Internet resources on the Russian securities market for additional information.

Skate Financial Network [http://www.skatefn.com] supplies financial information on European emerging markets. More than 2,000 securities are followed in the following sixteen countries:

- Bulgaria
- Croatia
- Cyprus
- Czech Republic
- Estonia
- Hungary
- Kazakhstan
- Latvia

- Lithuania
- Poland
- Romania
- Russia
- Slovakia
- Slovenia
- Turkey
- Ukraine

Each of the countries has its own section that includes a country profile and annual macroeconomic indicators for the most recent three years. The country profile includes items such as most developed industry sectors and the largest companies by revenue.

The following industries are covered:

- Chemical products
- Conglomerates
- Construction
- Construction materials
- Engineering
- Financial, insurance, real estate
- Food
- Hotels
- Information technologies
- Media and publishing
- Metals
- Oil and gas
- Power industry
- Telecommunications
- Wholesale and retail trade

Industry coverage includes a list of the companies covered by Skate, key market indicators, and key operating indicators. Profiles of the companies, in PDF format, are available only to paid subscribers.

It always helps to know how to contact the Central Bank in a country. Some of the Central Banks in this region are listed here:

- **The Croatian National Bank**
  http://www.hnb.hr

- **The National Bank of the Czech Republic**
  http://voskovec.radio.cz/gov-cr/bank.html

- **The Bank of Estonia**
  http://www.ee/epbe/en

- **The National Bank of Hungary**
  http://www.mnb.hu/index-a.htm

- **The Bank of Lithuania**
  http://www.lbank.lt/Eng/DEFAULT.HTM

- **The National Bank of Moldova**
  http://www.bnm.org/english/index.htm

- **The Central Bank of the Russian Federation**
  http://www.cbr.ru/eng

- **The National Bank of Slovakia**
  http://www.nbs.sk/INDEXA.HTM

- **The Bank of Slovenia**
  http://www.bsi.si/html/eng/index.html

These are the Central and Eastern European stock exchanges with a presence on the Internet:

- **Bulgaria—Bulgarian Stock Exchange**
  http://www.onlinebg.com

- **Croatia—Zagreb Stock Exchange**
  http://www.zse.hr

- **Cyprus—Cyprus Stock Exchange**
  http://www.cse.com.cy

- **Czech Republic—Prague Stock Exchange**
  http://stock.eunet.cz/bcpp_e.html

- **Estonia—Tallinn Stock Exchange**
  http://www.tse.ee/english/index.html

- **Greece—Athens Stock Exchange**
  http://www.ase.gr

- **Hungary—Budapest Stock Exchange**
  http://www.fornax.hu/fmon/stock/data/bethath.html

- **Latvia—Riga Stock Exchange**
  http://www.rfb.lv

- **Lithuania—National Stock Exchange of Lithuania**
  http://www.nse.lt

- **Macedonia—Macedonian Stock Exchange**
  http://www.mse.org.mk

- **Romania—Bucharest Stock Exchange**
  http://www.bse.ro

- **Russia—Federal Commission for the Securities Market**
  http://www.fedcom.ru/ewelcome.html

- **Slovakia—Bratislava Stock Exchange**
  http://www.bsse.sk/bsseApp/index.asp?LANG=EN&ITM=
  HOME

- **Slovenia—Ljubljana Stock Exchange**
  http://www.ljse.si/StrAng/PrvaStr/PrvaStr.asp

News Resources

One should always try to access local business publications, particularly in a region such as Central and Eastern Europe, which might not get a lot of coverage in the international business press. Yes, the countries in this area are in the news a great deal, but generally from a political perspective; the business climate in the individual countries and the companies located within them often get lost in the bigger picture. Additionally, with so many languages to take into consideration, finding business news in English can be quite a chore. Let's make the task a bit easier by looking at some of the resources for Central and Eastern European business news—some regional and some country specific.

Business Europa [http://www.business-europa.co.uk/bemag. html], a Central European business magazine, has a smattering of information at its site. Sample reports are available online for a couple of countries (Bulgaria and Ukraine, when I visited) and summary reports for the following countries:

- Albania
- Armenia
- Azerbaijan
- Belarus
- Bosnia-Herzegovina
- Croatia
- Czech Republic
- Estonia
- Georgia
- Hungary
- Latvia
- Lithuania
- Macedonia
- Moldova
- Poland
- Romania
- Russia
- Serbia & Montenegro
- Slovakia
- Slovenia
- Ukraine

Please note that the amount of information varies greatly by country. If, however, you have or plan on having ongoing projects in this region of the world, it's worthwhile to check out the site and consider a subscription to the print version of the magazine. A nine-issue subscription at the time of publication cost US$90.

- **Central Europe Review**
  http://www.ce-review.org/index.html

- **CEEBIZ.com**
  http://www.ceebiz.com
  A group of electronic newsletters covers IT & Telecom, Banking, Real Estate, and Capital Markets in Central Europe; paid subscription required. The site offers the ability to customize newsletters from other industry selections.

- **Central Europe Online**
  http://www.centraleurope.com
  A news-oriented portal for Central Europe focuses particularly on general and business news. In addition to the main regional section, it also has separate sections for: Croatia, Czech Republic, Hungary, Poland, Romania, Slovakia, Slovenia, and the Balkans (Albania, Bosnia, Bulgaria, Macedonia, and Yugoslavia).

- **Czech the News**
  http://www.czech.cz/washington/newslet/newslet.htm
  This site contains a monthly newsletter from the Embassy of
  the Czech Republic in Washington, DC, with archives to 1994.

- **Newspapers of the Czech Republic**
  http://www.columbia.edu/~js322/czech.html
  This site provides links to various Czech newspapers with
  notes in English.

- **Interfax**
  http://www.interfax-news.com
  Interfax provides business, political, and financial news for
  the countries in the region. Free daily headlines are available,
  as well as selected industry reports. All else requires a paid
  subscription.

- **The Moscow Times**
  http://www.themoscowtimes.com
  This site is updated daily and has a separate section for
  business news.

- **The Prague Post Online**
  http://www.praguepost.cz
  This site is updated weekly.

- **The Slovak Spectator**
  http://www.slovakspectator.sk
  Provides weekly news with archives to September 1999.

- **The St. Petersburg Times**
  http://www.sptimes.ru/cgi-bin/ home.cgi
  Publishes on Tuesdays and Fridays.

- **The Warsaw Voice**
  http://www.warsawvoice.com.pl
  Provides weekly Polish and Central European news with
  archives to 1996.

Poland

If you're interested in doing business in Poland, you're in luck.
Business information is more readily available here than for most

other countries in the region. Business Polska [http://www.
polska.net] is a great place to start. First, look at POLAND: Funda-
mental Facts, Figures, and Regulations (reached from the Investor's
Guide link on the main page). This PDF document runs forty-eight
pages and hits most of the important business highlights, including these segments:

- Average gross wages by sector
- Foreign trade
- Forms of legal business entities
- GDP structure by sector
- Import and export restrictions
- Industry production—output and trends
- Intellectual property protection
- Purchase of real estate by foreigners
- Sectors of foreign investment
- Taxes

Another useful publication at the site is *Business Opportunities in
Poland: A Guide for American Investors.* Topics covered include
Investment Risks, Taxes and Social Security Costs, Intellectual and
Industrial Property, and Commercial Relations Between the U.S.
and Poland. The section Examples of Sectoral Prospects for
American Investors gives brief overviews and some market informa-
tion on the following industries:

- Construction, including toll motorways and home and office
  construction
- Electronics
- Health, including medical equipment and pharmaceuticals
- Laboratory and scientific equipment
- Power industry
- Telecommunications

The publication's Annex provides an extensive list of useful contacts for those doing business in Poland.

Business Polska offers three different ways to search for Polish companies. The first is via a direct link to the CEEBICnet site (described earlier in the "U.S. Government Resources" section). The second is via a link to the American Chamber of Commerce in Poland site (described earlier in the "Chambers of Commerce and Industry" section). The final way is to choose a business sector and view a list of companies within that sector, many linked to company Web sites.

They also carry links to a number of other useful sites, including the Warsaw Stock Exchange, various domestic and international news sites, relevant chambers and business organizations, and market reports. The market reports come from CEEBICnet. The title of each report lists the publication date, so you can readily check for currency.

After you have thoroughly researched Poland for your client, try one more interesting point on this site: a link to Hotels Poland: Castles and Palaces [http://www.HotelsPoland.com/castle_palace]. Here you can make your own reservation for a stay in a castle in Poland. You will have more than twenty-five castles and palaces to choose from at rates ranging from US$29/night to around US$99/night. Cinderella, anyone?

Inside Poland [http://www.insidepoland.com.pl] is a very Yahoo!-like site for Poland with numerous subject categories to choose from, ranging from the more serious (Business, News, Government) to the more lighthearted (Weather, Travel, Photographs). The Business category, like all good business sites, offers a list of companies, sorted by city or sector. As I've come to expect for this part of the world, most entries offer nothing more than contact information. However, if you need to find someone "on the ground" in Poland to supplement your research, try one of the Business categories—Market Research.

If you have a client who plans to travel to Poland, use the Internet Service Provider category to locate a local ISP; there were 104 when I checked.

Inside Poland also has a free e-mail news service that provides local news from local sources under the following news categories:

• Corporate News

• Domestic and Political News

- Economic News

- International News

- Sports

Once you complete the free registration form, they will deliver your news via e-mail every afternoon.

Similar Inside … sites are available for many other countries in the region:

• Albania	• Macedonia
• Baltic States	• Moldova
• Belarus	• Yugoslavia
• Bosnia	• Romania
• Bulgaria	• Russia
• Croatia	• Slovakia
• Czech Republic	• Slovenia
• Hungary	• Ukraine

The Warsaw Business Journal compiles several lists of companies in Poland [http://www.wbj.pl/common/bol/default.asp?site=2]. Most company listings have links to the company's Web site. The lists include:

- Top 100 Companies

- Top Exporters

- Top Private Foreign Investors

- Top Women-Run Businesses

Several industry categories on the page can help you locate companies. Similar lists are available from the Prague Business Journal [http://www.pbj.cz/common/bol/default.asp?site=1] and the Budapest Business Journal [http://www.bbj.hu/common/bol/default.asp?site=3].

Greece

Invest in Greece (INVgr) [http://www.invgr.com] is a good mix of information on Greece. In order to reach some of the information, you must register at the site (it's free) and you will receive a user name and password via e-mail. The downside of this is that it can take a couple of days before you receive them, which could become a problem if time were of the essence.

Without registration, you can read stock market information including a list of the companies on the stock exchange, sorted by industry and carrying links to company Web sites. You can also view sections outlining economic indicators, an explanation of the Greek economy over the last two years, company news, useful links, and an archive of selected stories.

Much more is available after registration. There are company profiles and more detailed articles about Greek companies in the news.

Russia

Russia Today [http://www.russiatoday.com] is a good portal with which to start looking for business information on Russia. This searchable site updates daily with general and business news. The Business News section includes a Stock and Currencies area (current stock information, a currency converter, and exchange rate data), pertinent stories from PR Newswire, and ON24, with news in audio and video format. It also offers subscriptions to daily e-mail news updates.

The Country Info section is divided into several sections:

- Biographies—biographies of important politicians

- Constitution—the full-text of the Russian constitution

- Features—special articles and topics

- Government—information about the Federal Assembly, Federation Council, State Duma, and the Executive Branch

- Government Addresses—contact information for important government committees

- Hot Sites—links to Web sites in more than 20 categories and descriptions of their content. Additional links appear in the E-commerce section.

A good site for those interested in doing business in Russia is Russia at Your Fingertips [http://www.publications-etc.com/russia/index2.html]. While much of the site has not updated for the last nine to twelve months, some of the information offered will not change very rapidly. (When we last checked, a page at the site stated that the site is undergoing construction and will shortly convert into a business to business portal.)

Start with the Business FAQ section. Topics covered include the Russian Business Environment, Selling Products to Russia, Setting Up a Company in Russia, Buying from Russia, Selling Services in Russia, and Investing in Russia. Material seems very comprehensive and forthright.

The site has a small Russian/CIS Exporters Directory with, at last viewing, only a handful of companies listed. Each listing has a short statement describing the company and a link to its Web site. There are also articles on some of the major industries (see Figure 4.6) in Russia:

- Mining

- Oil & Gas

- Semiconductors

- Software

- Telecommunications

- Tourism

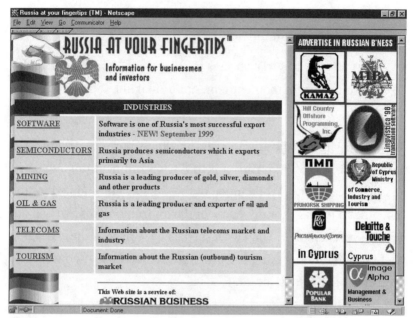

Figure 4.6   Industry Listings—Russia at Your Fingertips

Bucknell University has a page of U.S. firms in Russia [http://web3.departments.bucknell.edu/scripts/russian/usfirms]. You can search for companies by name, service, or product, or you can list all the companies alphabetically. Entries contain very cursory contact information, but do give some insight as to the companies already doing business in Russia.

Czech Republic

Czech Republic [http://www.czech.cz] has a good deal of basic information about the country. Exploring some of the links on the right side of the page, Basic Facts, Political System, Country & People, History of the Czech State, will provide overall background information on the Czech Republic. After exploring those areas, scroll down the page to the links with more concrete business information.

- Communication—Provides a general overview of media in the country; links to various news sources.

- Economy—Discussion of the country's economic situation

- Investment—Outlines the investment advantages to doing business with the Czech Republic and links to a Doing Business in the Czech Republic guide

- Other Czech Servers—Offers links to other Internet Czech resources

The Czech Info Center [http://www.muselik.com/czech/frame.html] has a searchable business directory. Some sections of the directory seemed still under construction, but much was already functional when last viewed. Other, more general, Czech information also appears on the site, such as travel, news, biographies, and even recipes.

Azerbaijan

Azerbaijan is not exactly a word that trips easily off the tongue; nor is it easy to spell. It's also not a country from which one would expect to find much business information. However, the State Statistical Committee of Azerbaijan Republic [http://www.statcom.baku-az. com] has some pretty amazing tables available at its site (see Figure 4.7):

State Statistical Committee of Azerbaijan Republic - Netscape

File Edit View Go Communicator Help

Employment by branches (thsd. person)					
Branches	1995 x)	1996 x)	1997 x)	1998 x)	in percent to total
Total	3613.0	3686.7	3691.1	3701.5	100
Industry	352.1	282.9	242.0	240.2	6.5
Agriculture and forestry	874.0	921.3	842.5	835.5	22.6
Construction	185.1	164.1	153.3	155.6	4.2
Transport and communication	159.1	168.3	166.3	168.3	4.5
Trade and public cate-ring, material and technical equipment supply and sales, procurement	396.2	456.6	602.8	704.0	19.0
Communal dwelling services, living subsis-tance contribution	81.8	86.1	94.6	95.5	2.6
Health care, physical training and social security	174.5	181.9	184.5	190.0	5.1
Education, culture and art	372.6	374.6	365.8	368.5	10.0
Science and scientific services	34.1	33.6	32.5	32.0	0.9
Credit, finance and insurance	14.2	14.0	10.5	11.0	0.3
General administrative organizations	66.6	68.9	67.8	68.0	1.8

Figure 4.7   Employment by Sector—State Statistical Committee of Azerbaijan

- Average monthly wages of employees of different professions and posts (in local currency)

- Employment by branches (meaning sector)

- Employment by ownership and type of establishment (state enterprise, private, cooperative, etc.)

- Indicators of industrial production

- Main indicators of construction

- Main trading partners

- Number of pensioners

Based in Washington, DC, the U.S.-Azerbaijan Council [http://ourworld.compuserve.com/homepages/usazerb] publishes the *Caspian Business Report* twice a month (archives at site back to November 1996) and *Caspian Crossroads Magazine* approximately once a quarter (archives at site back to Winter 1995). Subscription information for the hard-copy versions of both is available at the site. Take a look at the services offered by the Council. They could prove a valuable resource if the information you seek is not readily available.

A great set of links has been compiled at Azerbaijan Internet Links [http://resources.net.az]. For business purposes, the most useful areas are Economy and Azerbaijan in Internet. The Economy section has the following categories:

- Banks

- Communication

- Companies, Firms, and Consortiums

- Exchanges

- Fuel and Energy

- General Information

- Information Systems and Computers

- Insurance Companies

- International Economic Relations

- Privatization

• Transport

• Travel and Recreation, Hotels

Latvia

Interested in going to a virtual trade show? Check out Latvian Business Pages [http://www.expo.lv] for a different twist. On the main page, click on Online Exhibition and you go to the Exhibit Hall to see five categories of exhibits: Food, Consumer Goods, Industry, Transport, and Services. Choose any of the companies shown and you reach that company's "exhibit," most in English. For additional companies, click on Classificator. A very detailed Useful Business Links section not only covers Latvia extensively, it also includes Estonia, Lithuania, Kazakhstan, Kyrgyzstan, Tajikistan, Uzbekistan, Armenia, Belarus, Georgia, Moldova, Ukraine, and Russia.

The Latvian Business Directory [http://www.zl.lv/new1/region-eng.htm] claims that it has close to 60,000 businesses in its database. To begin, choose from twenty-five regions within Latvia. A search screen offers the option of searching by company name, city or district, street, product, or service. All entries in the database contain contact information. Some also contain a product/service description and a link to the company Web site. To reach a very extensive help section for searching, click on User Manual.

Estonia

Estonia may be a small country, but it is definitely dancing as fast as it can to build up its business economy. The Estonian Trade Council [http://www.ee/ETC], a nonprofit trade organization, has a pretty impressive Web site. It provides overviews of the food export, furniture, and engineering industries and offers a link to the Estonian Clothing and Home Textiles Importers Guide 1998.

You can look through the Trade Council's list of members alphabetically (browsing by activity does not appear to work), or you can use the search function. To test the search capabilities, I entered the term "furniture" and received three hits. Checking out the entries, I found contact information, year established, number of employees, activities, and products. Some entries also included export countries, turnover, and export turnover.

Ekspress Hotline [http://www.1182.ee/eng] has a very extensive Estonian Export Directory, searchable by company name and goods/services. Remember our previous cutlery searches? I decided to see whether or not Estonia had any cutlery manufacturers. Searching on "cutlery" returned three subcategories, one for "stainless steel cutlery." Following that link, one company appeared: Toprest Ltd. The company's entry included contact information, turnover, year founded, number of employees, and a brief description of the products offered (see Figure 4.8).

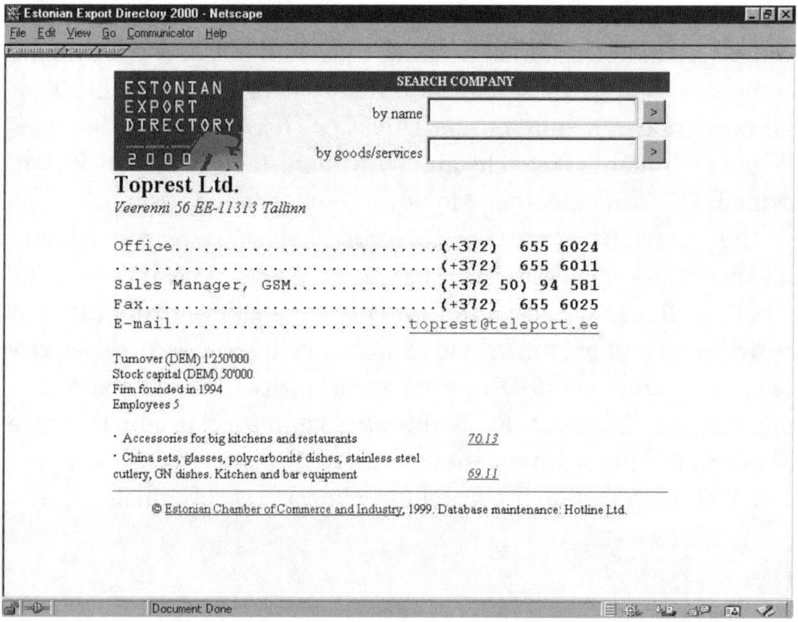

Figure 4.8   Company Directory Listing—Estonian Export Directory

Lithuania

Advantage Lithuania [http://www.lda.lt] is the Web site for the Lithuanian Development Agency (LDA). Start by clicking on Invest in Lithuania and you get Ten Reasons to Invest in Lithuania. On the left portion of the screen, you can explore the Country Profile, Business and Investment Climate, Legal Environment, Key Business Sectors, Foreign Trade, and Links and Resources. Each of the Key Business Sectors (wood processing, textiles, electronics, machinery and IT, food and agriculture, chemicals and pharmaceuticals, transportation infrastructure and distribution, financial services, and travel and tourism) includes a short industry overview and mentions the major foreign investors in the industry.

From the main page, choose Buy from Lithuania. Apparently the best products to acquire from Lithuania are textiles, furniture, chemicals, machinery and automotive components, electronics, and processed foods. You can also learn about Lithuanian trade conditions (taxes, tariffs, quotas, etc.), foreign trade statistics (see Figure 4.9), business opportunities, and the services of the Lithuanian Development Agency. The Exporters' Database, still under construction at my last visit, is now functional and searchable by company name, keyword or product code/HS code. For a free database, the entries are quite extensive. They include contact information (with the name of the appropriate individual), languages spoken, year founded, number of employees, turnover, export capacity (in percentages), major export partners (by country), business experience, and product descriptions sorted by HS code. As with many of the free databases, please bear in mind that inclusion is voluntary and the information provided by the companies is not verified. There is an outline of the services available through the LDA and points of contact. As in many cases, the personal approach

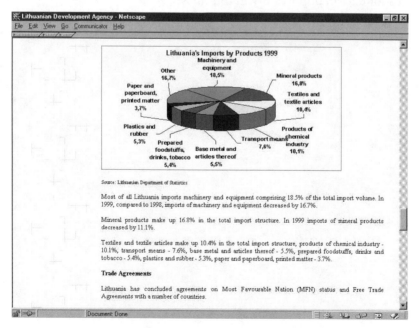

Figure 4.9   Lithuanian Imports by Product—Lithuanian Development Agency

may constitute the best route to follow for hard-to-find business information.

Most Central and Eastern European countries will have agencies similar to the LDA, which can seem like wonderful oases in deserts of business information. Using a search engine, try the phrases "investment promotion," "investment and export promotion," or "trade development" along with the name of a country. While you will undoubtedly get many irrelevant hits, you should easily find the right one in the search results.

Regional Wrap-Up

As stated in the beginning, Central and Eastern European business information is not easy to find. If you are lucky enough to find what you're looking for, be wary of the quality of the information. There are wonderful business opportunities in the region, but you will have to dig to find them. As always, consider supplementing open Web searches with the traditional online vendors—although you might not have much success there either for this region. But with the sites in this chapter in hand, you're in a good position to respond to an opportunity in this area.

CHAPTER 5

LATIN AMERICA AND THE CARIBBEAN

In the previous chapters, we traveled all around Europe and found ways to handle the intricacies of dealing with multiple languages and cultures. Now we turn to Latin American and Caribbean business information. Piece of cake, you say— basically one language and one culture. Nothing could be further from the truth. Sure, the major language is Spanish, but at the very least you will also find English, French, Portuguese, and some local Indian dialects.

Since the majority of the countries are Spanish-speaking, much of the rest of the world tends to view Latin America as one homogeneous entity with interchangeable countries. Wrong!

What is the definition of Latin America? Different people and organizations define the area and the term differently. On more than one occasion I've had colleagues call me to ask: "My business adviser wants me to look for information about the widget industry in Latin America. What does he mean by Latin America? Central America? Mexico? South America? Some combination of all three? Or a completely different grouping of countries?" To me, Latin America includes Mexico, Central America, South America, and the Spanish-speaking Caribbean countries of Cuba and the Dominican Republic. I generally also throw in Haiti, even though it is French-speaking, since it shares the island of Hispañola with the Dominican Republic.

When you tack on the Caribbean to complete the region, you add countries that have colonial roots in France, Africa, the Netherlands, and Great Britain. Of course, Brazil brings in the influence of Portugal. So much for homogeneity. Let's see if we can find some ways to muddle through this confusion and still find useful business information. We'll look at a selection of regional, government, and directory sites; specialized search engines; some country-specific sites for Argentina, Brazil, the Caribbean, and Guatemala; and more.

Search Engines and Directories

When I get the question asked in the Microsoft ads, "Where do you want to go today?," my answer is generally, "I don't know; probably someplace different than yesterday and maybe somewhere I've never been." Such is the curse (or blessing, depending upon your point of view) of the business searcher. Every day, every project differs. The challenge probably explains why so many of us enjoy what we do, but it also tends to make things a bit more difficult. Personally, I feel that directory sites are like Belgian chocolates—you can never have enough of them.

Start any Latin American search with the Latin American Network Information Center (LANIC) site of the University of Texas at Austin [http://lanic.utexas.edu]. LANIC, begun in 1992, focuses on the creation and maintenance of directories and guides to Internet-based resources on Latin America. Receiving countless awards over the years, the site covers thirty-six countries and fifty-one subjects. If I didn't have any leads to start a Latin American search, I would definitely begin here.

You have the option of starting with a country or a subject. I chose a country and tried El Salvador. This took me to the El Salvador page, divided into several sections: Academic Research Resources; Arts & Humanities; Economy; General; Government; Network & Information Services; News & Media; Other Resources; Portals, Directories & Search Sites; and Travel & Tourism. The sections, while not identical, are very similar from country to country and consist of numerous links (see Figures 5.1 & 5.2). As one would imagine, some countries have substantially more entries than others.

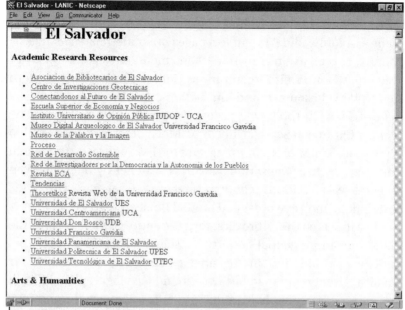

Figure 5.1   Excerpts from El Salvador Entry—Latin American
              Network Information Center

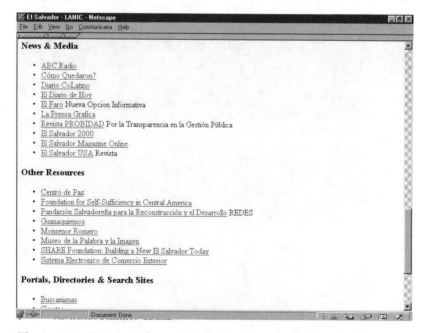

Figure 5.2   Excerpts from El Salvador Entry—Latin American
              Network Information Center

Depending upon your needs, you might also find it worthwhile to try the subject option. When I chose Economy as the subject and Trade as a subheading, I went to a page with trade-related listings by country, as well as links to Trade Agreements & Negotiations, Fair Trade and Non-Profit Organizations, Publications, Other Western Hemispheric Resources, and International Resources.

CaribSeek [http://www.caribseek.com] bills itself as "The Premier Caribbean Search Directory." Much of the site is devoted to "fluff" (tourism, sports, shopping, and the like); however, the search function may help the serious business searcher by offering seven different search options (country, category, subcategory, URL, title, description, and keywords) and limited Boolean searching.

You can search the entire directory, the entire Caribbean, only the islands, or an individual country or island. I decided to see what CaribSeek would find in the area of Business & Economy for Jamaica. Twenty-one matches were found (see Figure 5.3). Most of the sites seemed to hold good potential; Jamaica Promotions Corporation, Montego Bay Chamber of Commerce and Industry, and Export Jamaica looked particularly promising. The Office of the Registrar of Companies might also prove useful, depending upon one's needs.

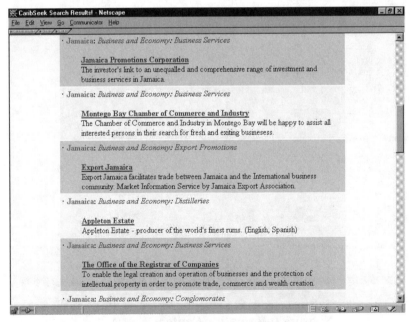

Figure 5.3   Partial Search Results—CaribSeek

Rhodes College in Memphis, Tennessee, produces several nice directories of international sites. Two pertain to our concerns: International Studies—Americas [http://blair.library.rhodes.edu/ishtmls/americas.html] covering North America, Central America, and the Caribbean and International Studies—South America [http://www.rhodes.edu/ishtmls/SAmerica.html]. The sites segment into general sites and country sites. Scrolling down the page of the Americas site (omitting the North American categories), one finds Caribbean, Island Links, Mexico, Central & Latin America—General Links, and Central & Latin America—Country Links. Similarly, the South America site separates into South America—General Links, and South America—Country Links. Many of these links take you to local newspapers (often in English), legal information, newsletters, and other Latin American directory sites. No value-added information appears at the site, nor is the information searchable (there's nothing to search), but as with many directory sites, it can help point you in the right direction.

The University of North Carolina at Charlotte offers VIBES—Virtual International Business and Economic Sources, a directory of Internet links, all in English and available free of charge. VIBES—Latin America [http://libweb.uncc.edu/ref-bus/reg.htm#latin] offers links to nearly thirty Latin American and Caribbean sites. Sources can also be found via individual country name.

@BRINT [http://www.brint.com], established in 1994, is a consulting firm that specializes in business technology and knowledge management. It refers to itself as a "virtual knowledge enterprise." The site contains a section entitled International Business & Technology that provides an extensive directory of sites. One section, Americas: Business & Technology [http://www.brint.com/Country.htm#IntAmerica], lists approximately twenty sites (including Canada) that would help people looking for Latin American business information. Some of the sites link to other, more specialized directories, while some sites link to specific studies such as Demographics and Behavior of the Chilean Internet Population.

Other directories and search engines for Latin America and the Caribbean include:

- **Caribbean Cyberspace**
  http://www.CaribbeanCyberspace.com
  Covers all Caribbean countries. Contains more fluff than
  business information, but is still worth checking.

- **Caribe Search**
  http://www.caribesearch.com
  Also Caribbean, this site can be searched in English, Spanish,
  French, German, Italian, and Portuguese.

- **Centramerica.com**
  http://directory.centramerica.com
  Information on this site covers Belize, Guatemala, El Salvador,
  Honduras, Nicaragua, Costa Rica, and Panama.

- **Central America on the Net**
  http://www.latinworld.com/centro
  Organized by country, each section is available in English,
  Spanish, and Portuguese.

- **Costa Rica Internet Directory**
  http://www.arweb.com/cr
  Contains a separate category for business.

- **EuroSeek Caribbean**
  http://webdir.euroseek.com/?ilang=en&catid=271
  Users can search by country or topic on this and the next two
  EuroSeek sites.

- **EuroSeek Central America**
  http://webdir.euroseek.com/?ilang=en&catid=266

- **EuroSeek South America**
  http://webdir.euroseek.com/?ilang=en&catid=265

- **Latin American/South American
  Search Engines and Directories**
  http://websearch.about.com/internet/websearch/
  msub12-m14.htm

- **South America on the Net**
  http://www.latinworld.com/sur/index.html

- **The Caribbean on the Net**
  http://www.latinworld.com/caribe/index.html

• **Yaguá Business**
http://www.yagua.com/cgi-local/categorias.cgi?categoria=
Comercio_y_Empresas
This site covers Paraguay; mostly in Spanish, some English.

Chambers of Commerce and Industry

We have already discussed (and I'm sure we will again) the use-fulness of Chambers of Commerce. Doing business research on Latin America is no exception. The region is home to the Association of American Chambers of Commerce in Latin America (AACCLA) [http://www.aaccla.org], founded in 1967. AACCLA has twenty-three members in twenty-one Latin American and Caribbean countries (Ecuador and Brazil each have two chapters). It represents more than 16,000 companies in the region and serves as an advocate for trade and investment with the United States.

Each AACCLA chapter has its own section of the site, which generally includes the following information:

• Contact Information

• Economic Outlook

• Link to the country's American Chamber (AmCham) site

• News—previous thirty days

• Publications

• Related Links

• Selected Government Contacts

• Statistical Snapshot—economic indicators, top trading partners

• Upcoming Events—trade shows, conferences

Be sure to check out individual AmCham sites (listed on the next page), as many of them contain pertinent business information. Information on important business issues in the region also resides here, such as background and up-to-the-minute information on the Free Trade Area of the Americas (FTAA) and the Caribbean Basin Initiative (CBI). AACCLA offers an extensive list of publications for sale, most within the $10 to $150 range.

- **American Chamber of Commerce in Argentina**
  http://www.amchamar.com.ar

- **American Chamber of Commerce of Bolivia**
  http://www.bolivianet.com/amcham

- **American Chamber of Commerce for Brazil, Rio de Janeiro**
  http://www.amchamrio.com.br (Portuguese only)

- **American Chamber of Commerce for Brazil, São Paulo**
  http://www.amcham.com.br/english

- **Chilean-American Chamber of Commerce**
  http://www.amchamchile.cl

- **Colombian-American Chamber of Commerce**
  http://www.amchamcolombia.com.co

- **Costa Rican-American Chamber of Commerce**
  http://www.amcham.co.cr

- **American Chamber of Commerce of the Dominican Republic**
  http://www.amcham.org.do

- **Ecuadorian-American Chamber of Commerce, Guayaquil**
  http://www.caecam.org/amcham.html

- **American Chamber of Commerce of El Salvador**
  http://www.amchamsal.com

- **American Chamber of Commerce in Guatemala**
  http://www8.bcity.com/amcham2

- **American Chamber of Commerce in Jamaica**
  http://www.amchamjamaica.org

- **American Chamber of Commerce of Nicaragua**
  http://amchamnic.com/index1.htm

- **American Chamber of Commerce and Industry of Panama**
  http://www.panamcham.com

- **American Chamber of Commerce of Trinidad & Tobago**
  http://www.amchamtt.com

- **Chamber of Commerce Uruguay-U.S.A.**
  http://www.zfm.com/amchamuru

- **Venezuelan-American Chamber of Commerce & Industry**
  http://www.venamcham.org/ingles/welcoeng.htm

Banking, Finance, and Stock Exchanges

The Center for Latin American Capital Markets [http://www. netrus.net/users/gmorles] has an interesting Web site that serves a variety of purposes. The Florida International University in Miami, Florida, hosts the Center. If you need to search for data on the capital markets of Latin America, the Research section of the site links to numerous studies. Another portion of the site, Exchanges, offers links to most of the Latin American stock exchanges currently online. Descriptions give an indication of what information appears on each site with the most important sites (in the opinion of the Center) highlighted. The News section links to numerous publications with descriptions in English. Some of the publications are general or regional, others are country-specific. A final section, General Economic Data, offers resources for Latin American economic data.

While on the subject of the stock exchanges within the region, here are links to those that have a Web site (not all sites are in English):

- **Argentina—Bolsa de Comercio de Buenos Aires**
  http://www.bcba.sba.com.ar/sib_i.htm

- **Barbados—Security Exchange of Barbados**
  http://www.cweek.com/sebact.html

- **Bermuda—Bermuda Stock Exchange**
  http://bsx.com/cgi-win/bsx.exe/bsxindex

- **Bolivia—Bolsa Boliviana de Valores**
  http://bolsa-valores-bolivia.com

- **Brazil—Rio de Janeiro Stock Exchange**
  http://www.bvrj.com.br

- **Brazil—São Paulo Stock Exchange**
  http://www.bovespa.com.br/indexi.htm

- **Cayman Islands—Cayman Islands Stock Exchange**
  http://www.csx.com.ky

- **Chile—Bolsa de Comercio de Santiago**
  http://www.bolsadesantiago.com/english/index.asp

- **Colombia—Bolsa de Occidente**
  http://www.bolsadeoccidente.com.co/0index_en.html

- **Colombia—Bolsa de Bogotá**
  http://www.bolsabogota.com.co

- **Ecuador—Bolsa de Valores de Guayaquil**
  http://www4.bvg.fin.ec/eng/default

- **Ecuador—Bolsa de Valores de Quito**
  http://www.ccbvq.com/bolsa/html/home.html

- **Honduras—Bolsa Centroamericana de Valores**
  http://www.bcv.hn

- **Jamaica—Jamaica Stock Exchange**
  http://www.jamstockex.com

- **Nicaragua—Bolsa de Valores de Nicaragua**
  http://www.bolsanic.com/engl.html

- **Paraguay—Bolsa de Valores de Asuncion**
  http://www.pdv.com.py/bolsa/index.html

- **Peru—Lima Stock Exchange**
  http://www.bvl.com.pe/homepage2.html

- **Trinidad and Tobago—Trinidad and Tobago
  Stock Exchange**
  http://stockex.co.tt

- **Venezuela—Caracas Stock Exchange**
  http://www.caracasstock.com/newpage/english/english.htm

In previous chapters, we've discussed the usefulness of Central Banks. Here are links to those in the region that have an Internet presence (again not all are in English):

- **Banco Central de la República de Argentina**
  http://www.bcra.gov.ar/english/e_english.htm

- **Central Bank of Barbados**
  http://www.centralbank.org.bb

- **Banco Central de Bolivia**
  http://www.bcb.gov.bo

- **Banco Central do Brasil**
  http://www.bcb.gov.br/defaulti.htm

- **Banco Central de Chile**
  http://www.bcentral.cl

- **Banco Central de la República—Colombia**
  http://www.banrep.gov.co/home4.htm

- **Banco Central de Costa Rica**
  http://www.bccr.fi.cr

- **Banco Central de la República Dominicana**
  http://www.bancentral.gov.do

- **Banco Central del Ecuador**
  http://www.bce.fin.ec

- **Banco Central de Reserva de El Salvador**
  http://www.bcr.gob.sv/ebcr000.htm

- **Banco de Guatemala**
  http://www.banguat.gob.gt/menugen.asp?kmenu=INDICE

- **Banco Central de Honduras**
  http://www.bch.hn

- **Bank of Jamaica**
  http://www.boj.org.jm/home30.html

- **Central Bank of the Netherlands Antilles**
  http://www.centralbank.an

- **Banco Central de Nicaragua**
  http://www.bcn.gob.ni

- **Central Reserve Bank of Peru**
  http://www.bcrp.gob.pe/english/e-Default.htm

- **Banco Central del Uruguay**
  http://www.bcu.gub.uy

- **Banco Central de Venezuela**
  http://www.bcv.org.ve

Yellow Pages

Below is a listing of Latin American Internet yellow pages directories. As you can see, some countries have more than one. Whenever possible, I have tried to point you to the English versions. However, there are still a few not available in English.

- **Argentina—Páginas Amarillas**
  http://www.paginasamarillas.com.ar

- **Argentina—Páginas Doradas**
  http://www.paginas-doradas.com.ar/PDPortal/guia_
  clasificada/guia_clasificada.asp

- **Bermuda Yellow Pages**
  http://www.bermudayp.com

- **Brazil Biz**
  http://www.brazilbiz.com.br/english

- **Chile—Las Amarillas de Internet**
  http://www.amarillas.cl

- **Chile Business Directory**
  http://www.chilnet.cl/consultas/abajoesp.asp

- **Colombian Yellow Pages**
  http://www.quehubo.com

- **Costa Rica Páginas Amarillas**
  http://www.costaricapages.com/local/localhome.htm

- **Páginas Amarillas de El Salvador**
  http://www.paginasamarillas.com/paginasamarillas/
  Salvador/Salvador.asp?NuevaB=2

- **Páginas Amarillas de Guatemala**
  http://www.paginasamarillas.com/paginasamarillas/
  guatemala/guatemala.asp

- **Páginas Amarillas de Panama**
  http://www.paginasamarillas.com/paginasamarillas/
  Panama/Panama.asp?NuevaB=4

- **Paraguay Páginas Amarillas**
  http://www.uninet.com.py/GUITEL/paginas_amarillas.html

- **Páginas Amarillas de Peru**
  http://www.paginasamarillas.telefonica.com.pe

- **Páginas Amarillas de Uruguay**
  http://www.guiatelefonica.com.uy/principal/index.htm

• **Venezuela—La Guia**

http://www.caveguias.com.ve

Local Government Resources

One should never overlook governments as good sources of business information and one site simplifies this resource for Latin America and the Caribbean. American Governments on the WWW [http://www.gksoft.com/govt/en/america.html] gathers all these sources on one easy-to-use location. This site is part of the Governments on the WWW series, online since June 1995.

Each regional section is broken up by country and lists the number of entries per country, along with the date of the last change. Click on a country to view a list of links for that country's government sites. Choosing Bolivia, we see numerous National Institutions including the National Congress, Ministry of Economic Development, Ministry of External Trade and Investment, and the National Institute of Statistics (see Figure 5.4). We also find links to Municipal Institutions (similar to state and local government offices), Bolivian consulates and embassies in other countries,

Figure 5.4   Partial Listing of Bolivian Resources—American Governments on the World Wide Web

Political Parties, and sites for Additional Information. While the number of listings for Bolivia is quite impressive (thirty), it pales in comparison to some of the other countries: Argentina (179), Brazil (357), and Chile (107).

The Organization of American States (OAS) Trade Unit has the Foreign Trade Information System or SICE from the Spanish acronym Sistema de Información al Comercio Exterior [http://www.sice.oas.org]. SICE provides a centralized location for public information and documents on trade in the Western Hemisphere in the four official languages of the OAS: English, Spanish, Portuguese, and French. The site is searchable in all four languages. While the site offers little in the way of value-added information, it can prove very useful in locating an abundance of Latin American and Caribbean trade information and is easy to navigate. These sections are also helpful:

- Trade Agreements—The texts of various multilateral, regional, free trade, bilateral, and other agreements appear here—many in English and Spanish, some only in Spanish. If you don't feel up to wading through an entire agreement, another section of the site offers summaries for many of the documents.

- Free Trade Area of the Americas (FTAA)—Just about anything you would want to know about the FTAA appears here. (A Free Trade Area is a region or a grouping of countries with no trade barriers between the countries. Import tariffs, quotas, and export subsidies are lifted for trade among the member countries.)

- Investment Treaties—Key points of bilateral investment agreements for twenty-five countries.

- Trade Related Links—Sorted by country, this site also links to Central Banks; various ministries such as Foreign Affairs and Economy, Industry, and Commerce; embassies; investment promotion agencies. It also provides links to tariff information, trade statistics (from official and nonofficial sources), and statistical agencies of various governments in the region.

- Intellectual Property Rights—Text of laws and regulations, directory of national authorities, and links to official sites in the region can be found here.

Exporter and Business Directories

Most countries in the region have at least one, and often more, exporters' or business directory sites. The sites are usually quite similar. Some can be searched by company name, product location, etc., and others offer alphabetical listings. Some even specialize in a particular industry. Start with these:

- **Bolivia Business Online**
  http://www.boliviabiz.com/business/company.htm
  Companies are listed alphabetically within sectors. The fifteen sectors include agriculture, communications, trade, and industry. Company listings link to company Web sites.

- **BrazilBiz**
  http://www.brazilbiz.com.br/english
  Individual industry sectors fall under the two broad headings of Products and Services. Company listings include contact information, link to company Web site, and brief company description (often in Portuguese).

- **DdeX Venezuela**
  http://www.ddex.com/index-e.html
  Search for exporters, products, and services alphabetically or by sector using the harmonized system. There is a separate section for engineering. Contact information and product listing are provided. The site also has an International Links section and an overview of Venezuela.

- **El Salvador Directory of Importers and Exporters**
  http://www.elsalvadortrade.com.sv/i_html/directorio.html
  Contains two directories, one for importers and one for exporters, that can be searched by product name or tariff code.

- **Haiti Business Directory**
  http://www.haitibusiness.com/INDEX.CFM?ACTION_
  RECHERCHE=RECHERCHE_ANGLAIS
  Companies are listed alphabetically by category in a combination of English and French.

- **Latin Export**
  http://www.latinexport.com
  This site covers Brazil, Argentina, Bolivia, Chile, Paraguay, and

Uruguay and contains four searchable directories: export companies, trading companies, service companies, and industry associations.

- **Latinvestor—Chilean Listed Companies**
http://www.latinvestor.com/listed%20companies/listed-ch.htm
Offers an alphabetical listing of Chilean companies on the Internet. Some companies have links to capsules at the Hoovers site.

- **Latinvestor—Colombian Listed Companies**
http://www.latinvestor.com/listed%20companies/listed-co.htm
Same as above for Colombian companies.

- **Peruvian Business Directory**
http://www.denperu.com/denexe/home-e.asp
Several search options are provided: alphabetical, company name, SIC, keyword, and more. Contact information offers Web site links, where available.

- **Trade Venezuela Trade Directory**
http://www.trade-venezuela.com/DIRENG.HTM
Alphabetical listing of companies; ten industries covered.

- **Uruguay.com**
http://www.uruguay.com/enlaces/yellow.html
This section of Uruguay.com site is called Yellow Pages but is really an alphabetical listing of companies in Uruguay. It includes brief description of companies and links to Web sites.

Guatemala

Guatemala is one of my favorite countries. Though I have never lived there, I have visited several times over the years. The climate is wonderful, earning it the nickname "Land of the Eternal Spring," and the textiles made there are outstanding. I normally don't like to shop, but turn me loose in Guatemala, and that's pretty much all I'll do. Traveling in Guatemala can be a bit dangerous, but if you use common sense and some caution, it's not too bad.

An ideal place to start Guatemalan business research, particularly when interested in investing in the country, is Guatemala Online [http://www.quetzalnet.com], which has been put together using some very impressive sources. (Quetzal, by the way, is both the national bird of Guatemala and the name of the currency.) Several organizations contribute to the content of Guatemala Online:

- The Guatemalan Ministry of Economy
- Guatemalan Development Foundation (FUNDESA)—a private, nonprofit institution that promotes Guatemalan trade and investment
- Chamber of Enterprise—composed of the principal chambers and business associations of the Guatemalan private sector
- AGEXPRONT—the Association of Exporters of Non-Traditional Products
- Central Bank of Guatemala
- INGUAT—the Guatemala Tourism Institute

The site begins with a narrative that asks and answers the question "Why invest in Guatemala?" and continues with a brief Country Profile and an Economic Overview. Just to demonstrate the wide variety of statistics and other information available at this site, here are some facts about Guatemala:

- Physicians Per Capita—4.7 per 10,000 persons
- Labor Force—2,500,000; 57.0% agriculture, 14.0% manufacturing, 13.0% services, 7.0% commerce, 4.0% construction, 3.0% transport, 0.8% utilities, 0.4% mining
- Telecommunications—fairly modern network centered in Guatemala City; 97,670 telephones; stations—91 AM, no FM, 25 TV, 15 shortwave; connection into Central American Microwave System; 1 Atlantic Ocean INTELSAT earth station
- National Libraries—100; Special Libraries—16

A Business Guidebook at the site, published by FUNDESA, provides information on various topics, including the legal framework for foreign investment, types of Guatemalan companies, taxation, and labor laws. Both traditional and nontraditional investment areas are discussed. The coverage outlines and explains the various local institutions involved in international trade and provides contact information for numerous public and private banks. It also carries an extensive section on tourism, but one really geared more to the vacationer than the business traveler.

Unfortunately, Guatemala Online's searchable Directory of Exporters seemed to have disappeared when last checked. The link now takes you directly to the previously mentioned AGEXPRONT [http://www.agexpront.com] site, where those interested in doing business in Guatemala can find further information. There are brief overviews and statistics on the seafood, agricultural, wood, handicrafts, apparel and textiles, and manufacturing sectors (see Figure 5.5). For each of the six sectors, they provide a short database of exporters with contact information and a brief product description. Databases are not searchable.

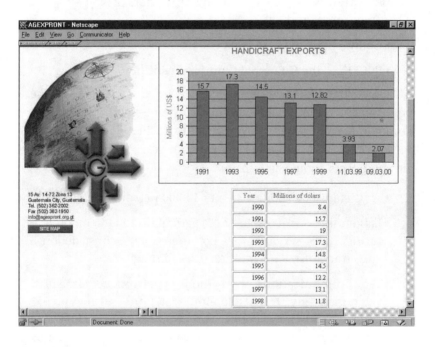

Figure 5.5   Guatemalan Handicraft Exports—AGEXPRONT

Argentina

Argentina differs somewhat from most of the other countries in South America. Although the people speak Spanish, a good portion of the population traces its ancestry to Italy and Germany. This gives the country more of a European or continental flair than you may find in other countries of the region. For this reason, many people prefer doing business here.

Fundación Invertir, a private organization of CEOs from leading Argentine enterprises and top government officials, has an amazing Web site [http://www.invertir.com]. It is one of the most comprehensive and useful country sites that I have seen. Fundación Invertir has a mandate to promote investment in Argentina and works closely with the Secretariat for Trade and Investments of the Ministry of Economy, Public Works and Services, as well as with other government agencies.

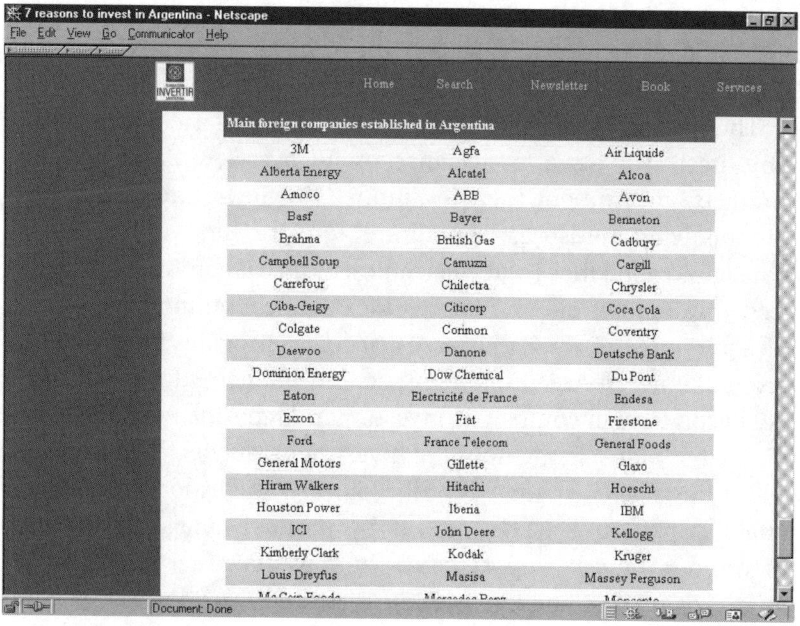

Figure 5.6   Foreign Companies in Argentina—Fundacion Invertir

The fully searchable site begins with some overview information on Argentina to help acquaint you with the country. The usual topline information appears in the Welcome to Argentina! section: population, GDP, geography, political system, why one should do business in the country, etc. There are brief summaries of the industries offering the best import and export opportunities, descriptions of industries with the greatest prospects for growth, and information on sectors undergoing privatization. There is also a list of the main foreign companies established in Argentina (see Figure 5.6).

The publication Argentina Monthly, available via e-mail, is published at the site (you can download it as a Word file), along with searchable archives going back to mid-1997. This newsletter covers not only current events, but often takes in-depth looks at one or more industries in Argentina. Additionally it offers mini-profiles of one or more companies in each issue.

A superb section on Economy and Statistics covers such topics as macroeconomic data, production and trade statistics (in the aggregate as well as by industry), and stock market and banking statistics. Much of the information appears in spreadsheet form that will automatically download into Excel. For some of the data, you exit the Fundación Invertir site, but the transfer occurs quickly and seamlessly, which makes it easy to return.

The section Investing in Argentina is almost a complete book unto itself. You get a foreign investment overview, along with key contacts, government agencies, industry reviews, and statistics for the following industries: agriculture, forestry and wood products, household appliances and electronics, industrial products and services, mining, petroleum and chemicals, telecommunications, textiles and apparel, and vehicles. The section provides hints and tips on marketing in Argentina, banking and finance information, and details on foreign companies investing in Argentina (which companies, what industries, amount of investment, and so forth).

Trading with Argentina describes import and export policies and offers import and export figures by product category. (In 1998, Argentina's largest import category was machinery and equipment—over US$10 billion; the category accounted for 32.6 percent of all imports.) If you definitely decide to do business in Argentina, the Business Contacts section may become the most useful section of all. To start with, it provides contact information for government agencies; trade offices; trade organizations; financial institutions; accounting, consulting, law, and market research firms; advertising agencies; transportation companies; radio and television stations; and newspapers. It also has corporate profiles of the companies affiliated with Fundación Invertir, including most of the largest companies in Argentina, and links to about a dozen directory sites where you can run searches looking for Argentine companies and/or products.

The balance of the site contains in-depth legal and tax information along with travel information and descriptions of business culture and business etiquette. If you can't find what you need here and you've exhausted all your other resources, Fundación Invertir will conduct in-country research for you. Available services and pricing are listed at the site.

Brazil

Brazil is a very interesting country and quite different from most of its neighbors, largely due to the language difference (Portuguese versus Spanish). While I can get by fairly well with Spanish, my complete lack of ability with Portuguese makes me quite a bit less comfortable when looking for Brazilian business information. Luckily, there are a number of sites in English to help overcome this barrier.

The Business section of Brazil InfoNet [http://www.brazilinfo. net/sky3/usbrazil2/public_html/business.html] has several areas that can get you started on your quest for information on business in Brazil. The Brazil InfoNet Business Directory is very similar to business directories we've seen elsewhere. Like many other directories, company listings are voluntary and fee-based so the information found in them isn't necessarily impartial. Categories covered include accounting, consulting, freight forwarders, Internet, legal, products, and telecommunications. Listings contain very brief company descriptions and links to company Web sites.

Brazil Newsstand links to several Brazil-oriented news publications in English; there are also quite a few in Portuguese. The English-language links reach these publications:

- Bloomberg News Latin America—covers the region, not just Brazil

- Business News Americas—also regional news

- Estado Brazil This Week—has a separate section for business news

- Gazeta Mercantil—also has a free e-mail business newsletter; subscription information at the site

- Latin News—Latin American newsletters concentrating on economic and political information

- Miami Herald—Internet edition focusing on Brazil

- Reuters—current news on Brazil

- Washington Post—articles on Brazil as well as links to Brazilian information

The Organizations section covers the following areas:

- Brazil/U.S. Business Council—a bilateral trade organization

- Brazilian Electrical and Electronics Industry Association

- Chambers of Commerce—links to Brazilian American chambers in the U.S. as well as other chambers within Brazil

- Government Resources—U.S. and Brazilian government sources

Some of the other offerings on Brazil InfoNet include links to U.S. Brazil, a company offering various services to businesses interested in Brazil and to Brazil TradeNet, a government office as well as a section for Trade Leads.

Brazil TradeNet is sponsored by the Brazilian Ministry of Foreign Relations [http://www.braziltradenet.gov.br/e/usrenglish.htm]. To find some overall Brazilian trade information, start with the Information About Brazil section, which has links to the following government sites (not all sites are in English):

- Ministry of Foreign Relations—an overview of Brazil, its economy, political structure, and culture

- Ministry of Foreign Relations: Mercosur—foreign trade statistics and economic data for Brazil and the other Mercosur countries (Mercosur is a Latin American trading block created by the Treaty of Asunción in March 1991. Argentina, Brazil, Paraguay, and Uruguay are members of Mercosur; Chile and Bolivia became associate members in 1996 and 1997 respectively.)

- IBGE, The Brazilian Institute of Geography and Statistics— up-to-date statistics and geographical data

• Governo do Brasil—links to all branches of the Brazilian government, including links for all ministries and most government agencies

• Ministry of Development and Foreign Trade—foreign trade statistics and economic data

• Banco Central—Brazil's Central Bank

• BNDES, The National Bank for Economic and Social Development—a state-owned development bank with information on investment opportunities in Brazil

• EMBRATUR—the Brazilian government's tourism board

The Investments section provides a mechanism for registering investment opportunities, both demands and offers. Two useful documents are available here for download in Word or PDF formats; the Legal Guide for the Foreign Investor in Brazil and Company Formation in Brazil.

The Virtual Showroom is pretty interesting. Products from the software, toy, furniture, jewelry, handicraft, and clothing sectors are featured. Each sector has a brief market overview along with a multitude of pictures of items offered for export and ordering information. (Look at the jewelry in Figure 5.7.)

If you register at the site, you gain free access to a searchable directory. (Warning: it might take several days for your registration to process. I registered on a Saturday and could not access the directory until the following Wednesday. Unfortunately, you do not receive a message advising that your registration has been processed. You just need to keep trying to access the database.) The directory may be searched by product or service code (there is a cascading list to help you choose the correct code, much like an SIC), company name or abbreviation, or the Brazilian state in which the company is located. Once you have narrowed your search, a list of companies from which to choose appears. Company listings carry good topline information:

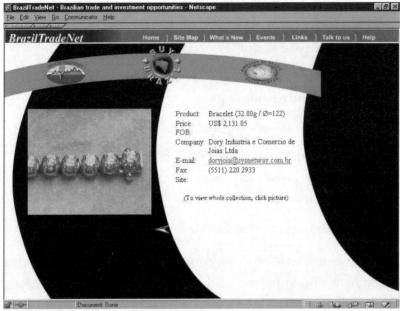

Figure 5.7   Jewelry for Export—Brazil TradeNet Virtual Showroom

- The company's full name and any abbreviations or acronyms used

- Contact information, including a contact name

- Language(s) to use in correspondence with the company

- The company's e-mail address and Web site URL

- A list of all the company's products and services by eight digit code (again, similar to SIC) and a notation as to the availability of individual products for export

- The markets to which the company exports and the markets of interest (not available for all companies)

The Brazilianist [http://www.brazilianist.com] is an interesting online publication. Started in 1996 with a target audience of investors, business people, and multinational companies entering or operating in the Brazilian marketplace, it was originally available in both print and online versions. In 1999 it became completely Internet based and now publishes three to four times a year. Upon review, the site appears to have a U.S. and Canadian focus, rather than global.

The most recent issue of *The Brazilianist* is posted at the site, with links to the full text of the articles. A Businesses in Brazil section has brief articles on the Brazilian activities of foreign companies. For example, the Spring 2000 issue discussed an expansion by Marriott Hotels, the acquisition by PSINet of a Brazilian ISP, and the launch by IMS Health of a new report that will track sales to Brazilian hospitals by pharmaceutical wholesalers.

Archives to *The Brazilianist* extend back to Winter 1996, but they are not posted at the site. Instead, you may request an archived article via an e-mail message after perusing a list of all past articles. You then receive the article via e-mail.

Companies may list themselves for free at the site or pay to upgrade for an expanded listing. The areas of advertising, associations, consultants, importers and exporters, and manufacturers/suppliers/distributors are represented in the Affiliates section. Note that not all of the companies listed are actually located in Brazil; many are U.S. or Canadian companies that conduct business in Brazil. Events such as Fenasoft 2000, an information technology show, are described in the Events section. The Classified section has brief ads for companies offering or looking for products and services. (Unfortunately, you will have to scroll past the occasional personal ad, such as the American male in his thirties looking for a Brazilian woman to marry.)

Some interesting Brazilian Internet statistics appeared on the main page the last time I visited the site:

- 9% of the population have access to the Internet
- 56% of them are men, 44% women
- 84% belong to the upper or middle class
- 47% are heavy users, accessing the Internet almost every day
- 27% are afraid of using credit cards to buy online

Caribbean

The Caribbean is a difficult area to research, comprising, as it does, a multitude of very small countries, all with different heritages. Sue Evan-Wong, an information professional with Carib Info in Antigua, sums it up when she says that one "needs to be aware that the Caribbean is very much divided according to each respective island's colonial experience—there is not enough cooperation between the English/French/Spanish/Dutch-speaking Caribbean and each group considers itself *the* Caribbean. When I get requests for information on 'the Caribbean' through my home page, I always have to ask what they mean by 'the Caribbean.'" Fortunately, she has a plethora of suggestions as to some basic resources useful for tackling the region.

If you have an ongoing interest in the Caribbean, you might want to stay on top of any business news that impacts the area. Bookmark the site for the Caribbean News Agency (CANA) [http://www. cananews.com] and check it at least once a week. CANA, a nonprofit cooperative owned by twelve private- and public-sector media houses, covers news and information from the CARICOM (Caribbean Community and Common Market) countries. The News section covers regional stories and keeps only a week's worth of stories posted; the Business section covers business news and has about a four-month archive. The Business section also contains short country profiles for the following countries:

• Anguilla	• Jamaica
• Antigua & Barbuda	• Montserrat
• Bahamas	• St. Kitts
• Barbados	• St. Lucia
• Belize	• St. Maarten
• British Virgin Islands	• St. Vincent
• Cayman Islands	• Suriname
• Dominica	• Trinidad & Tobago
• Grenada	• Turks and Caicos Islands
• Guyana	• Unites States Virgin Islands

Each country profile has three main sections:

• Economic Profile—quick overviews of the tourism, construction, agriculture, and financial sectors, along with a brief forecast

• History

• Quick Look—population, capital city, size, climate, currency

There is also information from the stock exchanges of Barbados, Bahamas, Jamaica, and Trinidad.

Back on the main page of the site, you will also find links to more than thirty Caribbean newspapers and about a dozen other Caribbean source links.

Another site with news—and more—is Caribbean Week [http://www.cweek.com]. One advantage, you can search the entire site with a search engine that even supports Boolean searching. You can find a week's worth of news stories, sorted by country, by clicking on Today's News, as well as stock market information for the exchanges in Barbados, Trinidad, Tobago, and Jamaica in the Stock Exchanges section. Newsstand brings up a page with links to numerous newspapers in the region. The Caribbean Week link allows you to choose from various sections of the newspaper, including Front Page, News & Briefs, and Business & Briefs. Business & Briefs has the text of all articles that have appeared in the section going back to August 1997. If you need information on a particular country, click on the country's name in the left frame to access the country's archives. It includes most of the countries in Latin America and the Caribbean.

The site also carries Business Guides for all the countries covered. Each guide includes an Economic Report and contact information (hyperlinked when possible) for government offices, banks, attorneys, accountants, consultants, transportation companies, free zones, and more (see Figure 5.8).

The Eastern Caribbean Investment Promotion Service (ECIPS) [http://www.ecips.com] is an agency of the Organization of Eastern Caribbean States (OECS). OECS countries consist of Anguilla, Antigua and Barbuda, British Virgin Islands, Commonwealth of Dominica, Grenada, Montserrat, St. Kitts and Nevis, St. Lucia and St. Vincent, and the Grenadines. These islands are important resources for anyone interested in apparel manufacturing, electronics assembly, information processing, and hotel and tourism development.

The ECIPS site lists synopses of investment benefits and selected economic, demographic, and tourism statistics. As ECIPS offers a range of services free of charge to potential investors, you can obtain additional information by contacting them directly.

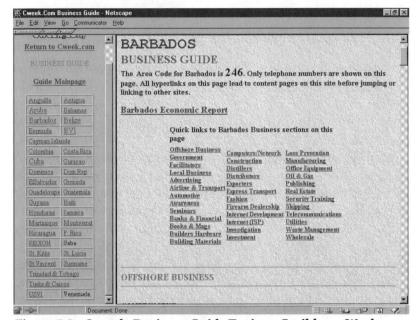

Figure 5.8   Sample Business Guide Topics—Caribbean Week

The Tourism and Industrial Development Company of Trinidad and Tobago Limited (TIDCO) [http://www.tidco.co.tt] maintains several sites, some with sections useful to those interested in doing business in Trinidad and Tobago. The Investing in Trinidad and Tobago site [http://www.investtnt.com] is probably the most useful. The Economy at a Glance portion includes a snapshot of the country and the capital (Port of Spain) and various economic indicators from 1993 through 1998. It also has charts and tables showing major trading partners, the ethnic makeup of the country, and an outline of the financial system. The Country Profile section details the political system and trade agreements, and provides brief overviews of the energy, manufacturing, agricultural, recreational marine, tourism, and entertainment sectors. It also lists the following as Emerging Sectors:

- Entertainment
- Environmental Services
- Financial Services
- Furniture, Joinery Products, and Wood Processing

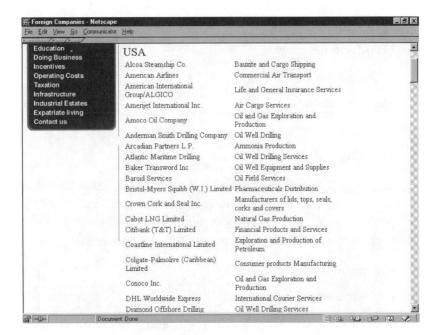

Figure 5.9   U.S. Companies in Trinidad & Tobago—Tourism & Industrial Development Company of Trinidad & Tobago (TIDCO)

• Information Technology Services

• Recreational Marine Services

• Tourism and Hospitality

Foreign Companies lists some of the companies already operating in Trinidad and Tobago. For a more extensive listing, sorted by country, scroll down the page and click on individual country names. Figure 5.9 shows a partial listing of U.S. companies with operations in the country. Other countries represented include Japan, India, United Kingdom, Australia, Canada, Guyana, Bermuda, Antigua, Jamaica, Barbados, Venezuela, Mexico, Germany, France, Italy, Finland, the Netherlands, and Switzerland. A lot of trading partners for two such small islands!

This section also includes a short, streaming video clip of an executive giving a testimonial on doing business here.

The Investment Opportunities section provides a briefing on six sectors considered ripe for investment:

- Chemicals, Pharmaceuticals, and Plastics

- Food and Beverage

- Information Technology

- Leisure Marine

- Metal Processing

- Printing and Packaging

The Doing Business section has a Business Guide that includes information on establishing a business, income tax, value-added tax, procedures, and other business requirements.

Other portions of the site discuss the following topics:

- Infrastructure

- Investment incentives

- Operating costs—includes electricity and water rates, along with labor rates for various jobs in different business sectors

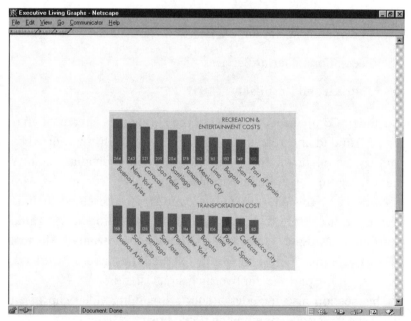

Figure 5.10   Comparative Living Expenses—Tourism & Industrial Development Company of Trinidad & Tobago (TIDCO)

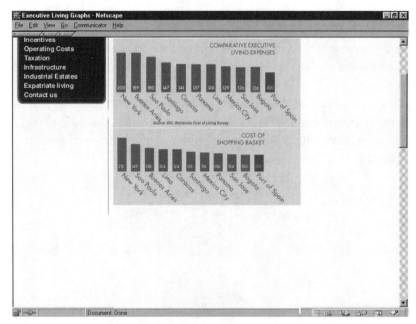

Figure 5.11   More Comparative Living Expenses—Tourism & Industrial Development Company of Trinidad & Tobago (TIDCO)

- Quality of life for expatriates—has interesting graphs comparing cost of living with other cities in Latin America and the Caribbean (see Figures 5.10 and 5.11)

- Tax system—with some industry specifics

TIDCO's Trade Information site [http://www.tradetnt.com] didn't prove as useful as I had hoped. I found quite a few dead links. However, it is much improved since my last visit and therefore earned a mention here. Useful items include trade statistics, transportation information, a description of the country's major industrial and commercial areas, a link to the Ministry of Trade and Industry, links to several local newspapers, and a searchable company database that contains the usual contact information, along with a listing of the company's products, services, year established, and number of employees. Additional company information appears at the Virtual Trade Fair portion of the site.

If the TIDCO sites have sparked your interest in Trinidad and Tobago, you might want to check out the Trinidad and Tobago Manufacturers Association site [http://www.ttma.com] for further information about local companies.

Regional Wrap-Up

By now you should have recognized the disparity of the many countries in the region. Hopefully, however, we have not discouraged you and you will use our suggestions as good starting points for Latin American and Caribbean business information. If you use one or more of the traditional online services (whenever possible) and complement them with some of the resources we've discussed here, you should find what you need.

CHAPTER 6

THE MIDDLE EAST AND NORTH AFRICA

The Middle East and North Africa represents another exotic locale for us to explore. During my research for this chapter, I came across so many definitions of this region that my head was spinning. Some sources go as far east as Afghanistan; others as far south into Africa as Djibouti and Somalia; others north to Turkey. To further complicate matters, the definition problem is not restricted to geography; religion and culture also come into play. Some sources refer to the Arab Middle East or the Muslim Middle East.

For most readers, researching this region leads us into new territory and into dealing with cultures very different from our own. We will need more background research into standard business practices, customs, and mores. To help in that endeavor, in this chapter we will cover the region in general and look at Bahrain, Egypt, Israel, Lebanon, Morocco, Palestine, Saudi Arabia, and the Sudan individually.

One word of caution before we begin examining ways to extract meaningful business information from this mysterious part of the world. Much of the time, I found the Web sites for the Middle East painfully slow to load. If you're a Free Cell addict (and you know who you are), this is a good opportunity to work on your playing strategy while waiting for Web pages to fully load.

Regional Resources

ArabNet [http://www.arab.net] is a comprehensive site for the Arab portion of the Middle East and North Africa (see Figure 6.1). It is owned and operated by ArabNet Technology (ANT), part of the Saudi Research and Marketing Group, a publisher of leading newspapers and magazines in Saudi Arabia. The site covers the following countries:

• Algeria	• Morocco
• Bahrain	• Oman
• Comoros	• Palestine
• Djibouti	• Qatar
• Egypt	• Saudi Arabia
• Iraq	• Somalia
• Jordan	• Sudan
• Kuwait	• Syria
• Lebanon	• Tunisia
• Libya	• United Arab Emirates
• Mauritania	• Yemen

Figure 6.1   Portion of ArabNet Home Page

On the right-hand section of the screen (scroll past the Arabic portion, unless you happen to read Arabic), you will see links to numerous regional news articles. Bear in mind, however, that these news articles are written from an Arabic point of view.

The center portion of the page is Country Data and features the names and flags of the covered countries. A great deal of information appears on the country sites, and for most countries, the links to other sites are quite extensive and impressive. As expected, some countries offer more details than others. For example, there is far more information on Egypt than Jordan. The information falls into nine categories:

- Business

- Culture

- Geography

- Government

- History

- Links to Other Sites

- Overview

- Tour Guide

- Transport

Each category, in turn, has various subcategories. Egypt's Business category includes Economy, Trade, Industry, Agriculture, Fishing, Petroleum & Minerals, and Currency. Information is brief, but sometimes quite interesting. For example, you may not know that in the 1990s, there were 1.6 million donkeys and 4.8 million goats in Egypt.

Back on the main page of the ArabNet site, the left side is entitled A-Z Directory and offers a grab bag of information, including links to numerous companies, organizations, and a potpourri of other things. A-Z of Camels answers more questions than you ever thought to ask about camels. One of the more useful links, The Saudi 100, lists the top 100 Saudi companies ranked by turnover. The list may be viewed by company name or by rank. Company profiles are extensive for a free site and include turnover and percent change from the previous year, assets, capital, number of employees,

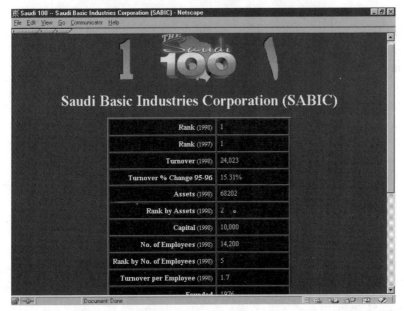

Figure 6.2   Partial Description of the Top Company in the Saudi 100—ArabNet

turnover per employee, year founded, activity, legal status, chief executive, and telephone and fax numbers (see Figure 6.2).

Returning once again to ArabNet's main page, you will see an icon near the top labeled Middle East Internet Directory (MEID). This icon links to a list of companies trading and operating in the Middle East and North Africa. As with most free directories of this type, companies choose to be included, which tends to under-represent the market as a whole.

The directory lists companies alphabetically and by category. These categories are covered:

- Arts & Culture
- Business & Economy
- Construction
- Education
- Health
- Information Technology & Communications
- Manufacturing & Processing

- Media & Printing

- Miscellaneous

- Retail & Trading

- Services

- Sports & Leisure

- Transport & Shipping

- Travel & Tourism

Listings include typical directory information with some data unusual for a free directory, such as capital, trade license number, executives' names, shareholders, members of the Board of Directors, bankers, products, and brand names.

On the bottom of the MEID page appears a link for the Top 100 Arab Banks. While the information here is a bit old (rankings from 1996), it's a good starting point for banking information. Banks rank by capital, assets, and profits.

One last feature to note about the ArabNet site is its searchability, although it doesn't appear to support Boolean searching.

Arab World Online [http://www.awo.net] is a joint venture of the National U.S.-Arab Chamber of Commerce (NUSACC) and Multitasking Online. The main page contains headlines of current news articles and links to the full text. Three of the more interesting and relevant sections of the site are listed here:

- Business: Banks—Best Opportunities for Investment and Export, and Investment Climate are worth reviewing in this section.

- Commercial Directory—Here you will find the Arab World Online Commercial Directory Database where you can search for companies that fit your criteria. You can also retrieve a list of NUSACC members.

- Country Information—Twenty-two countries are listed here, each with seven sections of information: Country Profile; Government Contacts; Private Sector Listings; Import, Export, Trade Balance Statistics with the U.S.; Articles; Exchange Rate; and Links to Related Sites (see Figure 6.3).

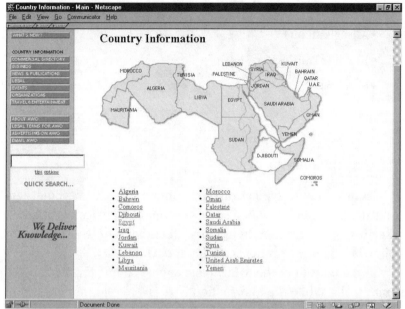

Figure 6.3   Map of Countries Covered by Arab World Online

Directories

Like most of the rest of the world, this area of the world has some regional directory sites worth exploring. In the case of the Middle East, I would encourage you to explore more than just the business sections of the directories. Customs and culture differ greatly in this part of the world and will definitely affect the conduct of business. The more well-versed you are in the ways of the region, the better positioned you will be to infiltrate the business community.

Start with the Web site for The Center for Middle Eastern Studies at the University of Texas at Austin [http://menic. utexas.edu/menic.html]. You can choose from the following subject categories:

- Ancient History

- Arts and Humanities

- Business and Finance

- Cultures and Groups

- Education

- Energy

- Government and Politics

- Maps and Travel

- News and Media

- Regional Information

- Religion

- Society

You can also choose to look at all of the listings for a particular country by selecting one of the countries from the list on the left side of the page; the list contains twenty-three countries from Afghanistan to Yemen.

The Al Mashriq—the Levant site [http://almashriq.hiof.no] covers "cultural riches from the countries of the Eastern Mediterranean," defined as Egypt, Israel, Jordan, Lebanon, Palestine, Syria, and Turkey. In addition to the country-specific links, other topics covered include business, education, environment, politics, and software. Some less "serious" topics are also addressed, such as food, arts and crafts, and humor.

Al-Murshid [http://www.murshid.com] provides a searchable index of Arab and Middle Eastern sites. Topics include the following:

- Arts and Literature

- Business and Economy

- Computers and Internet

- Countries and Regions

- Education

- Entertainment

- Health

- News and Media

- Politics and Law

- Recreation and Sports

- Reference

• Sciences

• Society and Culture

You can drill down easily through the various levels of the index to find what you need. For example, if you want to find companies within a particular industry, follow Business and Economy to Companies and choose an industry sector (see Figure 6.4). It lists companies, each with a link to its Web site.

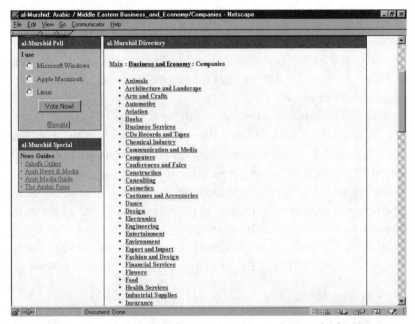

Figure 6.4   Examples of Industry Sectors—Al-Murshid Directory

If you or your client plans to travel to the region, you can find information on local ISPs and Internet cafes via the Computers and Internet link. You can also drill down by country to retrieve country-specific links sorted by category.

Here are several other good directories to try:

• **1001 Sites.com**
http://www.1001sites.com
A searchable site organized by topic and country.

- **ArabInfo.org**
  http://www.arab-trade.com
  Covers more than twenty countries in the region; also has links to newspapers (in English and Arabic).

- **Arabist**
  http://www.arabist.com
  This directory covers most of the Arab countries in the Middle East.

- **EgyptSearch.com**
  http://www.egyptsearch.com

- **EuroSeek.com**
  http://webdir.euroseek.com/?ilang=en&catid=264
  In addition to a Business and Economy category, the site has separate listings for Bahrain, Cyprus, Egypt, Iran, Iraq, Israel, Jordan, Kuwait, Lebanon, Libya, Oman, Palestine, Qatar, Saudi Arabia, Syria, Turkey, and the United Arab Emirates.

- **iGuide**
  http://www.iguide.co.il
  This searchable directory site focuses on Israel.

- **Lebanon Online**
  http://www.lol.com.lb/index.shtml
  This Lebanese directory also has news.

- **Libanis**
  http://libanis.com
  Another Lebanese directory site.

- **Middle East Directory**
  http://www.middleeastdirectory.com
  Try several sections here for business information: Business & Finance, Associations, Computers & Technology, Health & Medicine, Internet, and News & Media.

- **The Middle East Information Network**
  http://www.mideastinfo.com
  In addition to a Business category, this site also has separate country sections and is searchable.

Search Engines

There aren't very many search engines dedicated to this region of the world. Several sites that purported to be search engines had notices on the site such as "Coming Soon." So it appears that more are on their way; it's just a matter of time.

- **Arab Sites.com**
  http://arabsites.com/index.html

- **Cyprus 2000**
  http://www.cyprus2000.com/search

- **Lebanese Sites Search Engine**
  http://www.netgate.com.lb/bigbang

- **Robby—The Hellenic Search Engine**
  http://www.robby.gr

- **Search Egypt Web**
  http://Search.EgyptWeb.com/#SearchTable

Yellow Pages

Unfortunately, this part of the world has few online yellow pages sites. All except one of the following are in English:

- **Bahrain Yellow Pages**
  http://www.bahrainyellowpages.com

- **Cyprus Yellow Pages**
  http://www.cyprusyellowpages.com

- **Iran Yellow Pages**
  http://www.iranyellowpages.net

- **Israel Golden Pages**
  http://www.yellowpages.co.il/yp/yp.cgi?lang=E&clear=1

- **Lebanon Internet Yellow Pages**
  http://www.yellowpages.com.lb

- **Morocco Yellow Pages**
  http://www.maroc.net/yp

- **Palestine Yellow Pages**
  http://www.palestine-yellowpages.com

- **Tunisia Yellow Pages (French only)**
  http://www.pagesjaunes.com.tn

- **United Arab Emirates Internet Yellow Pages**
  http://uae-ypages.com/html/1.htm

Banking, Finance, and Stock Exchanges

Historically, the people of the Middle East have always been thought of as businesspeople and merchants. Therefore, it should come as no surprise to find a multitude of information in the areas of banking, finance, and the stock market. There are numerous good banking and financial sites for the region, many with useful and hard-to-find value-added information.

The site for The Emirates Bank Group [http://emiratesbank.com/ebg] bills itself as "The voice ... on the economy and the financial industry in the U.A.E. (United Arab Emirates) and the G.C.C. (Gulf Cooperation Council)." The first page of the site lists headlines and links to the full text of several top news stories. The news updates daily. For further news impacting the economic and financial sectors, click on Gulf Highlights to receive a partial list of countries in the region with links to additional stories.

Going back to the main page, choose Financial Highlights from the drop-down menu on the right. (Note: The print for the drop-down menu is extremely small and difficult to read.) Here are some of the options:

- Stockline—a brief review of the market (EMNEX—Emirates Equity Index) and a comparison among various sectors

- News & Views—the Daily Treasury Report that includes international interbank exchange rates and interest rates, selected international market indicators, and news highlights

- Faxline—exchange rates, deposit rates, and Gulf currency exchange rates

- Treasury Newsletter—a financial review of the previous week

A drop-down menu on the main page of the site offers additional information on the individual banks composing the Emirates Bank Group.

HSBC Bank Middle East [http://www.hsbc.com/cgi-bin/bvsm/hsbc/scripts/hsbc_main.jsp] has a great Business Profile of the United Arab Emirates in PDF format. (This would be a good time to return phone calls or attend to paperwork, as this document really takes a long time to download.) For those of you as geographically challenged as I am, it helpfully lists the seven Emirates that compose the U.A.E.:

- Abu Dhabi

- Ajman

- Dubai

- Fujairah

- Ras Al Khaimah

- Sharjah

- Umm Al Quwain

The comprehensive Business Profile covers a variety of topics, including the following:

- An overview of the economy with a discussion of efforts to diversify in order to reduce dependence on oil and gas

- Major exports by product and destination

- Major imports by product and country of origin

- GDP by industry sector

- An overview of business law

- Information on free trade zones

- Intellectual property protection

- Work permits

- Contact information for government offices and chambers of commerce

Similar HSBC Bank Business Profiles exist for the following Middle Eastern countries (all of which are available at http://www.hsbc.com):

- Bahrain
- Egypt
- Jordan
- Lebanon
- Oman
- Qatar

The National Bank of Kuwait [http://www.nbk.com] has some interesting documents in the Economics & Markets section of the site, all of which you can receive at no charge via e-mail subscription or view at the site. There is the Daily Money Market Report, the Weekly Money Market Report (only available in Arabic), the Monthly Newsletter, and the NBK Quarterly Report (previous four quarters are available at the site in PDF format.) The NBK Quarterly Report provides a lot of detail in its various sections, which will vary somewhat from quarter to quarter, such as:

- Foreign trade (including regional trade)
- Breakout of non-oil exports
- Labor force, including an educational profile of the labor force
- Sector overviews: Oil; Construction, Real Estate, and Housing; Money and Banking; and the Stock Market
- Special report on Kuwait and the Euro
- Key Economic and Financial Indicators

The site for the Jordan Kuwait Bank [http://www.jordan-kuwait-bank.com] mainly contains information about the bank itself, including an annual report. The Quarterly Bulletin link leads to a few overview articles on the economic and financial sectors of Jordan and Kuwait. Following the Banking Services link allows you to connect directly to the site for the Amman Financial Market

(AFM) [http://www.access2arabia.com/afm]. Two sections of the AFM site have particular interest. The first is the Daily Report of the AFM. This report (about three months behind during my last site visit) lists current market information by listed company sorted into the following sectors: banking, insurance, service, industry, parallel market, and the complete market. The other useful section is the list of brokers accredited by the AFM; the listings include contact information.

Israel's Mizrahi Bank [http://www.mizrahi.co.il] provides a wealth of financial information for the business searcher. Follow the Capital Market link and you just might find what you need in one of the three choices listed.

The Capital Market Research Department of the bank compiles the first section, Corporate Survey and Valuation Appraisal. It carries valuations of more than twenty Israeli companies. Each valuation includes slightly different information, but generally includes company financials, SWOT analysis (strengths, weaknesses, opportunities, and threats), three- to five-year income forecasts, and competitors (see Figure 6.5).

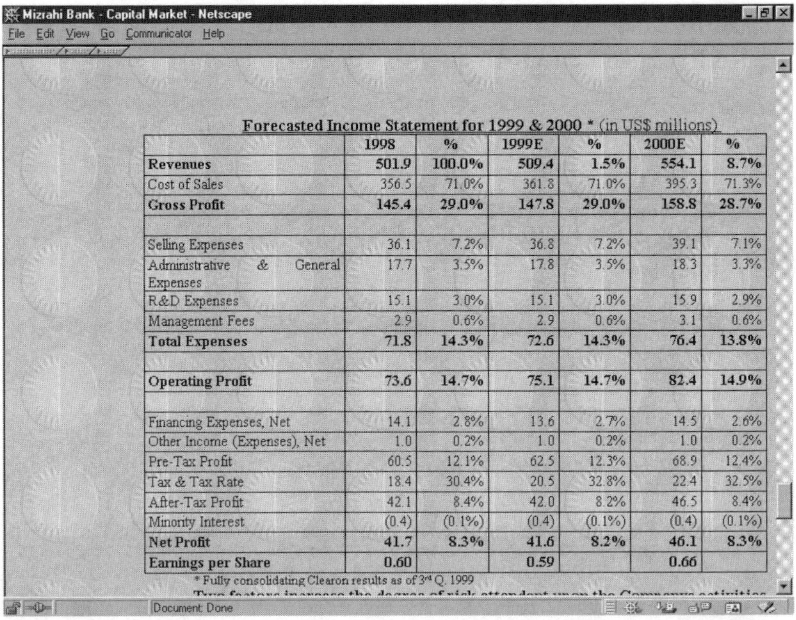

Forecasted Income Statement for 1999 & 2000 * (in US$ millions)

	1998	%	1999E	%	2000E	%
Revenues	**501.9**	**100.0%**	**509.4**	**1.5%**	**554.1**	**8.7%**
Cost of Sales	356.5	71.0%	361.8	71.0%	395.3	71.3%
Gross Profit	**145.4**	**29.0%**	**147.8**	**29.0%**	**158.8**	**28.7%**
Selling Expenses	36.1	7.2%	36.8	7.2%	39.1	7.1%
Administrative & General Expenses	17.7	3.5%	17.8	3.5%	18.3	3.3%
R&D Expenses	15.1	3.0%	15.1	3.0%	15.9	2.9%
Management Fees	2.9	0.6%	2.9	0.6%	3.1	0.6%
Total Expenses	**71.8**	**14.3%**	**72.6**	**14.3%**	**76.4**	**13.8%**
Operating Profit	**73.6**	**14.7%**	**75.1**	**14.7%**	**82.4**	**14.9%**
Financing Expenses, Net	14.1	2.8%	13.6	2.7%	14.5	2.6%
Other Income (Expenses), Net	1.0	0.2%	1.0	0.2%	1.0	0.2%
Pre-Tax Profit	60.5	12.1%	62.5	12.3%	68.9	12.4%
Tax & Tax Rate	18.4	30.4%	20.5	32.8%	22.4	32.5%
After-Tax Profit	42.1	8.4%	42.0	8.2%	46.5	8.4%
Minority Interest	(0.4)	(0.1%)	(0.4)	(0.1%)	(0.4)	(0.1%)
Net Profit	**41.7**	**8.3%**	**41.6**	**8.2%**	**46.1**	**8.3%**
Earnings per Share	**0.60**		**0.59**		**0.66**	

* Fully consolidating Clearon results as of 3rd Q. 1999

Figure 6.5 Company's Forecasted Income Statement Prepared by Mizrahi Bank

Next the Survey of Israel's Capital and Financial Markets basically reviews economic factors affecting Israel's capital market. While the site's instructions expected posting of the previous month's report, when I last visited the site, the posted report was about a year old.

Lastly, this site links to the Tel Aviv Stock Exchange (TASE) [http://www.tase.co.il/buildpage.cgi]. While the information provided by TASE is publicly available, those of us outside Israel can find it difficult to track down. Along with the usual information one would expect to find at a stock exchange site, it has market data for all listed companies sorted by sixteen sectors. One can also find the companies with the most actively traded shares.

The Members List contains all banks and brokerage firms belonging to TASE, along with contact information and links to their sites.

The site is a bit confusing, so if you still haven't found the nugget you seek, keep checking different areas of the site. You could find the information buried somewhere.

For another useful Israeli bank site, try Bank Hapoalim [http://www2.bankhapoalim.co.il/national/index.html]. This site's pertinent sections include the following:

- Capital Markets—contains the Weekly and Daily Reviews of the Israeli Capital Market and special financial updates, including analysis, for a handful of Israeli companies

- Israel Economy—the Economic Developments in 2000 and Forecast for 2001 and Monthly Update Reports

- Exchange Rates—comparison of the Israeli shekel to more than thirty foreign currencies (Check the date before you use the data; sometimes it's very current and sometimes several months old.)

Another site jointly sponsored by Bank Hapoalim and Standard & Poor's [http://www.standardpoor.co.il/bankhapoalim] contains profiles of the leading Tel Aviv Stock Exchange companies, as well as Israeli companies traded on the NASDAQ, NYSE, AMEX, and London Stock Exchange. You can select profiles by company name, industry, or stock exchange. As a point of interest, each of the stock exchanges contains the following number of company profiles:

- AMEX—2

- London Stock Exchange—2

- NASDAQ—36

- NYSE—5

- TASE—62

There are forms at the site to order annual reports for close to 100 Israeli companies and a copy of the Standard & Poor's Directory of Public Companies & Financial Institutions—Israel. All publications are free.

We've already mentioned a few of the stock exchanges in the region. Here are the URLs for some of the others:

- **Bahrain—Bahrain Stock Exchange**
  http://www.bahrainstock.com

- **Egypt—Cairo & Alexandria Stock Exchanges**
  http://www.egyptse.com

- **Iran—Tehran Stock Exchange**
  http://www.neda.net/tse

- **Kuwait—Kuwaiti Stock Prices (not the actual exchange)**
  http://www.alsadon.com/rates.html

- **Lebanon—Beirut Stock Exchange**
  http://www.bse.com.lb

- **Morocco—Casablanca Stock Exchange**
  http://www.casablanca-bourse.com/homeen.html

- **Palestine—Palestine Securities Exchange**
  http://www.p-s-e.com

- **Tunisia—Tunis Stock Exchange**
  http://www.tunisie.com/BusinessInfo/stock.html

- **Turkey—Istanbul Stock Exchange**
  http://www.ise.org

Chambers of Commerce and Industry

Only a small number of the few AmChams in the region have Web sites and even those offer very little useful information, which I found quite disappointing. However, there are several other Chambers to be found.

American Chambers of Commerce (AmChams)

- **American Chamber of Commerce of Egypt**
  http://www.amcham.org.eg

- **Israel-America Chamber of Commerce & Industry**
  http://www.amcham.co.il

- **The American Chamber of Commerce in Morocco**
  http://www.amcham-morocco.com

Other Chambers (Not AmChams)

- **Arab Chambers of Commerce Offices in the Arab World**
  http://www.awo.net/commerce/arabcoc/coc.asp

- **National U.S.-Arab Chamber of Commerce**
  http://www.nusacc.org

- **Bahrain Chamber of Commerce and Industry**
  http://www.bahchamber.com

- **Chamber of Commerce and Industry—
  Haifa and Northern Israel**
  http://haifachamber.com

- **Federation of Israeli Chambers of Commerce**
  http://www.chamber.org.il

- **Federation of Jordanian Chambers of Commerce**
  http://www.fjcc.com

- **Amman Chamber of Industry (Jordan)**
  http://www.aci.org.jo

- **Chamber of Commerce and Industry—Beirut (Lebanon)**
  http://www.ccib.org.lb

- **Palestinian Chambers of Commerce, Industry, and Agriculture**
  http://www.pal-chambers.com

- **Palestine Chamber of Commerce**
  http://www.g77tin.org/pccghp.html

- **Council of Saudi Chambers of Commerce and Industry**
  http://www.awo.net/saudicouncil

- **Jeddah Chamber of Commerce and Industry (Saudi Arabia)**
  http://www.awo.net/commerce/arabcoc/home.asp

- **Riyadh Chamber of Commerce and Industry (Saudi Arabia)**
  http://www.riyadh-chamber.org

- **U.S.-Saudi Arabian Business Council**
  http://www.us-saudi-business.org

- **Federation of Syrian Chambers of Commerce**
  http://www.fedcommsyr.org

- **Abu Dhabi Chamber of Commerce and Industry (United Arab Emirates)**
  http://www.adcci-uae.com

- **Ajman Chamber of Commerce and Industry (United Arab Emirates)**
  http://www.ajcci.co.ae/ajcci.htm

- **Sharjah Chamber of Commerce and Industry (United Arab Emirates)**
  http://www.sharjah.gov.ae/scci

News Resources

Globes, Israel's largest business newspaper for more than fifteen years, launched Israel's Business Arena [http://www.globes.co.il/serveen] in August 1995 as an online English edition of the newspaper. The site updates daily (Sunday through Thursday) at 6 P.M. Israel time.

Near the bottom of the column, the heading Features appears. This includes links to stories concerning the real estate market and a Standard & Poor's annual review of Israel's economy and capital markets.

An entire section of Israel's Business Arena is devoted to high-tech companies with news stories, a profile of a different high tech start-up company each week, an article on How Israeli High-Tech Happened, and a Start-Up Guide (including information on finding start-ups, business incubators, government and legal framework for high-tech start-ups, and links to the Israel Start-Up Companies Promotion Center and Messer—The Israel Idea Promotion Center). An archive of the start-up company profiles sorts into the following categories:

- Agriculture

- Communication

- Computing and Internet

- Education and Services

- Industrial Processes and Products

- Medical and Biotech

- Transport

The entire Israel's Business Arena site is searchable. Using the Advanced Search function, you can search back to November 30, 1995. Free registration is required.

Arabia.On.Line [http://www.arabia.com] offers a good bit of news, along with other information. In the center of the page, you will find headlines and links for the full text of current news stories in various categories, such as news, business, and technology. To find more news, follow the News link in the box near the top of the page.

Choosing the Business link brings current and recent news stories relating to business, covering areas such as Oil and Energy, Banks and Funds, Stocks and Currency, and IT Business. Country-specific links with business news are available for these countries:

• Algeria	• Kuwait
• Bahrain	• Lebanon
• Egypt	• Libya
• Iraq	• Morocco
• Jordan	• Oman

- Palestine
- Qatar
- Saudi Arabia
- Sudan

- Syria
- Tunisia
- United Arab Emirates
- Yemen

The Technology link takes you to another Web site, Arabian Business.com [http://www.itp.net/corporate/current/9747835099 8941.htm], a site with technology and Internet news of the region.

In case you still haven't had your fill of Middle Eastern news, I have one last source to suggest: Middle East Economic Survey (MEES) [http://www.mees.com], a weekly newsletter on the Middle East and North Africa. Published for the last forty years, it covers finance and banking, oil, and politics, among other topics. One of the pages at the MEES site, Newspapers and News Agencies [http://www.mees.com/dotcom/newspapers/index. html], lists news sites for seventeen countries. It also identifies the language of the site, with Arabic, French, and English the most common.

Palestine

Arab Supernet [http://www.a-supernet.net/default.asp], a Palestinian business exchange, can help identify Palestinian companies. Online since January 1998, Arab Supernet makes it easy to search for companies, organizations, or foreign organizations in Palestine. The site has one downside; companies must subscribe to be listed. It's obviously not a comprehensive (or unbiased) list of companies. On the other hand, it's free and just might have companies not listed elsewhere.

To search the site, scroll down to the box about halfway down the page. There are nine company types from which to choose:

- Agents
- Business Organizations
- Financial Services
- Industry Sector
- Information Technology

- Real Estate and Construction

- Services

- Tourism Services

- Trade & Investments

To test the site, let's choose Industry Sector as the company type. An extensive listing of companies appears. Scrolling through and choosing Nassar Investment Company, we see the company address, phone and fax numbers, and e-mail address. A short description lets us know Nassar Investment manufactures building materials, in particular, stone, granite, and marble works. Clicking on the company name takes us to a page with options for more company data (see Figure 6.6). The About link at the top of the page presents a paragraph describing Nassar Investment in more detail. The company's home page, containing a product catalog and product photos, is also available.

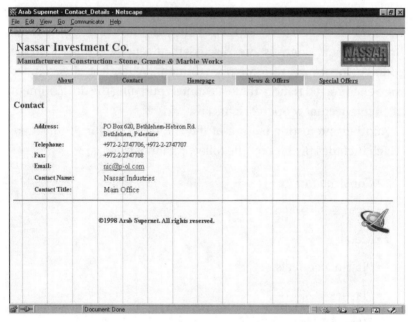

Figure 6.6   Company Contact Information from Arab Supernet

Back on the main page, you can also search for Organizations (civil, educational, local governments) and Foreign Organizations (consulates and diplomatic missions, media agencies, and press offices).

Near the bottom of the page, you will find a Made in Palestine link. Clicking on this takes you to a list of four product categories:

- Arts & Handicrafts

- Food & Beverages

- Footwear

- Health & Medical

Choosing one of them will bring up a table with item names, product description, and the producer, plus a link to the producer's listing in the database, similar to that displayed previously in Figure 6.6.

PALTRADE [http://www.paltrade.org] is the Web site for the Palestine Trade Center and has several sections designed to help those interested in conducting business in or with Palestine. Follow the Country Profile link to Market Profile. Here you will find a long document (also available in PDF format) covering critical areas such as Market Access, Investment Climate, and Foreign Trade. Import/Export controls are discussed at length, along with the country's openness to foreign investment. When last checked, we were encouraged to note that Palestine is pursuing the development of an intellectual property rights law.

Another interesting feature of the site is the Sector Profile area, which includes profiles on the following industries:

- Construction

- Food & Beverage

- Metal

- Pharmaceuticals

- Plastics

- Stone & Marble

- Textiles & Garments

Other sections to check are Directory, Import/Export Guide, and Links We Like.

Lebanon

If you need to look for companies in Beirut, go to Lebanon.com [http://www.lebanon.com]. Scroll down almost to the bottom of the page, click on Lebanon.com Business Directory, and click again on Enter Directory and Lebanon.com to reach the directory. On the left, you can choose to view by category or company name. Choosing View by Category displays all available categories (more than eighty), from Accounting to Waterproofing. As an example, selecting Telecommunications reveals nine companies. The third company on the list, Pesco Telecom S.A.L., provides the following information (see Figure 6.7):

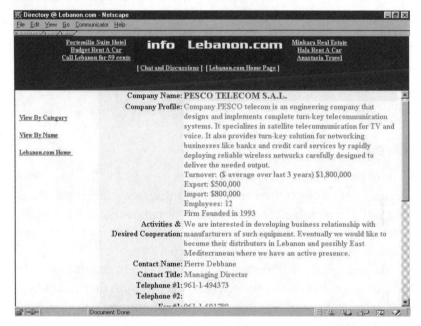

Figure 6.7   Portion of Company Profile—Lebanon.com

- Activities & Desired Cooperation—company goals

- Company Profile—includes company description, turnover, export and import figures, number of employees, and year founded

- Contact Name and Contact Title

- E-Mail Link—to use the e-mail link, you must register at the site; registration is free

- Telephone and Fax Numbers

Some company entries also include street address and Web site URL.

Lebanon.com provides other useful services for the international business searcher. The main page contains links to current local news stories. A link at the bottom of the page ostensibly takes you to government sites, but the link has never worked for me. In the middle of the page on the right-hand side, a drop-down menu offers one choice entitled Beirut Stock Exchange. Here you will find an overview and history of the exchange, as well as a link to daily stock prices. Along with daily stock bulletins, it carries weekly and monthly bulletins, a monthly market capitalization summary, and various summary reports for the previous year.

Another site to use when looking for Lebanese companies is IDREL [http://www.idrel.com.lb]. While not much value-added information appears here, if you scroll about halfway down the page, you will find the heading Companies. Approximately thirty sectors are listed here. Clicking on any one of them will take you to a list of companies in that sector. Unfortunately, the site provides no information about the companies, but each name links to that company's Web site.

Israel

Interested in the electronics industry in Israel? Try the Israel Association of Electronics Industries [http://www.iaei.org.il]. Here you will find a profile of Israel's electronics industry covering topics such as Sales and Exports, Sales per Employee, and Sales and Exports by Industry Groups (see Figure 6.8).

The site contains information on employment opportunities in electronics industries: companies and the positions they want filled. It also has links to other affiliated organizations and pertinent government offices.

One can look for companies (close to 200 of them) within seven major sectors:

- Industrial Equipment

- Information Services

- Medical Equipment

- Military and Defense Equipment

- Passive Components

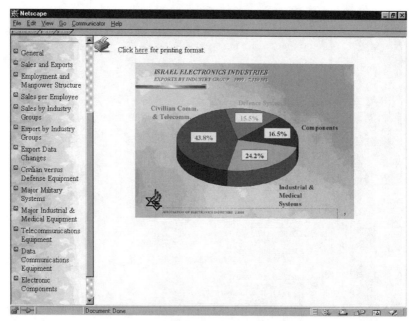

Figure 6.8   Electronics Exports by Industry—Israel Association of Electronics Industries

- Semiconductors, Active Components, and Power Supplies

- Telecommunications and Data Communications

You can search by company name, turnover, number of employees, or choose a company from the list on the left of the screen. Company information generally includes managing partner, address, phone and fax numbers, turnover, number of employees, main business area, link to Web site, and number of engineers and technicians.

US-IBEX—U.S. Israel Business Exchange [http://www.israelemb.org/economic/economic_frame.htm] has a section U.S. Companies in Israel with a very extensive list of companies. Minimal information is supplied, but you will find the nature of the company's business, e.g., whether it is a wholly owned subsidiary, if it only has representation in the country, what percentage of an Israeli company is owned, or if it has merged or acquired another company.

The Israel Foreign Ministry [http://www.israel-mfa.gov.il/mfa/go.asp?MFAH00kj0] has compiled a wonderfully useful page of links. The Economics and Business section provides links for information on business incubators, various trade associations, financial

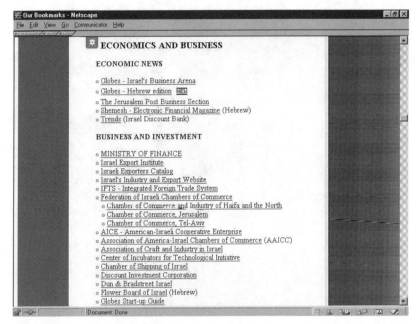

Figure 6.9   Section of the Business Links from the Israel Foreign Ministry

information, and more (see Figure 6.9). The site also links to just about every Israeli government office, including local governments, with remarkable currency. When I last visited the site, it had been updated only three days previously.

Egypt

The Egypt State Information Service (SIS) [http://www.uk. sis.gov.eg] offers a great deal of information to acquaint you with the country. The Yearbook 1999 covers the country from top to bottom—from Land & People and History to Economy, Agriculture, Industry, and Energy. Reading the Yearbook we learn that Egypt's economic development plan considers the chemical industry most important, followed by engineering and food. The site also links to the SIS internal search engine that appears relatively sophisticated. First you choose whether you would like to do a Global Search or a Subject Search. Choosing the Subject Search, some relevant options include Business, Communication, Industry, and News.

I don't know when I've seen a more helpful and well thought out online publication than Business Today Egypt Online [http://www.

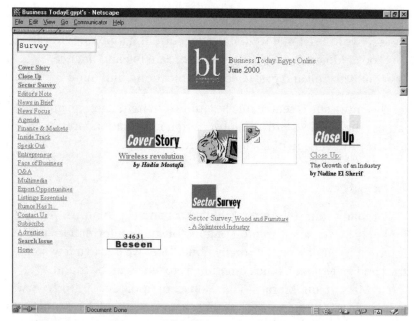

Figure 6.10 Home Page of Business Today Egypt Online

businesstoday-eg.com]. It's a very nice, up-to-date overview of business in Egypt. On the front page you see links to three different articles. When I last visited the site, they had an overview of the wood and furniture industry (Sector Survey), a report on the flower industry (Close Up), and a cover story on the wireless revolution in Egypt (see Figure 6.10).

These sections are also included in the publication:

- Agenda—dates and descriptions of upcoming conferences and exhibitions held in Egypt

- Entrepreneur—an interview with one of Egypt's up and coming businesspeople

- Face of Business—a background article on a local business

- Listings Essentials—list of the most important contacts for business services and offices in Cairo and Alexandria, including airlines, chambers of commerce, government offices, ministries, and conference organizers

- Multimedia—discussion of various Internet and e-commerce issues

- News Focus—provides a bit more detail on a few industries

- News in Brief—short updates on current happenings in various industries such as agriculture, banking and finance, industry, oil and gas, telecommunications, and more

The entire site is searchable but, unfortunately, it has no archived issues. The site does provide subscription information for the counterpart print version of *Business Today*.

Morocco

For many countries in the Middle East and North Africa, you will find only a very small amount of good business information on the Internet; in some cases, virtually none. Here we'll take a few countries and give them a quick mention as to what can be found.

La Maison du Maroc—The House of Morocco [http://www. maroc.net] is an interesting site that seems to suffer from a touch of schizophrenia. All of the links in the Menu are labeled in English; News, Magazines & E-zines, Culture, Education, etc. But, many of those links lead to information that's only in French. And, some pages mix French and English (see Figure 6.11).

Figure 6.11   The House of Morocco Site

The Maroc Search link leads to a business directory with fourteen categories including Computers & Internet and Business & Economy. You may use the search form or use the direct links to find companies that meet your criteria. However, as mentioned previously, your results may be a mixture of French and English. Some companies have a French name with an English description and others have an English name with a French description. And then, of course, there are companies that are consistently either French or English language. Each company entry leads to the company Web site.

Sudan

Sudan.Net [http://www.sudan.net] offers some cursory information about the Sudan. To get up to speed on the country, I would suggest starting with Fast Facts on Sudan. Here you will learn about the country's electrical consumption, imports and exports, communications system, and more. For further information, try Sudanese Related Links.

Bahrain

The Bahrain Promotions and Marketing Board (BPMB) [http://www.bpmb.com] is an independent government agency organized to attract business to Bahrain. Bahrain Focus contains business articles, as well as some focusing on local companies and their activities. The site also has a nice Hot Links section that displays a variety of Bahrain related links. It appears that the site is still under construction, as some of the most promising sections, Feature, Newsline, and Doing Business in Bahrain, were not yet complete at press time. Those interested in Bahrain should remember this site for future reference.

Saudi Arabia

The U.S.-Saudi Arabian Business Council [http://www.us-saudi-business.org] has a very well thought out site. The section on the Saudi Arabian Economy is very thorough and includes brief overviews of the following industries:

- Agriculture
- Construction

- Healthcare

- Mining

- Oil

- Petrochemicals

- Power and Energy

- Transportation and Communication

Doing Business in Saudi Arabia covers topics such as how to operate in Saudi Arabia, leading sectors for U.S. exports and investments, and the business infrastructure. Other important areas to review include Business Regulations and Procedures, Joint Ventures, and Key Contacts. The Key Contacts section contains major Saudi Arabian companies, Saudi Arabian agencies, organizations, government ministries, and much more.

Regional Wrap-Up

Well, we're more than halfway through our virtual journey, and the Middle East and North African region may seem no easier than the other regions we've traversed so far. But, by now, patterns should be emerging and your level of comfort with international business research should be rising.

CHAPTER 7

Sub-Saharan Africa

Sub-Saharan Africa is quite a bit different from the other areas of the world we've visited so far. The entire region is composed of developing countries, which makes the task of the business researcher infinitely harder. While most of the countries are interested in cultivating trade and investment opportunities, issues such as infant mortality, poverty, and starvation may be more pressing. When organizations face the decision of either dedicating funds to development programs or putting up a Web site to attract investors, development usually wins hands down.

This doesn't mean that there's nothing out there. It does mean, however, that we may need to set our goals a little lower when looking for business information in this region. For example, for most of Africa, it is extremely difficult, if not impossible, to find very current information. Numbers in the three-to-five-year range, if you can find them, will often be as good as it gets. We need to be more creative. We also may need to extrapolate data more than we usually do.

Since a good portion of the useful sites for this region cover multiple countries, we will not go into as much detail on individual countries. Countries covered individually are Botswana, Ethiopia, Swaziland, Uganda, Zambia, and Zimbabwe.

Directories

By now everyone should know what I think of directory sites— can't search without 'em. Stanford University Libraries & Academic

Information Resources has a site called Africa South of the Sahara—Selected Internet Resources [http://www-sul.stanford.edu/depts/ssrg/africa] that provides a good starting point for Sub-Saharan African information. From the main page, you may choose, among other things, Countries/Regions, Topics, Search the Africa Pages, and Breaking News. After choosing a country or a region, you get an extensive listing of current news and other links. The site offers almost fifty countries from which to choose in the following six regions:

- Central Africa

- East Africa

- Horn of Africa

- Indian Ocean Islands

- Southern Africa

- West Africa

The Topics section offers Business and Current Events as two of the choices and, again, long lists of Sub-Saharan African links appear. You can search the entire site, though not with Boolean techniques.

The J. Murrey Atkins Library & Information Services of the University of North Carolina at Charlotte has a directory site, a portion of which covers Africa [http://libweb.uncc.edu/ref-bus/reg.htm]. There are links here for numerous sites, including newsletters and newspapers, the Central Bank of West African States, the African Development Bank Group, and other metasites.

The Electronic African Bookworm [http://www.hanszell.co.uk/indexlink.htm] bills itself as a Web navigator. The site has four sections: Africa, African Studies, African Book World & Press, and Resources for Writers.

You can search the entire site and the results returned will point you to the section of the site where you can find the appropriate link(s). One of the first sections of the site is Africa: General, Educational, and Commercial Resources, which includes African search engines. Depending on your needs, some of the links that bear further examination include Africa Homepage, Africa Online, African Governments on the WWW, Ananzi, Rubani, and my personal favorite (for its name), Zebra. A print version of The Electronic African Bookworm is available with details for obtaining it found at the site.

Columbia University Libraries has compiled the African Studies Internet Resources [http://www.cc.columbia.edu/cu/libraries/in div/area/Africa]. This searchable site divides into numerous categories, some rather general and some more specific, such as region and country, organization, and topic (which includes business and economic information). For those sites that defy categorization, turn to the link entitled Other Africa-Related Resource Collections.

Other directory sites include the following:

- **African Studies Center University of Pennsylvania**
  http://www.sas.upenn.edu/African_Studies/Home_Page/
  Country.html

- **EuroSeek.com—Africa**
  http://webdir.euroseek.com/?ilang=en&catid=263

- **Harambee Africa Links**
  http://www.harambee.co.uk/links.htm

- **Index on Africa**
  http://www.africaindex.africainfo.no/pages

- **Jump Start**
  http://www.mg.co.za/mg/jump/j-africa.htm

- **NewAfrica.com**
  http://www.newafrica.com

Search Engines

Only a few search engines specialize in this region and most of them cover just one country, as opposed to the whole region. Here are a few worth trying:

- **AAA Matilda Angola**
  http://aaa.com.au/images/logos/searches/ao.shtml
  Angola search engine

- **Aardvark**
  http://www.aardvark.co.za
  South African search engine

- **Ananzi**
  http://www.ananzi.co.za
  South African search engine

- **Max**
  http://www01.max.co.za
  South African search engine

- **WoYaa**
  http://www.woyaa.com
  Covers all of Africa; can search by country or category

Chambers of Commerce and Industry

Disappointingly, there are very few American Chambers of Commerce (AmChams) in Sub-Saharan Africa, and it appears that, so far, only one has an Internet presence:

- **U.S.-Angola Chamber of Commerce**
  http://www.us-angola.org

Let's hope this will change in the near future, since AmChams can be such a good source of business information. Here are some of the other chamber and chamber-like sites available:

- **Cameroon Chamber of Commerce and Industry**
  http://www.g77tin.org/ccimhp.html

- **Addis Ababa (Ethiopia) Chamber of Commerce**
  http://www.addischamber.com
  Economic statistics, trade show information, local companies seeking foreign partners

- **Mauritius Chamber of Commerce and Industry**
  http://www.mcci.org
  Investment and Business section with profiles of the agricultural, manufacturing, and tourism sectors, trade statistics, stock market information, and import/export issues

- **Uganda National Chamber of Commerce and Industry**
  http://www.uganda.co.ug/commerce.htm

- **Confederation of Zimbabwe Industries**
  http://www.czi.org.zw
  Business news, links to member companies' Web sites, useful links section

- **South African Chamber of Business**
  http://www.sacob.co.za
  Economic information, text of monthly newsletter

- **The Alberton (South Africa) Chamber of Commerce and Industry**
  http://www.alberton.com
  List of chamber members by industry

- **Johannesburg Chamber of Commerce and Industry**
  http://www.jcci.co.za
  News, publications for sale, trade opportunities, monthly newsletter online

- **Bloemfontein (South Africa) Chamber of Commerce and Industry**
  http://www.bcci.co.za

- **Cape (South Africa) Chamber of Commerce and Industry**
  http://www.capechamber.co.za
  News, searchable membership database, exporter/importer database, Business Guide

- **Durban (South Africa) Chamber of Commerce and Industry**
  http://www.durbanchamber.co.za
  Searchable membership database, publications for sale

- **Greater Germiston (South Africa) Chamber of Commerce and Industry**
  http://www.ggcci.co.za

- **Pietermaritzburg (South Africa) Chamber of Commerce and Industries**
  http://www.pcci.org.za

- **Port Elizabeth (South Africa) Regional Chamber of Commerce and Industry**
  http://www.pechamber.org.za
  News, online member directory

- **Eurochamber of Commerce in Southern Africa**
  http://www.eurochamber.co.za

- **Ghana National Chamber of Commerce**
  http://www.g77tin.org/gncchp.html

Banking, Finance, and Stock Exchanges

The dearth of information available for this region holds true for the financial area as well. There are very few stock exchanges and central banks on the Internet. Here are the ones that currently have a Web presence:

Stock Exchanges

- **Botswana—Botswana Stock Exchange**
  http://mbendi.co.za/exbo.htm

- **Ghana—Ghana Stock Exchange**
  http://www.gse.com.gh

- **Mauritius—The Stock Exchange of Mauritius**
  http://www.semdex.com

- **Nigeria—Nigerian Stock Exchange**
  http://www.nse.com.ng

- **South Africa—The Johannesburg Stock Exchange**
  http://www.jse.co.za

- **Zambia—Lusaka Stock Exchange**
  http://www.pangaeapartners.com/luseinfo.htm

- **Zimbabwe—Zimbabwe Stock Exchange**
  http://www.zse.co.zw

Central Banks

- **Central Bank of the West African States**
  http://www.bceao.int/internet/bcweb.nsf/pages/us
  Covers the countries of Benin, Burkina Faso, Guinea Bissau, Côte d'Ivoire, Mali, Niger, Senegal, and Togo.

- **South African Reserve Bank**
  http://www.resbank.co.za
  Be certain to check the *Economic Information* section.

- **Central Bank of Swaziland**
  http://www.centralbank.sz/cbs.html

- **The Bank of Zambia**
  http://www.boz.zm

- **The Central Bank of Kenya**
  http://www.africaonline.co.ke/cbk/index.html

- **Banco Nacional de Angola**
  http://www.ebonet.net/bna/bna.htm

- **Central Bank of Lesotho**
  http://www.centralbank.org.ls

- **Banco de Mozambique**
  http://www.bancomoc.mz

Yellow Pages

Currently there are very few Yellow Pages directories online. The following should cover most, if not all, of the ones currently available:

- **Ethiopia Yellow Pages**
  http://www.ethioyellowpages.com/pages/ethiopia.html

- **Ghana Yellow Pages**
  http://www.ghanaforum.com/directory.htm

- **Kenya Yellow Pages**
  http://www.postel.co.ke

- **Nigeria Yellow Pages**
  http://www.yellowpages.com.ng

- **South Africa Internet Directory**
  http://iafrica.com/directories/business/index.htm

- **South Africa—EasyInfo Internet Directory**
  http://www.easyinfo.co.za

News Resources

Financial Mail [http://www.fm.co.za] is the online version of a weekly South African newspaper. The print version started forty years ago. The online counterpart has existed for more than three years. You can search both the current issue and the archives to find general South African news and details on South Africa's budget (current year and the previous two years), including analysis. However, for the serious business searcher, both offer a great deal more.

Start by clicking on Top Companies in the left column to find extensive information on the top industrial companies in South Africa—some of it in handy chart form. Here you will find highlights on the electronics, information technology, telecommunications, retail, hotel and leisure, food, and media sectors; mining houses; and the gold industry. Essays on South African mergers and acquisitions and foreign investment, profiles of five companies, and four specially "featured" companies are also supplied.

Going back to the main Financial Mail page, this time choose Special Reports and Surveys. This section contains overviews of more than fifty South African industries and sectors, including accountants and attorneys, banking, cell phones, forestry, and information technology. When I visited the site, no report was older than three years; some were less than a month old.

African Business Information Services (AfBIS) [http://www.afbis.com] initially looked more promising than it turned out to be, but I still think it is worth a quick mention. AfBIS is an independent private organization formed in 1998 to provide information on African economies and to help companies and individuals around the world gain a better understanding of Africa. If you need some top African news stories, check here. AfBIS has articles, reports, and analyses on the African economy and other general African business issues. Additionally, the full text of *Newswatch*, a weekly Nigerian magazine, is featured.

Other sites with regional and/or country news include these:

- **AfricaNet.com**
  http://www.africanet.com

- **Africa News Online**
  http://www.africanews.org

- **E&P Media Links Online Directory—Africa**
  http://emedia1.mediainfo.com/emedia/africa.htm

- **Ghana Classifieds**
  http://www.ghanaclassifieds.com

- **Ghana Review International**
  http://212.67.202.38/~gri

- **International Political Economy Network—News Links**
  http://csf.colorado.edu/ipe/africa.html

- **NewsAfrica.com**
  http://www.africanews.com

- **Nigeria.com Daily News**
  http://www.nigeria.com

U.S. Government Resources

The United States Agency for International Development (USAID) site [http://www.info.usaid.gov] has some interesting sections with Sub-Saharan African business information. Rather than showing how to navigate through the site, let's go directly to the more relevant areas. USAID has published the third Internet edition of U.S. Merchandise Trade with Developing Countries, a report presenting statistics on U.S. trade with developing countries and regions for the years 1988 to 1998. Enter http://www.info.usaid.gov /economic_growth/trdweb/africa.html into your browser and you go straight to the current section on Sub-Saharan Africa. Here you will find information on trading partners, exports, imports, and trade statistics, along with some very useful graphs (see Figure 7.1).

This same Web page lists tables available for downloading in Excel format. The tables contain detailed information on exports and imports by country and product using the U.N. Standard International Trade Classifications (SITC). If you do not find data available here for your commodity of interest, you can request the construction of a table using custom criteria.

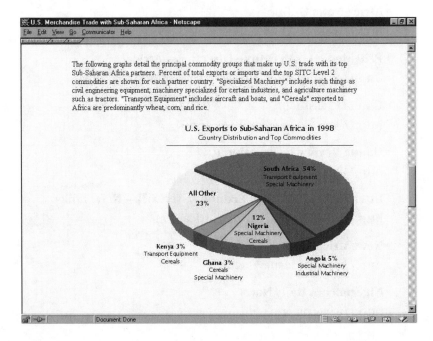

Figure 7.1   U.S. Exports to Sub-Saharan Africa 1998—USAID

USAID's Africa Bureau Information Center has compiled the Internet Resource Guide—Selected Sites with Special Reference to Africa [http://www.info.usaid.gov/regions/afr/abic/guides/afrsites. htm]. This guide is a directory of Africa-related Internet sites. While not all sites will help the business searcher, you should scroll through them to see what they offer.

USAID has a Global Technology Network (GTN) [http://www. usgtn.org], designed to provide small and medium-sized U.S. companies with business opportunities in the developing world. Working in conjunction with other U.S. government agencies, GTN focuses on four sectors: agribusiness, information technology, environment and energy, and health. Companies registering with GTN receive trade leads in their sector of interest. You can find the African Regional Information at http://www.usgtn.org/Africa%20FG/Africa %20Homepage.html. This page explains some of the services available to U.S. businesses interested in working with Africa, including market trend analyses and business counseling. The GTN Africa

Overview [http://www.usgtn.org/Africa%20FG/Africa%20Overview %20(long).html] lists the countries that currently have a GTN office: Botswana, Ghana, Kenya, Madagascar, Mali, Mozambique, Namibia, Nigeria, Rwanda, Senegal, South Africa, Tanzania, Uganda, Zambia, and Zimbabwe. The site contains fact sheets on all of these countries.

Regional Resources

The MBendi AfroPaedia site [http://www.mbendi.co.za] is produced by MBendi Information Services (Pty) Ltd., an African consulting firm founded in 1995 specializing in Internet strategy, Africa, and the African oil industry. (MBendi is a composite African language word meaning "the knowledge that brings wisdom.")

Clicking on the Countries link, you will see a list of all the countries in Africa. Choose a country and you get an information profile with the following sub-topics (with some variation in topics from one country to another):

- Basic Country Data
- Business Opportunities and Challenges
- Demographics
- Doing Business In …
- Economy
- Exporting/Importing Guide
- Investment Profile (automatically links to Ernst & Young site with business and taxation information)
- Industries
- Key Statistics
- Legal Profile
- Manufacturing
- Map of Country
- News and Views
- Politics
- Stock Exchange
- Trading Profile

Each of these sections provides detailed information designed to help those interested in doing business in the country. For example, the Industries section contains profiles of the country's leading industries (see Figure 7.2).

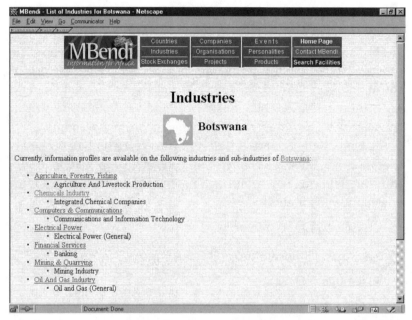

Figure 7.2   Botswana Industry Section—Mbendi

An abundance of other information also appears in this section. You may search for a company by its name, owner's name, industry, type of facility or business, or location. A list of companies, presumably those registered with MBendi, contains company overviews of varying lengths, as well as a list of local organizations, including unions, government ministries, chambers of commerce, and stock exchanges. Personalities is an interestingly named section; it refers to searching for a person to find his or her organization and position within the organization. You can also search for publications, events, listed companies, and more.

If you don't know the country in which a particular company is located, start at MBendi's main page and choose Companies. From here you can move to an alphabetical list of the companies in the database with country location attached. Choosing Industries will bring up a list of all African industries with available profiles. They even specify Comprehensive, Summary, and Outline profiles. Similarly, you can look for organizations, personalities, stock exchanges, products, and services throughout Africa.

News & Views takes you to a detailed search screen for African news. In addition to searching by keyword(s), you can also choose the type of news item (news, press release, FAQ), news topic, country, and industry—all with drop-down menus. Many of the documents appear to come from the Ernst & Young Africa Group, while others come from the MBendi and other organizations' Web sites.

The Common Market for Eastern and Southern Africa (COMESA) [http://www.comesa.int] consists of twenty-one countries in the region. (Note: A few of these countries were covered previously in Chapter 6: The Middle East and North Africa.)

• Angola	• Malawi
• Burundi	• Mauritius
• Comoros	• Namibia
• Democratic Republic of Congo	• Rwanda
• Djibouti	• Seychelles
• Egypt	• Sudan
• Eritrea	• Swaziland
• Ethiopia	• Tanzania
• Kenya	• Uganda
• Madagascar	• Zambia
	• Zimbabwe

Established in 1994, it replaced the Preferential Trade Area for Eastern and Southern Africa. The COMESA site has lots of trade, investment, and general business information for the region. Let's explore some areas on the site.

Starting with Information by State we find separate listings for each country in the region. Choosing Kenya as an example, we see such categories of information as Maps of Kenya, Basic Country Data, World Factbook Data, Banking/Economic Details, Stock Exchange, Investment Information, Import/Export Boards, Trade and Industry Information, Statistics for Traders, Customs

Regulations, Transport, Communications, Natural Resources/ Agriculture, Travel Requirements, Currency Converter, Kenyan News Sources, Useful Links, COMESA Contacts, and Local Internet Service Providers.

Banking/Economic Details provides in-depth information on the monetary and banking system, macroeconomic indicators, and banking contacts. For instance, we discovered that seventy-five to eighty percent of the labor force works in agriculture, tea and coffee are the primary exports, and machinery and transportation equipment are the primary imports.

The Investment Information section provides links to two guides on doing business in Kenya, a guide to investing in Kenya, and an extensive business directory listing companies alphabetically by sector and including contact information. If you need to know which companies in Kenya deal in coffee, you can find them easily here. A description of Kenya export programs and a link to the Ministry of Commerce and Industry appear in the Import/Export Boards area.

Back on the main COMESA page, go to Trade & Customs and then Trade Databases. The first listing is the Online Directory of Companies in the COMESA Region. Click on this to enter the database. This Directory of Producers allows you to choose all of the COMESA countries or any one of them and to specify the commodity. I chose to look for coffee in any country and received a lengthy listing of companies, sorted by country. Clicking on Paul Ries, one of the companies under Ethiopia, I received a listing for the company, including number of employees, contact information, and year established (1885!) (see Figure 7.3). At this section of the site, external links connect you to product directories for Kenya, Mauritius, Namibia, Tanzania, Uganda, Zambia, and Southern Africa.

Another useful section of the COMESA site is the Commerce & Industry portion. Here you will find overviews of the metal and engineering sectors.

Doing Business leads to several useful guides, in particular, Doing Business with COMESA: The Handbook, and legal guides to establishing business in Malawi, Mauritius, Rwanda, Sudan, Swaziland, Tanzania, Uganda, Zambia, and Zimbabwe.

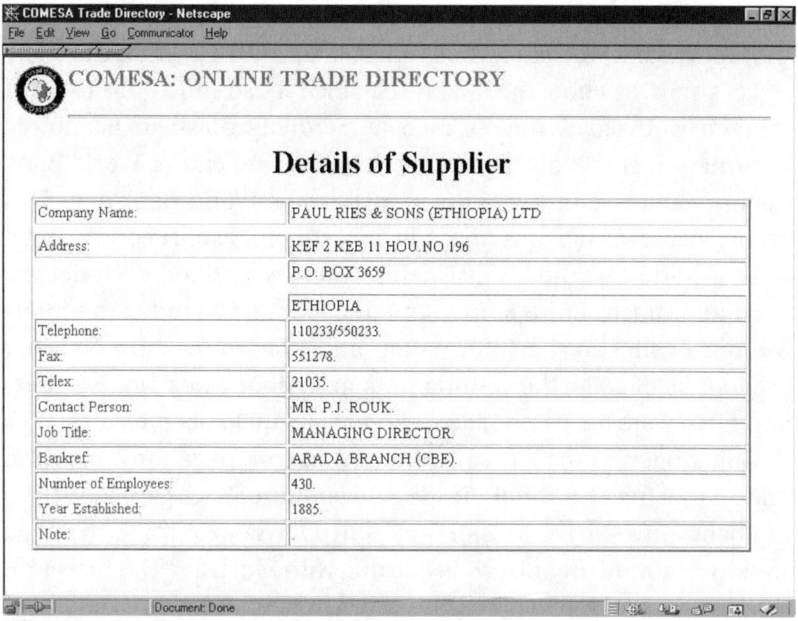

COMESA Trade Directory - Netscape

File Edit View Go Communicator Help

COMESA: ONLINE TRADE DIRECTORY

Details of Supplier

Company Name:	PAUL RIES & SONS (ETHIOPIA) LTD
Address:	KEF 2 KEB 11 HOU.NO 196
	P.O. BOX 3659
	ETHIOPIA
Telephone:	110233/550233.
Fax:	551278.
Telex:	21035.
Contact Person:	MR. P.J. ROUK.
Job Title:	MANAGING DIRECTOR.
Bankref:	ARADA BRANCH (CBE).
Number of Employees:	430.
Year Established:	1885.
Note:	.

Document: Done

Figure 7.3 Company Directory Listing—COMESA

The Africa Business Network [http://www.ifc.org/abn] is a service of the International Finance Corporation (IFC), a member of the World Bank Group. (The IFC is the largest multilateral source of loan and equity financing for private sector projects in the developing world.) This site, which covers most of Sub-Saharan Africa, brings together information from the IFC and its partners, offered to help stimulate private investment in Africa.

Stop first at the Country Information Center, where you will find a list of the countries covered. As with most good sites, there is a consistent layout from country to country, which helps to speed up the learning curve for using the site. For each country, the sections covered are:

- Additional Contacts
- Business Information
- Economic Information
- General
- Internet Information and Web Sites
- Newspapers and Publications
- Travel and Tourism

Many links take you to pages on either the main IFC Web site or the World Bank Web site, while others take you away from the site.

Let's start by choosing a country. Since it's so much fun to say, I thought we'd check out Zimbabwe. Scrolling down to Economic Information and choosing Competitiveness Indicators: World Bank Report, we arrive at a lengthy report on the World Bank site. This report includes statistics on trade, investment, export competitiveness, export structure, infrastructure, literacy, and more. Under the heading Infrastructure & Investment Climate, I found some interesting statistics in the Information and Communication Network section. As of 1996, the waiting time for a phone line was 7.2 years and there were 6.7 personal computers per 1,000 people.

Going back to the Africa Business Network page for Zimbabwe and choosing National Trade Development Organisation of Zimbabwe, we arrive at ZimTrade [http://www.zimtrade.co.zw], a trade promotion organization. Starting with ZimTrade Databases on the left side of the page, we find three choices: Company Database, Foreign Buyer/Seller Database, and Trade Statistics. Choosing Complex Search, a search screen gives the following search options:

- Current market

- Established before or established after

- Major sector

- Nature of business

- Number of employees greater than or less than

- Product category

- Product name

- Product/HS code

- Sector

Company listings include contact information, as well as a link to a list of the company's export products.

Back on the main page, the Investment Climate link brings up detailed information about investing in Zimbabwe. If this still doesn't answer all your questions, you can get more information through the Zimbabwe Investment Centre, accessible at this point. There you will find brief information on mining, manufacturing, agro-industry, tourism, and construction—all industries considered to have strong potential for the foreign investor. Address, phone, fax, and e-mail contacts are listed for those requiring further information.

ZimTrade also includes the following information:

- Current exchange rates for 16 countries

- A link to the Zimbabwe Stock Exchange

- Import and export statistics; the top products for import and export as well as the major import and export markets (see Figure 7.4)

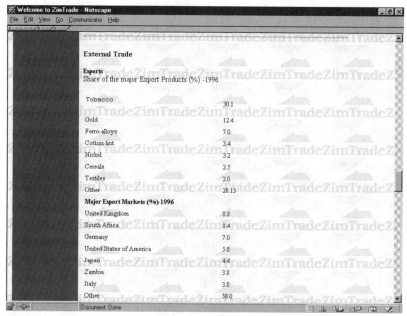

Figure 7.4   Zimbabwe Export Statistics—ZimTrade

- Profiles of the manufacturing, mining, commercial agriculture, tobacco, horticulture, and arts and crafts industries

- Business opportunities: companies interested in buying products and companies looking for joint ventures

- An online version of ZimTrade's quarterly publication containing additional trade information and a profile of a prominent Zimbabwean company

- ZimTrade products for sale, such as a company profile database on diskette, an export directory, etc.

Returning again to Zimbabwe's page on the Africa Business Network and choosing the link under Newspapers & Publications, we arrive at the Zimbabwe version of AfricaNews Online [http://www.africanews.org]. Published by the Africa News Service, a twenty-five-year-old nonprofit organization, this news service uses more than sixty sources for information. Here we find the full text of news stories from the previous week. You can also link to stories about other African regions or countries.

One last Africa Business Network link remains for us to explore: the Internet Connectivity Profile. Here you will find a history of the Internet infrastructure in Zimbabwe, along with a listing of ISPs operating in the country and the approximate costs for Internet service.

Africa Dot Com [http://africa.com], which refers to itself as the "gateway to all that's African on the World Wide Web," is largely a collection of links. From here, you can link to many online newspapers and magazines, as well as sites dealing with African politics, history, education, religion, health, travel and tourism, and sports. Since Africa Dot Com is very frame-intensive, I would suggest going directly to the Business section, the most useful portion of the site for our purposes [http://africa.com/business.html], rather than following the direct link. Here you will find a large selection of links, including some for general business information, trade, and real estate, along with numerous country-specific sites for South Africa, Nigeria, and Zimbabwe. The site is currently undergoing revision and at the moment is not quite as useful as it has been in the past. Hopefully, completion of the site revision will remedy this problem.

Anyone who wants to do business in Africa should know about the Corporate Council on Africa (CCA) [http://www.africacncl.org]. This nonprofit organization is composed of American corporations and individuals dedicated to developing the African private sector and strengthening the commercial relationship between the U.S. and Africa. It organizes trade missions to Africa and is heavily involved in trade and investment issues. While the CCA Web site is very general and only describes its programs, if you need African business information, you might phone them at 202/835-1115 to see what resources might exist.

Business Directories

As with the other regions of the world, sites set up as business directories enable the businessperson to find companies within a particular industry or service. Some directories link directly to the company Web sites; other sites include a brief description of the companies within the database.

To locate companies in a particular line of business, use Braby's Red Index [http://www.redindex.com], a Southern Africa business-to-business directory. More than seventy percent of the companies listed in the Braby database are small and medium-sized businesses. Braby's covers the following countries:

- Angola
- Botswana
- Lesotho
- Madagascar
- Malawi
- Mauritius
- Mozambique
- Namibia
- Seychelles
- South Africa
- Swaziland
- Tanzania
- Zambia
- Zimbabwe

From the main page, you may search the entire region or individual countries by category or business name. Using the Expanded Search option, you may also search by phone or fax number and limit the search to companies with an e-mail address or Web site.

Searching the diamond industry, I received a short Classification Directory that allowed me to choose a more expanded directory. In addition to diamond mining, it lists numerous related industries such as diamond & jewelry valuators, diamond drilling & cutting equipment, diamond sorters, and so on. Choosing diamond mines produced a list of several company names, along with region and phone number. Clicking on any of the companies will yield a typical directory listing, albeit some proved a bit more comprehensive than others.

Here are some of the other business directories for Sub-Saharan Africa:

- **Buy SA.com**
  http://www.1023.co.za
  Search all of South Africa or a particular region of the country; search by category and/or keyword.

- **East Africa Sources Trade Directory**
  http://www.eastafrica-sources.com/cgi-bin/w3-msql/
  trading_directory/index.html?ID=GUEST
  Kenya, Uganda, and Tanzania are included.

- **GhanaWeb Directory of Businesses**
  http://www.ghanaweb.com/main/overview.php3?CAT=B]
  Find Ghanain businesses in the finance, import/export, Internet, hotel, manufacturing, travel and tourism, real estate, retail, and service industry areas.

- **Internext Gateway to South Africa**
  http://www.zaworm.co.za
  This site provides a brief description of the companies in the database, as well as a link to the company's Web site. Also includes affiliated organizations.

- **KenyaWeb**
  http://www.kenyaweb.com
  Search for businesses in Kenya at this site. It also has a good section with an overview of the country's economy.

- **Southern Africa Directory**
  http://www.sadirectory.co.za
  This directory offers the capability to search Angola, Botswana, Lesotho, Malawi, Mozambique, Namibia, South Africa, Swaziland, Zambia, or Zimbabwe individually or together. You can drill down to find the sector you wish to search and it returns Web site links.

- **South Africa Online Business Directory**
  http://www.southafrica.co.za/busfin
  Choose from twenty business categories. Results include a brief company description and a Web site link.

Zambia

Zambia's first ISP, ZamNet [http://www.zamnet.zm], is a good place to start for information on Zambia. While it offers little "value-added" information, it does point to a number of other good sites. From here, you can link to several different news sites, a country overview, the Zambia Legal Information Institute (ZamLII), and the government site, State House. This site appears to be expanding, so bookmark it and recheck it whenever you need information on Zambia.

ZamNet also has a section called Zambian Business WWW Pages [http://www.zamnet.zm/zamnet/zambus/zambushome.html]. This section links to various Zambian businesses, as well as to the Zambian Privatization Agency, the Zambia Revenue Authority, the Development Bank of Zambia, and more.

The Export Board of Zambia [http://www.zamnet.zm/zamnet/zambus/ebz/ebz.htm] provides an overview of the country and the government structure. The following additional information is offered by the Export Board of Zambia:

- Brief descriptions of the country's most important sectors: mining, agriculture, manufacturing, forestry, tourism, and handicrafts

- General economic information

- Import/Export procedures

- Links to trade related organizations and ministries

- List of Zambian export companies by industry; contact information is provided, but no links.

- Trade regulations

The Zambia Investment Center [http://www.zic.org.zm] was established to promote and facilitate investment in Zambia. Its site provides a good discussion of the investment situation in the country. A monthly newsletter available at the site outlines recent investments in the country. Archives to the newsletter go as far back as July 1998; however, there is no search function.

Other sections of the site discuss the following information:

- Basic economic indicators

- Investment climate and the incentives offered, necessary procedures and permits, and investment opportunities

- Key facts and statistics about the country

- Major exports (copper and cobalt) and major imports (crude oil, chemicals, machinery, iron, steel, and manufactured goods)

- The country's economic history and an overview of the current economic situation

- Zambia and world trade

Botswana

The Government of Botswana [http://www.gov.bw/home.html] has a site that offers some good insight into the country, both past and present (see Figure 7.5). The Business and Investment section discusses the overall economic situation in Botswana and includes information on taxation, customs, the workforce, and investment incentives. In the Gem of Africa section, we learn that the high growth sectors for Botswana are transport and communications—in particular telecommunications, air transport, rail transport, and road transport. The site also features news from the Botswana Press

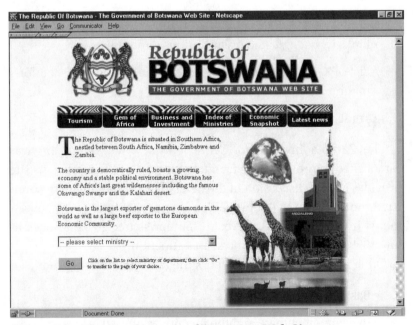

Figure 7.5   The Government of Botswana Web Site

Agency which updates daily except on Saturdays and Sundays. News archives go back to January 1999, but they are not searchable. All articles are listed by date of publication only. Finally, the site offers links to sixteen different government ministries and agencies including the Ministry of Agriculture, Ministry of Commerce and Industry, and the Department of Foreign Affairs.

Zimbabwe

We looked at Zimbabwe previously when we explored ZimTrade. For a bit more information, let's now look at the site for the High Commission of the Republic of Zimbabwe in Ottawa, Canada [http://www.DocuWeb.ca/Zimbabwe/index.html]. Follow the Doing Business in Zimbabwe link for investment information and an explanation of the Zimbabwe Investment Centre, established in 1990 to help simplify the investment procedure. The Trade section describes the various international trade agreements in which Zimbabwe participates. Exchange controls and tax issues are outlined and eleven Sectors to Watch are listed including these six:

- Building and construction materials
- Chemical and chemical products
- Engineering products
- Metallurgy and metal products
- Textiles, clothing, leather, and footwear
- Wood-based products

Ethiopia

If you have an interest in doing business with Ethiopia, stop by the site for the Ethiopian Embassy in Washington, DC, [http://www.ethiopianembassy.org] and begin with the Fast Facts section to bring yourself up to speed on the country in general. The News section updates daily and includes press statements, daily news, speeches and interviews, and reports and opinions. If you're uncertain as to the rapport between the U.S. and Ethiopia, click on Government and then on U.S.-Ethiopia Relations for the details.

Brief industry profiles for the following industry sectors may be found in the Economy and Business area:

- Agriculture

- Banking, Finance & Insurance

- Education and Health

- Energy

- Manufacturing

- Mining

- Telecommunications

- Transport

- Travel & Tourism

The Investment Guide to Ethiopia, prepared by PriceWater-houseCoopers under the direction of UNCTAD (United Nations Conference on Trade and Development) and the International Chamber of Commerce in cooperation with the Ethiopian Investment Authority, is quite complete and even provides a list of current investors (company name, country of ownership, type of business, and address).

Before leaving this site, check out the list of Web Resources. It has links to the Ethiopian Privatization Agency, Ethiopian Telecommunications Corporation, and more.

Angola

The Business and Economics section of the Embassy of the Republic of Angola's Web site [http://www.angola.org] has the following sector profiles:

- Agriculture—includes coffee, forestry, fruits, vegetables, oil seeds, and livestock

- Energy—includes oil and hydro-electric

- Fisheries

- Manufacturing and Industry—light and heavy industry

- Mining—includes diamonds and other minerals

- Services—Business & Banking

- Telecommunications

- Tourism

- Transportation—includes railways, ports, shipping, and air transport

Some of these profiles are a few years old; however, given the dearth of information for the Sub-Saharan African countries, older information is better than no information.

Swaziland

Swazi.com [http://www.swazi.com] could be considered your link to all things related to Swaziland. While there is little value-added information here, the site provides links to a great deal of useful information. Some of the sites accessible from Swazi.com include:

- The official Web site of the Swaziland government

- The Swaziland Business Yearbook 2000—A Commercial Guide—This resource includes an analysis of the country's investment climate and incentives, as well as overviews of the manufacturing, arts and crafts, agriculture, geology and mining, construction, transport and freight, and communications sectors.

- Several Swazi and South African news publications

- The Swaziland Business Directory—the usual type of directory for locating companies

Uganda

Uganda Home Page [http://www.uganda.co.ug] bills itself as a comprehensive guide to Uganda. Most links on the main page take you to other sites about Uganda, with only a small amount of actual content on the site. It does link to business directories, various government sites, associations, news organizations, and more.

Regional Wrap-Up

Africa is often called "the Dark Continent," and now we know why. There simply isn't an abundance of illuminating business information. In fact, most business in Africa occurs in South Africa. (Approximately eighty percent of the total GDP of Sub-Saharan Africa is generated in South Africa.) Africa does hold remarkable promise for the future, though. There are numerous projects underway to increase the telecommunications infrastructure that will result in more telephone service and improved Internet access. Free trade zones have also sprung up that will dramatically increase trade and investment opportunities.

However, for the time being, when faced with a project involving this region, I would strongly advise against relying solely, or even primarily, on Internet sources. This is one case where I would suggest thoroughly checking the traditional online services. I would also recommend spending the time to pick up the phone and call some of the organizations mentioned here or others that turn up in the course of searching. *Do not* underestimate the time that will be involved in an African project or you will be sorely disappointed at the outcome. Tailor your expectations and hope for the best.

CHAPTER 8

MEXICO AND CANADA

While Mexico and Canada are certainly very different countries, from a U.S. point of view, their common thread is NAFTA, the North American Free Trade Agreement. NAFTA, implemented in January 1994, formed a free trade area for the U.S., Canada, and Mexico. In effect, it formalized long-standing trade trends and helped eliminate the remaining trade barriers between the three countries. It was unique as the only trade agreement in the world linking a developing country (Mexico) with two of the most highly industrialized countries (Canada and the U.S.) in the world.

NAFTA

Before getting into the specifics of each country, you might start by checking some useful sites for further information on NAFTA.

- **LANIC—University of Texas at Austin's Latin American Network Information Center—NAFTA Resources**
  http://www.lanic.utexas.edu/la/Mexico/nafta/index.html

- **NAFTA Customs**
  http://www.nafta-customs.org

- **NAFTA Secretariat**
  http://www.nafta-sec-alena.org

- **SECOFI-NAFTA**
  http://www.naftaworks.org

- **VIBES—Virtual International Business & Economic Sources—University of North Carolina at Charlotte**
  http://libweb.uncc.edu/ref-bus/reg.htm#nafta

Let's take a look at each country individually, beginning with Mexico.

MEXICO

To some, it might seem strange to cover Mexico separately from the rest of Latin America. As a country, it certainly has a great deal in common with many of the other countries in the region; the major difference is the proximity to the U.S. People from the U.S. are constantly flowing in and out of Mexico for touring, shopping, visiting, and so on. Additionally, because Mexico is a member of NAFTA, there is continual trade back and forth across the border. U.S. and Mexican companies do business together on a daily basis. Mexico is not part of Central America or South America; technically it falls within the geographical boundaries of North America. Because of all of these factors, the influence of the U.S. is greater in Mexico than in the other Latin American countries.

However, when conducting business research on Mexico, don't rely solely on Mexico-specific sources; many of the Latin American sources will include Mexico as well.

Directories

As usual, let's begin our search with some good, solid directory sites.

- **EuroSeek—Mexico**
  http://webdir.euroseek.com/?ilang=en&catid=26584
  Relevant categories include Business & Economy, News & Media, Government, and Science & Environment.

- **Mexico Channel**
  http://www.trace-sc.com
  Start with the Business Center; it has close to twenty categories, each with numerous sub-categories. Categories include Agri-Business, Business Organizations, Industrial Parks, In-Bond Plants, Legislation, Trade Data & Info, and more (see Figure 8.1). Government Online provides links to

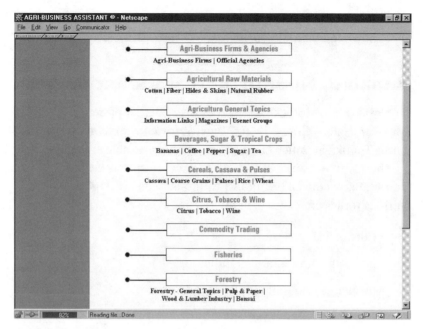

Figure 8.1   Agri-Business Subcategories—Mexico Channel

official government sites and press releases, international organizations, and foreign embassies and consulates. Mexico Today includes links for News & Media, Politics & Politicians, and Education & Research, as well as some less "serious" topics such as Traveling and Sports & Entertainment. Mexico Channel also has its own, built-in Yellow Pages Directory.

Search Engines

There are several search engines dedicated to Mexico; however, a good number of them are available only in Spanish. As Mexico is often included in the general Latin American search engines, don't forget to check the ones listed in the chapter on Latin America and the Caribbean.

- **Explore Mexico**
  http://www.explore-mex.com
  Subjects are in English; however, subcategories and results are in Spanish.

• **Yahoo!—Mexico**
http://dir.yahoo.com/regional/countries/mexico

Banking, Finance, and Stock Exchanges

Mexico has one stock exchange with an Internet presence, the Bolsa Mexicana de Valores [http://www.bmv.com.mx/bmving/index. html]. Thankfully, much of the information is available in English.

The Central Bank, Banco de México [http://www.banxico.org. mx/siteBanxicoINGLES/index.html], also has an English Web site. Various topics are covered here:

• Currency descriptions

• Economic and financial indicators

• Exchange rate policy

• Foreign exchange market

• Location of currency exchange centers

• Monetary policies

Mexico Online [http://www.mexonline.com/banks.htm] has a Bank and Finance Directory. This directory includes a guide to banking in Mexico and a guide to the Mexican stock market. It also lists several Mexican banks, along with links to the bank sites. For additional banks, check the BankSITE Global Directory [http://www.banksite. com/intbanks/north_america_banks.htm]. Scroll about halfway down the page and you will find the section for Mexico.

Investing in Mexico

If you have interest in investing in Mexico, don't miss the site for the Mexican Investment Board [http://www.mib.org.mx]. Start with the Country Profile section for a good general overview of the country. The Country Profile covers the standard topics: geography, currency, demographics, government, etc. There's also a short video to view.

From here, proceed to the Investing in Mexico section, which covers the following topics and more:

• Anti-trust

• Corporate forms

- Directories of banks, brokerage firms, law firms, accounting and consulting firms, economic development offices in each Mexican state

- Environmental legislation and investment opportunities in the environment and natural resources sectors

- Intellectual property law

- Investment opportunities

- Labor regulations

- Legal system, including an unofficial translation of Foreign Investment Law

- Taxes

Next, check in with the *What's New* section, which really has some meaty material, including investment projections for the year 2000 and lengthy studies of the maquiladora export industry, the electrical and electronics industry, and the textile industry (see Figure 8.2). (The term *maquiladora* was originally associated with the milling process. In Mexico, it evolved into a word for another type of processing; the assembly of imported component parts for re-export. U.S. firms, with the

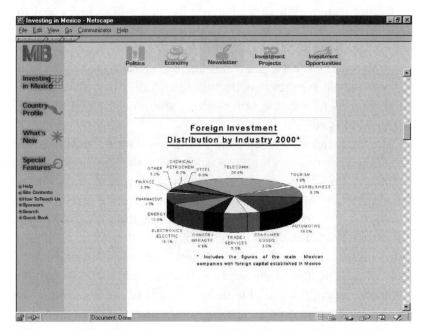

Figure 8.2 Foreign Investment Distribution by Industry— Mexican Investment Board

support of the Mexican government, set up assembly plants in Mexico. The U.S. firms were then allowed to import components and raw materials duty-free as long as the finished product was re-exported to the U.S.)

BANCOMEXT, the Mexican Bank for Foreign Trade [http://www.mexico-trade.com] was founded in 1937 to facilitate foreign investment in Mexico. The primary goal of the BANCOMEXT Web site is to maintain a One-Stop Mexico Information Center for U.S. companies interested in or actively doing business with Mexico. Information found at the site includes:

- A searchable directory of Mexican exporters

- A Mexican investment guide written by a Mexican law firm

- Trade leads

- Links for regional and state information, Mexican news sources, legal resources, universities, government agencies, and more

- A Basic Guide for Foreign Investors

A monthly newsletter is available at the site, with archives back to October 1997. Follow the link called Apparel Industry Information Center and you will find several detailed industry studies on the automotive, chemical & pharmaceutical, electric & electronic, iron & steel, plastic & rubber goods, and textile industries. There is no indication as to why the link to these studies only mentions the apparel industry.

The Mexican Intelligence Report [http://www.mex-i-co.com] has some good information for those scouting out the Mexican business climate. A monthly newsletter posted at the site focuses on business development in Mexico. You may subscribe at the site to receive the newsletter (at no charge) via e-mail on a monthly basis. The Industries link takes you to profiles of the agribusiness, construction, health care, automotive, energy, and telecommunications industries. The Company Profiles include contact information, company description, topline financials, officers, and subsidiaries. Unfortunately, the profiles are not searchable; the companies are merely listed alphabetically. And finally, the Markets section describes the business environment in each of the Mexican states.

Chambers of Commerce and Industry

The American Chamber of Commerce of Mexico, A.C. [http://www.amcham.com.mx/amchamber/english/index21.html] has many useful publications. Unfortunately, they are not available for viewing at the site, only for purchase.

- Business Mexico—Published monthly, it contains current event sections on banking and finance, environment, management and industry, and investment summaries. Four times a year they publish a telecommunications and technology section.

- Business Planning—An annual in-depth analysis of the Mexican economy, with projections on key variables, this publication includes the results of an AmCham survey describing what AmCham member companies plan in terms of investment, prices, salary increases, new hiring, and financing alternatives. Another section deals with sectoral data on the volume and value of specific manufactured products.

- Directory of American Companies in Mexico—This publication includes close to 7,000 companies.

- Surveys of Salaries and Benefits—This is an annual publication.

The directory of members at the site breaks out into the following categories:

- Chemicals
- Construction/Building, Real Estate
- Financial, Credit, and Insurance
- Food and Beverages/Agriculture
- Health and Environment
- Industrial Machinery, Supplies, and Assembly
- Management, Human Resources, and Training
- Office and Household Supplies
- Paper, Printing, and Packaging

- Personal Articles, Recreation, and Gifts

- Petroleum, Petrochemicals, and Minerals

- Retail and Direct Sales

- Services: Business and General

- Telecommunications/Electronics

- Textiles and Clothing

- Trade Services

- Transportation, Couriers, and Warehousing

Only contact information (name and phone number) is available for the individual companies. For further information, you would need to purchase the annual AmCham Membership Directory. You can cheat a bit on this, however. The area of the site called New Members lists full contact information and type of business for all new AmCham members.

Back on the main page of the site, following a flashing link near the bottom called What's News will lead to many useful sections:

- Economic Indicator—GDP, inflation, unemployment, and more from 1995 through projections for 2001

- Exchange Rate

- NAFTA—Detailed results of a survey of AmCham members identifying the effects of NAFTA five years after its implementation

- Quick Links—Links to Economy, Trade, Finance, and Investment sites, NAFTA-related sites, Mexican news, government, infrastructure, transportation, telecommunications sites, and more

Mexico has two other AmCham chapters with an Internet presence; the American Chamber of Commerce of Mexico—Guadalajara Chapter [http://www.amchamgdl.com.mx/english/framesidx.html] and the American Chamber of Commerce of Mexico—Monterrey Chapter [http://www.usmcoc.org/monterrey.html].

Business Directories

Of the directory sites for finding businesses in Mexico, some are more useful than others, for a variety of reasons. Try these when looking for businesses in Mexico:

- **Mexico Web**
  http://mexico.web.com.mx/english
  Try the Companies category, which has about seventeen sub-categories. The one problem with this site: while the search categories are in English, the subcategories and the results returned are in Spanish.

- **The Mx International—Mexico**
  http://www.mxsearch.com/mexico
  It has the same drawback as **Mexico Web**—the search categories are in English but the results are returned in Spanish.

- **Mexico Online**
  http://www.mexonline.com/business.htm
  Follow the Business link, then choose from the following: Alphabetical Business Directory, Bank and Finance, Classifieds Online, Consulting Services, Customs Brokers & Freight Forwarders, Health & Medicine, Information Resources, Insurance & Legal Services, Maquila Master Supplier Directory, NAFTA Trade Directory, and Professional Contacts Network. The results returned will link to company Web sites. This business directory actually has some value-added information including guides to Mexican banking, information on the stock market, starting a business in Mexico, and legal information.

- **Information Mexico—Business**
  http://www.mexicosi.com
  This site has a business directory with eighteen categories (see Figure 8.3). Listings include contact information and a good description of the company's business. The site also has a Doing Business with Mexico Guide that includes a Business Overview, the Economy in Brief, and Foreign Trade. The Business Tips section carries useful little cultural pointers. Some of the information at the site is a bit old (in particular the economic data and

trade show section); however, due to the nature of the rest of the information, the data could still be valid.

- **Infosel Cdmex**
  http://cdmex.infosel.com
  Broad categories are Manufacturers and Professional Services, with each splitting into numerous subcategories. Company results include contact information, URL, number of employees, year established, names and titles of primary contacts, list of products, and a description of the company's activities. The site is also searchable.

- **MexSearch Yellow Pages**
  http://www.yellow.com.mx/indexs.html
  Since I could only find one online yellow pages directory for Mexico and the yellow pages are used much the same as the business directories, I thought I'd include it here.

Association and Industry Resources

There are a few English-language sites for associations in Mexico. And, as we all know by now, associations can be a good source of industry information.

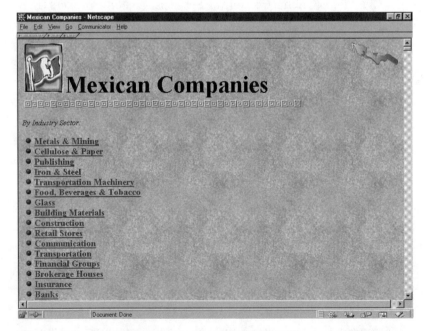

Figure 8.3   Sample Industry Sectors from Information Mexico

ANIQ, Asociación Nacional de la Industria Química or the National Association of the Chemical Industry [http://www.aniq. org.mx/iindex.htm] ostensibly has a listing of members sorted by various industry sectors; however, it was still under construction when we last checked. The site offers a nice overview of the Mexican chemical and petrochemical industry. Until the site construction is completed, there really isn't much else there. If you have an interest in the chemical industry, I would periodically check back to see if more content has been added to the site.

According to the Consejo Mexicano del Café—the Mexican Coffee Council [http://www.sagar.gob.mx/cmc/cafe01in.htm], Mexico is the world's fifth largest coffee producer, after Brazil, Colombia, Indonesia, and Vietnam (see Figure 8.4). That was news to me. I knew about Brazil and Colombia, but Indonesia and Vietnam were big surprises. I also didn't realize that Mexico was in the top five. As we can see from Figure 8.5, the U.S. is the biggest export market for Mexican coffee with Japan a distant second.

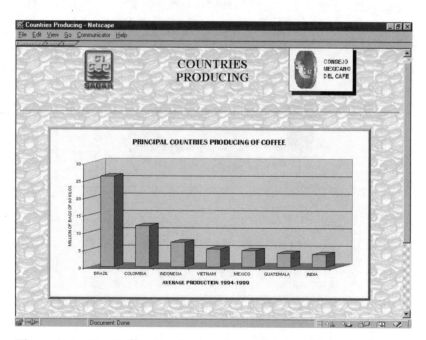

Figure 8.4   Top Coffee Producing Countries—Mexican Coffee Council

This site is chock full (sorry, couldn't resist the coffee pun) of just about everything you could possibly want to know about the Mexican coffee market. Here are samples of what you can find:

- Mexico's principal coffee producing states and how much each produced annually for each of the last five growing seasons

- The different types and qualities of coffee and how much of each is exported

- How much coffee is produced versus how much is exported

- The monetary value of the exported coffee

- Domestic (Mexican) coffee consumption

- Which countries import organic coffee

- Daily coffee prices

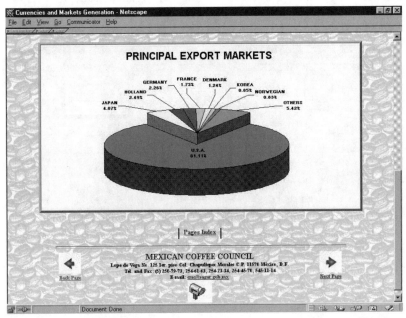

Figure 8.5 Principal Coffee Export Markets—Mexican Coffee Council

The Mexican Coffee Council's site is impressively current. When I last visited, none of the statistics were more than a month old.

The Mexican Bank for Foreign Trade (BANCOMEXT), in conjunction with its office in Montreal, has created a site focusing on the

Mexican textile industry [http://www.mexicanshowroom.com]. The site begins with a general economic and export overview of Mexico and then gets into the specifics of the textile and apparel industry. Industry questions answered at the site include these:

- Location of the textile and apparel industry within Mexico

- The size of the market

- Export targets for Mexican textiles and apparel

- Industry growth since the implementation of NAFTA

- Types of textiles and apparel produced in Mexico

- Foreign countries investing in the Mexican textile and apparel industry

- Segments of the industry receiving direct foreign investment (see Figure 8.6)

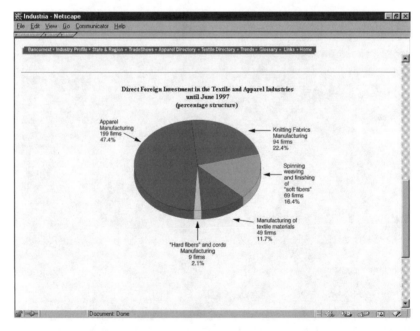

Figure 8.6   Foreign Direct Investment—Mexican Textile & Apparel Industry

The site also has two searchable directories: one for textile manufacturers and one for apparel manufacturers. Both sites may be searched by company name, product, label, brand, contact person, and other fields. The entries contain contact information and annual sales. Some companies also have photos and specifications of major products. And, for the fashion-forward individual, there is also a section on Fashion Trends.

The Mexican Mining Information Centre [http://www.mexmin. com] was created by the Ministry of Trade and Industrial Development to promote and modernize Mexico's mining industry. The site starts out, as so many sites do, with an Outlook section. This covers the gamut of topics from the obligatory country overview and the economic environment to items such as trade agreements, direct foreign investment, privatization, and the financial and labor environment. Following the Outlook comes an Industry Profile that discusses mining legislation and Mexican mining production. There is also a 1998 Industry Report that goes into further detail (see Figure 8.7). The rest of site covers regional mining data, details on mining projects, and a searchable directory of mining and exploration companies.

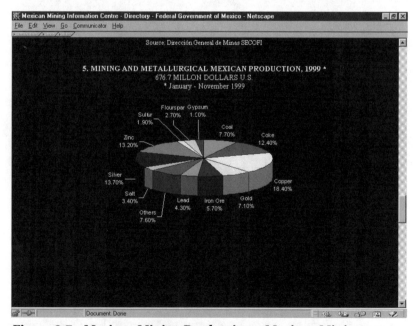

**Figure 8.7 Mexican Mining Production—Mexican Mining
Information Centre**

CANADA

Canada, even more so than Mexico, seems to live in the shadow of the U.S. It is a large, industrialized country and most of the population speaks English. People from the U.S. would most likely have no more trouble finding their way around in a Canadian city than they would in an unknown city in the U.S. I wouldn't be surprised if many people in the rest of the world viewed the U.S. and Canada interchangeably.

There are some differences, though. While both countries have origins in Great Britain, Canada also has a strong heritage from France, which makes for sharp cultural differences. The U.S. and Canada have different forms of federal government. For starters, the U.S. has a President and Canada has a Prime Minister. Of course, that's only a small example; the differences go much deeper.

To do business in Canada means needing to research and consider a whole other set of laws, rules, regulations, taxes, and more. The following sites should help to answer some of your Canadian business questions.

Directories

Canada has a number of good directory sites. The National Library of Canada [http://www.nlc-bnc.ca/caninfo/ecaninfo.htm] offers one that can sort by subject or alphabetically. Personally, I think it is easier to work with when sorted by subject. The directory divides into ten subjects with subcategories under each. Scrolling down the page, we see that each subject contains several subcategories, along with a notation as to the number of entries for each subcategory. Depending upon the specifics of your search, some of these subcategories might be worth trying:

- Commerce, communication, telecommunication, transportation
- Economics
- General subjects, general works
- Journalism, publishers, and publishing
- Law
- Library science, information science
- Political science

Another interesting directory has been compiled by the Canadian consulting firm Hal Doran Associates: Internet Sources for Journalists and Broadcasters [http://www.synapse.net/~radio/welcome.html]. Follow the Subject link and then the Business and Finance link to get to the most useful section [http://www.synapse.net/~radio/business.htm]. Here you will find numerous business sites under the headings of Business, Banks and Credit Unions, Finance and Investment, Business Media, and Other Business sites.

Other Canadian directories to try include the following:

- **Canadian Links**
  http://www.canadian-links.com
  Search by topic or geographic region.

- **Canadian Webs**
  http://www.canadianwebs.com

- **Canadopedia**
  http://www.canadopedia.com

- **EuroSeek Canada**
  http://webdir.euroseek.com/top/catid=87439/ilang=en

- **GDSourcing—A Reference Point for Canadian Statistics**
  http://www.gdsourcing.com/about.htm
  This site specializes in Canadian statistical sites.

- **Price's List of Lists—Canadian Business**
  http://gwis2.circ.gwu.edu/~gprice/listof.htm#CanadianBusiness
  What could possibly be said about Gary Price's List of Lists that hasn't been said countless times before? Price comes through again, with a directory-style set of URLs for various lists related to Canadian business.

- **Sympatico.ca**
  http://www1.sympatico.ca

- **Yahoo! Regional Canada**
  http://dir.yahoo.com/regional/countries/canada

- **Yahoo! Canada**
  http://ca.yahoo.com
  I'm unclear as to the difference between the two Yahoo! directories, but they are set up differently. If you belong to the "leave no stone unturned" school, you just might want to take a look at both of them.

Figure 8.8   Sample Canada.com Directory Choices

Search Engines

Moving on to search engines, a few focus specifically on Canada and are useful for business research. Canada.com [http://www.canada.com/home] is a search engine, but also has additional information. On the main page of the site, there are links to current news stories. Scrolling to the bottom of the page, there are links to numerous Canadian news sites. Canada.com also functions as a directory site, with several predetermined categories and subcategories. Clicking on Browse Directories on the main page, then Business & Finance, then Data & Statistics, we see that we will still need to choose from National, By Province, or By Territory. Choosing By Province, we then receive a list of the Canadian provinces from which to choose (see Figure 8.8). Selecting any one of the provinces will return a list of links to business and financial statistical data for that province.

Maple Square [http://www.maplesquare.com] is another Canadian search engine that also has a directory function. Launched in early 1996, Maple Square adds over 100 sites daily—at least that's what it states at the site. The directory portion of the site has quite a few interesting subcategories under the Business and Money and Computers and Internet headings that could help with business research.

Canada also has a couple of regional search engines: MyBC.com [http://www.mybc.com] for British Columbia and Alberta.com [http://www.alberta.com] for, of course, Alberta.

A final Canadian search engine to try is AltaVista Canada [http://www.altavistacanada.com/cgi-bin/query]. If you are at all familiar with searching AltaVista, you should have no difficulties searching the Canadian version.

Yellow Pages

As one might expect, Canada has several online Yellow Pages directories, some for the whole country and some for particular regions:

- **Canada Yellow Pages**
  http://canadayellowpages.com

- **Canadian Yellow Business Directory**
  http://www.yellow.ca

- **Canada 411**
  http://canada411.sympatico.ca

- **Yellow Pages.ca**
  http://www.yellowpages.ca/bin/cgidir.dll?mem=800&MG=

- **WorldPages.com**
  http://www.worldpages.com/bus

- **QuebecTel's Yellow Pages**
  http://pagesjaunesqctel.com/eindex.html

- **Mysask.com**
  http://www.mysask.com
  A yellow pages for Saskatchewan

- **myWinnipeg.com**
  http://www.mywinnipeg.com
  A yellow pages for Winnipeg

Chambers of Commerce and Industry

While Canada does not have an AmCham chapter, there are many other chambers of commerce within the country. Let's look at some of the larger Canadian chambers.

- **The Canadian Chamber of Commerce**
  http://www.chamber.ca/newpages/main.html
  This chamber has offices in Ottawa, Toronto, and Montreal. It maintains an online library of news releases relating to important business issues, as well as a section of links to various Canadian government sites.

- **British Columbia Chamber of Commerce**
  http://www.bcchamber.org
  Items available here include a list of corporate members with phone and fax numbers, press releases and articles, business links, and the current issue of chamber newsletter.

- **Calgary Chamber of Commerce**
  http://www.calgarychamber.com
  Daily business headlines and business resources links are presented. A notation indicated they planned to post the membership list shortly.

- **Niagara Falls Chamber of Commerce**
  http://www.nflschamber.com
  The membership list is searchable by company name or category (list of categories provided). You'll also find useful links.

- **Ottawa Board of Trade**
  http://www.board-of-trade.org
  This site contains a searchable membership directory, local government links, economic development links, and press releases.

- **Ontario Chamber of Commerce**
  http://www.occ.on.ca
  Profiles of recent winners of the Outstanding Business Achievement Award and press releases are available here.

Associations

Most business searchers, whether conducting domestic or international research, check to find any associations relevant to the industry being researched. Canada, much like the U.S., has numerous associations; many with Web sites. Here is a potpourri of industry association sites:

- **Aerospace Industries Association of Canada**
  http://www.aiac.ca

- **Canadian Association of Petroleum Producers**
  http://www.capp.ca/capframe.html

- **Canadian Bankers Association**
  http://www.cba.ca

- **Canadian Chemical Producers' Association**
  http://www.ccpa.ca/english/index.html

- **Canadian Electricity Association**
  http://www.canelect.ca/connections_online/home.htm

- **Canadian Gas Association**
  http://www.cga.ca

- **Canadian Petroleum Perspective**
  http://www.mossr.com

- **Canadian Soft Drink Association**
  http://www.softdrink.ca

- **Canadian Steel Producers Association**
  http://www.canadiansteel.ca

- **Mining Association of Canada**
  http://www.mining.ca/english

- **Petroleum Services Association of Canada**
  http://www.psac.ca

Lists

As we saw in the first chapter, lists of various types help us in doing company or industry research. To know the top five (fill in the blank) or how many companies in industry X take their place in the top 100 of some list or another can often prove useful. Luckily, a number of those lists for Canada are compiled and available on the Web.

The *Globe and National Report on Business Magazine* [http://www.robmagazine.com] pulls together several business lists for us, many accessible from one page of the site [http://www.robmagazine.com/top1000/index.html] (see Figure 8.9):

- Top 1000 Canadian Companies—by profits

- Top 300 Private Canadian Companies—by revenue

- Top 50 Canadian Companies—by five year profit growth (%)

- Top 50 Canadian Companies—by five year stock growth (%)

- Top 50 Canadian Companies—by five year revenue growth (%)

- Top 50 Canadian Companies—by number of employees

- Top 50 Canadian Companies—by R&D expenditures

- Top 50 Canadian CEOs—by total compensation

For all companies listed, the site provides a short profile that includes a company description, contact information, major officers, and topline financials.

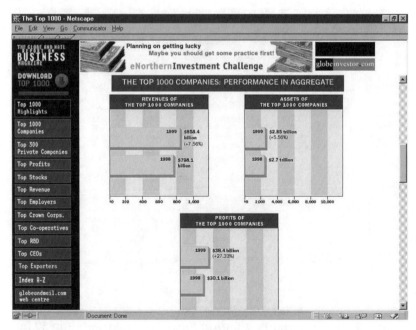

Figure 8.9   Excerpts from Top 1000 List—*Globe and National Report on Business Magazine*

Deloitte & Touche Canada [http://www.deloitte.ca/en/industries/HiTech/Fast50_99ranking.ASP] annually publishes the Canadian Technology Fast 50 list. It bases the rankings on revenue growth over the last five years. There is also a link to the previous year's list [http://www.deloitte.ca/en/industries/HiTech/Fast55_98ranking.ASP]. Each company's entry includes the CEO name, city and province of location, five-year growth rate, and a link to the company's Web site.

Canadian Business Magazine [http://www.canbus.com/CB500/p500.htm] publishes the Performance 2000, comprising three different lists:

- Growth Leaders

- Highest Return to Investors

- Top 50 in Sales

The lists are searchable; however, other than rank on each list, little other information appears (see Figure 8.10).

	THE FIRST 50		
	SALES RANK	COMPANY	PERFORMANCE RANK
			% change 3 year
	'99 '98		sales growth
	1 1	General Motors of Canada Ltd. (auto)	1296
	2 2	BCE Inc. (tele)	-
	3 3	Ford Motor Co. of Canada Ltd. (auto)	919
	4 4	Nortel Networks Corp.*1 (tele)	365
	5 8	Chrysler Canada Ltd. (auto)	700
	6 7	Canadian Imperial Bank of Commerce (fs)	763
	7 5	Royal Bank of Canada (fs)	1000
	8 9	Bank of Montreal (fs)	790
	9 10	TransCanada PipeLines Ltd. (o&g)	-
	10 12	Bank of Nova Scotia (fs)	916
	11 24	Power Corp. of Canada (div)	404
	12 26	Power Financial Corp. (div)	391
	13 11	George Weston Ltd. (div)	1039
	14 29	Great-West Lifeco Inc. (div)	380
	15 14	Sun Life Assurance Co. of Canada (fs)	931
	16 6	Seagram Co. Ltd.* (div)	-
	17 18	Loblaw Cos. Ltd. (food)	984
	18 16	Alcan Aluminium Ltd.* (mng)	818
	19 25	Bombardier Inc. (manu)	624
	20 -	Sobeys Canada Inc.2 (food)	-
	21 44	Toronto-Dominion Bank (fs)	1037
	22 19	Manulife Financial (fs)	1029

Figure 8.10 **Excerpt of *Canadian Business Magazine*'s Top 50 in Sales List**

Profit, The Magazine for Canadian Entrepreneurs, publishes a list of the 200 fastest growing Canadian companies [http://www.profit100.com/1999/99home.htm]. In addition to the information in the table for each company (see Figure 8.11), it carries a nice write-up several paragraphs long on each company.

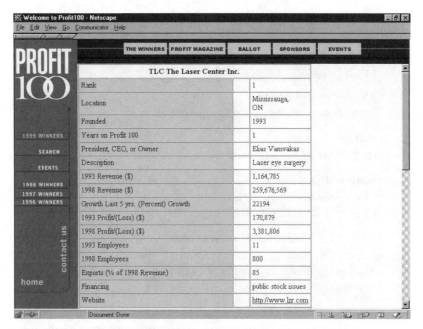

Figure 8.11   Sample Entry from *Profit*'s List of 200 Fastest Growing Canadian Companies

Business Directories

For each region of the world, we've looked at business directories, those compilations that help, in one way or another, to identify companies in particular industries, those that export or import, etc. Canada, of course, due to its size and as an industrialized nation, certainly has its fair share of those directories. When you look for companies, start with these business directories:

- **Alcanseek**
  http://www.alcanseek.com
  Includes Alaska

- **CanadaOne**
  http://www.canadaone.com/business/index.html#businesses

- **Canadian Business Directory**
  http://www.cdnbusinessdirectory.com
  Can search by province

- **Canadian Exporters Catalogue**
  http://www.canadianexporterscatalogue.com

- **Canadian Trade Index**
  http://www.ctidirectory.com

- **Marketplace.ca**
  http://www.marketplace.ca

- **The Montreal Page**
  http://www.pagemontreal.qc.ca/english

- **Ontario Online**
  http://www.OOL-inc.com

- **Search BC.com**
  http://www.searchbc.com
  Only British Columbia

- **Strategis—Canadian Business Map**
  http://strategis.ic.gc.ca/scdt/bizmap/nav.html
  Also useful in identifying associations, stock exchanges,
  and more

- **Strategis—Company Directories**
  http://strategis.ic.gc.ca/sc_coinf/engdoc/homepage.html

- **SurfOttowa.com**
  http://www.surfottawa.com

- **VanLink**
  http://www.vanlink.com
  Only Vancouver

Banking, Finance, and Stock Exchanges

If I were interested in doing business either in Canada or with a Canadian company, one of the first bits of information I would want would be a good economic overview. Strategis, the Canadian government's Internet site for business, offers a good Regional Economic Overview [http://strategis.ic.gc.ca/sc_ecnmy/mera/engdoc/09.html], updated every quarter. The Canadian Department of Finance [http://www.fin.gc.ca/fin-eng.html] site also warrants a quick look. I recommend investigating these investment sites:

• **Advice for Investors**
http://www.fin-info.com

• **About.com's Investing in Canada Links**
http://investingcanada.about.com/money/
investingcanada/msub45.htm?once=true&

• **About.com's Canadian High Tech Investing Links**
http://investingcanada.about.com/money/
investingcanada/msub28.htm?once=true&

For banking information, begin with the Office of the Superintendent of Financial Institutions [http://www.osfi-bsif.gc.ca/eng/default. asp?ref=home]. This site carries a good deal of information designed to help safeguard your financial dealings. One should also look at the site from Canada's central bank, The Bank of Canada [http://www.bank -banque-canada.ca/english].

Asset Rank	Bank	Country (Year End)	Assets ($millions CDN)	Pre-Tax Profit ($millions CDN)	Pre-Tax Return on Assets (%)
1	Deutsche Bank	Germany (12/98)	1,123,194	7,226	0.64
2	UBS	Switzerland (12/98)	1,051,663	4,534	0.43
3	Citigroup	U.S. (12/98)	1,025,227	14,212	1.39
4	BankAmerica Corp.	U.S. (12/98)	947,087	12,340	1.30
5	Bank of Tokyo-Mitsubishi	Japan (03/99)	918,017	239	0.03
6	ABN AMRO Bank	Netherlands (12/98)	772,970	5,183	0.67
7	HSBC Holdings	U.K. (12/98)	743,122	10,106	1.36
8	Credit Suisse Group	Switzerland (12/98)	726,758	3,129	0.43
9	Credit Agricole Group	France (12/98)	700,775	5,773	0.82
10	Societe Generale	France (12/98)	686,221	3,079	0.45
11	Sumitomo Bank	Japan (03/99)	674,195	(9,666)	(1.43)
12	Dresdner Bank	Germany (12/98)	655,119	2,398	0.37
13	Sanwa Bank	Japan (03/99)	641,491	(8,243)	(1.28)
14	Westdeutsche Landesbank Girozentrale	Germany (12/98)	626,157	1,431	0.23
15	Norinchukin Bank	Japan (03/99)	625,010	1,231	0.20
16	Dai-Ichi Kangyo Bank	Japan (03/99)	608,220	(8,335)	(1.37)
17	Industrial & Commercial Bank of China	China (12/98)	599,847	639	0.11
18	Sakura Bank	Japan (03/99)	597,119	(8,994)	(1.51)
19	Commerzbank	Germany (12/98)	584,738	2,222	0.38
20	Banque Nationale de Paris	France (12./98)	581,191	2,666	0.46
21	Industrial Bank of Japan	Japan (03/99)	567,925	(3,263)	(0.57)
22	Chase Manhattan Corp.	U.S. (12/98)	560,996	9,169	1.63
23	Fuji Bank	Japan (03/99)	549,279	(8,461)	(1.54)
24	Barclays Bank	U.K. (12/98)	541,818	4,893	0.90
25	Hypo Vereinsbank	Germany (12/98)	517,024	4,198	0.81
26	ING Bank Group	Netherlands (12/98)	501,102	1,403	0.28
27	Fortis Banking Group	Belgium (12/98)	496,125	3,206	0.65
28	National Westminster Bank	U.K. (12/98)	474,435	5,463	1.15
29	Paribas	France (12/98)	474,348	2,581	0.54

Figure 8.12   Portion of Top 150 Banks Worldwide—Canadian Bankers Association

Canadian Bankers Association (CBA), mentioned earlier, has compiled a very useful page of links for financial, economic, and banking information [http://www.cba.ca/eng/links_index.htm]. The CBA has also graciously compiled a list of the Top 150 Banks Worldwide by Size of Assets [http://www.cba.ca/eng/Statistics/ Stats/bankrankings.htm]. This list is useful both for Canadian banking information (by scrolling through the list and pulling out the Canadian banks) and on a global basis in identifying the largest banks throughout the world (see Figure 8.12).

If looking for a bank for business dealings, check the Canada portion of the North America Bank Directory of Bank Web Sites [http://www.banksite.com/intbanks/north_america_banks.htm].

SEDAR, the System for Electronic Document Analysis and Retrieval [http://www.sedar.com/homepage.htm] serves much the same function as EDGAR, the Electronic Data Gathering, Analysis, and Retrieval System, in the U.S. SEDAR has profiles of Canadian public companies and mutual fund groups, along with links to public filings (see Figure 8.13). The SEDAR site is searchable and very user friendly.

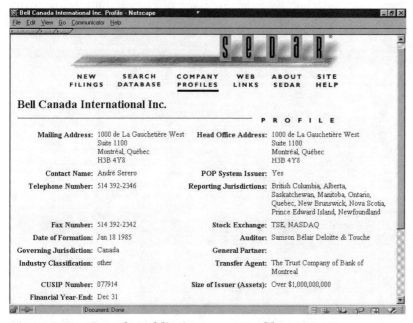

Figure 8.13   Sample Public Company Profile—SEDAR

This seems as good a time as any to mention the various Canadian exchanges with an Internet presence:

- **Alberta Stock Exchange Market Quotes**
  http://www.telenium.ca/ASE/index.html

- **Canadian Venture Exchange**
  http://www.cdnx.ca

- **Montreal Exchange**
  http://www.me.org

- **Toronto Stock Exchange Market Quotes**
  http://www.telenium.ca/TSE/index.html

- **Winnipeg Commodity Exchange**
  http://www.wce.mb.ca/market/_activepages/market.htm

- **Winnipeg Stock Exchange**
  http://www.wse.ca/start.html

Business News

Canada, of course, has countless Internet sources for news in general and business news in particular. In the U.S., Canadian business news is often interspersed with our own. If you happen to be at a loss as to where to go on the Internet for Canadian business news or just need a quick reminder where to look, here are some ideas:

- **Canadian Business Magazine**
  http://www.canadianbusiness.com/index.shtml
  Previously discussed for its Performance 2000 lists, *Canadian Business Magazine* is strictly devoted to business issues. While the entire print issue is not posted at the site, there are selected articles and the site is searchable. Additionally, there is a resource section with statistics and research links. Stories are divided into several categories: Investing, E-commerce & Technology, Business News, Executive Development, and Travel & Leisure.

- **Canadian Corporate News (CCN)**
  http://www.cdn-news.com/company/index.html
  The CCN site is searchable by company name, stock symbol, keyword, or industry. Links move you to both today's news and the past week's news.

- **The Financial Post—Canoe Money**
  http://www.canoe.ca/FP/home.html
  Financial, technology, mergers and acquisitions, agriculture, economic, world news, and more is offered. The site also has stock market, mutual fund, and banking information.

- **Canada NewsWire**
  http://www.newswire.ca

On this searchable site of news releases; you can search by category, date, industry, keyword, organization, stock symbol, or subject. It also includes government releases and claims to have over 175,000 releases in its database.

- **The Globe and Mail**
  http://www.globeandmail.ca
  This major Canadian newspaper makes much of its content available at the Web site. Selected stories from the current issue as well as the previous seven days' issues are available and searchable.

- **Maclean's Online**
  http://www.macleans.ca/index.stm
  Publishes weekly with about a year and a half's worth of archives at the site. According to a statement at the site, only those who subscribe to the print version can access the full text of the articles; others will only receive the first paragraph. However, I tried several different articles, including some from various archived issues, and could always view them in full text.

- **Silicon Valley North**
  http://www.silvan.com
  High-tech news for British Columbia, Alberta, Toronto, and Ottawa is presented.

In addition to the above-listed online magazines and newspapers, some sites provide only links to news sites. Here are a few of those:

- **NewsCentral—Canadian Newspapers A-M**
  http://www.all-links.com/newscentral/northamerica/canada.html

- **NewsCentral—Canadian Newspapers N-Z**
  http://www.all-links.com/newscentral/northamerica/canada2.html

- **Canada's Information Resource Center**
  http://circ.micromedia.on.ca

Industry Resources

While the main purpose of the Invest in Canada Web site [http://napoleon.ic.gc.ca/scdt/bizinvst/interface2.nsf/engdoc/0.html] is to convince you to invest in Canada, in order to do so, it has compiled a number of very helpful industry overviews and profiles (see Figure 8.14). These industries are among the ones covered:

- Aerospace

- Agri-food

- Automotive

- Chemicals

- Pharmaceutical

- Software

- Telecommunications

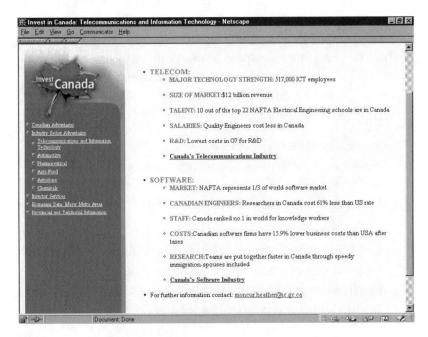

Figure 8.14   Portion of Telecommunications and Software Industry Profiles

The Research Department of the Canadian Broadcasting Corporation [http://www3.cbc.ca/research/hpenglish.html] regularly conducts studies on the broadcast/telecommunications industry and will often make them available free of charge. When I last visited the site, some of the studies were a bit old (three to four years), but others were less than a year old. Sample titles include

"Does Radio Have a Future: Trends in North American Radio," "What Will We Watch? A Forecast of Viewing Habits In 10 Years," and "Measuring the Use of the Internet—The Future of New Media."

Earlier, I mentioned Strategis [http://strategis.ic.gc.ca/engdoc/main.html], the Canadian government's Internet site for business. I saved a more in-depth look at Strategis for last, as it is really the "mother lode" of industry information; the site contains over two million documents and includes reports, economic data, trade data, market analysis, and company information. I find that, until you're very familiar with the site, it's best to work from the Site Map rather than any of the menus. You might also want to work in text-only mode, as opposed to graphical.

The first section covered is Company Directories, which includes two databases and a links area. The searchable databases are Canadian Companies Capabilities and Federal Corporations Data Online. The Canadian Business Map's Company Directories is an extensive list of links to other business directories on the Internet.

The Trade and Investment section definitely covers a lot of territory. These relevant portions are included:

- International Business Analysis—Special Reports—Periodic reports on a variety of trade-related topics such as A Report on Foreign Investment Barriers and Data on Trade and Investment in Canada

- International Business Opportunities—Trade Strategies and Action Plan—Overviews of the Agriculture, Food, and Beverages; Automotive; Bio-Industries; Building Products; Electrical Power, Equipment, and Services; Environmental; Health; Information Technologies and Communications; and Plastics industries from the point of view of international trade

- International Business Opportunities—Canadian Importers Database

- Trade Statistics—Trade Data Online—Imports and exports by product (HS Codes) and industry (SIC Codes)

- Trade and Investment Policy—Policies, negotiations, and trade agreements

When you move into Business Information by Sector, you'll find these sectors covered:

- Advanced Materials
- Aerospace & Defense
- Assistive Devices
- Automotive & Transportation Industries
- Bio-Industries
- Chemicals
- Consumer Products
- Environmental Affairs
- Forest Industries & Building Products
- Health Industries
- Information Technology & Telecommunications
- Manufacturing & Processing Technologies Metals & Minerals Processing
- Plastics
- Rubber
- Services Industries & Capital Projects

Each industry overview is structured a bit differently; however, they all brim over with useful information.

Strategis' Economic Analysis and Statistics section starts out with several economic periodicals. It also contains links to some of the industry and trade information discussed previously, as well as a mechanism for comparing U.S. and Canadian economic growth trends. The Research, Technology, and Innovation section offers access to the Canadian patent database, links for industry research, and other directories.

The Canadian Intellectual Property Office, bankruptcy statistics, and Investment Canada may all be reached in the Licences, Legislation, and Regulations section. The Canadian Trademarks Database has a link in the Consumer Information section.

Some sections of Strategis, such as Canadian Industry Statistics [http://strategis.ic.gc.ca/sc_ecnmy/sio/homepage.html], are difficult to find if you don't know exactly where to look. The section contains over twenty industry sectors, listed by two-digit SIC. Choose any of the sectors and you will then have the choice of the four-digit SIC subsectors. Each subsector overview contains the same seven topics (see Figure 8.15):

- Definition
- Employment
- Investment
- Major Players
- Preface
- Production
- Trade

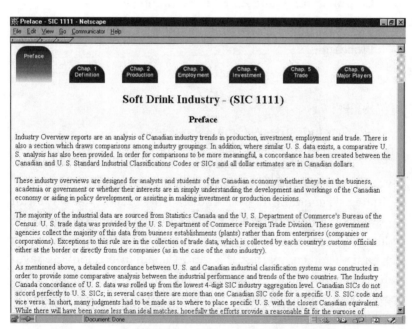

Figure 8.15   Portion of Soft Drink Industry Overview—Strategis

Strategis has many other useful sections. If you're serious about doing business in Canada or with a Canadian company, spend some time to familiarize yourself with the site; it's easy to overlook key areas. As an added bonus, Strategis offers a free e-mail bulletin, Headlines, listing every new document published on Strategis that week.

Regional Wrap-Up

Searching Canada and Mexico may have been a bit more comfortable, as they're so close to home for many of us. And, with Canada, we have the added advantage of knowing that most, if not all, of the information will be available in English. Due to NAFTA, and Mexico's proximity to the U.S., more and more information on Mexico should also appear in English as time goes on.

CHAPTER 9

ASIA AND THE PACIFIC

Our global excursion is almost finished, but we have one very large region left to cover: Asia and the Pacific. While those of us in the Western Hemisphere tend to lump together all of the countries in the Eastern Hemisphere, we couldn't be more wrong. There are many languages, multiple dialects, a diversity of religious beliefs, and social norms and customs that fundamentally differ from country to country. The region contains a vast mix of developing countries, very under-developed countries, newly industrializing states such as Thailand, Korea, and Indonesia, and highly developed, first-world countries such as Japan and Australia.

Asia and Pacific business coverage has very few one-size-fits-all sources. When you need business information on more than one country, you will generally have to use multiple sources. In addition to regional resources, we will cover country-specific sources for Australia, Hong Kong, India, Indonesia, Japan, Nepal, New Zealand, and Singapore. With such a vast and diverse region, what follows is merely the tip of the iceberg.

Directories

The Australian National University Library [http://anulib.anu. edu.au] has a good directory section for Asia/Pacific Internet Resources [http://anulib.anu.edu.au/clusters/ap/subjects/subjects. html]. You can browse the directory either by subject or by country/region. Other relevant directory sections of this library include the following:

- Business Administration
  http://anulib.anu.edu.au/clusters/ssh/subjects/busadmin.html

- Commerce
  http://anulib.anu.edu.au/clusters/ssh/subjects/commerce.html

- Economics
  http://anulib.anu.edu.au/clusters/ssh/subjects/economics.html

- Statistics
  http://anulib.anu.edu.au/clusters/ssh/subjects/statistics.html

The University of Texas at Austin comes to the rescue again with another in its series of international directories. ASNIC, the Asian Studies Network Information Center [http://asnic.utexas.edu/asnic.html] has several extremely useful sections:

- **The All Asia Links**
  http://asnic.utexas.edu/asnic/pages/allasia.html

- **Asia-Pacific Links**
  http://asnic.utexas.edu/asnic/pages/AsiaPac.html

- **East Asia Links**
  http://asnic.utexas.edu/asnic/pages/EAsia.html
  This site is particularly useful for links to sources for English language news.

- **Countries of Asia**
  http://asnic.utexas.edu/asnic/pages/countries.html
  Covers the following countries individually: Bangladesh, China, India, Indonesia, Japan, Laos, Malaysia, Mongolia, Myanmar (Burma), Nepal, Pakistan, Philippines, Singapore, South Korea, Sri Lanka, Taiwan, Thailand, Tibet, and Vietnam.

- **South Asia Links**
  http://asnic.utexas.edu/asnic/pages/SAsia.html

- **Southeast Asia Links**
  http://asnic.utexas.edu/asnic/pages/SEAsia.html

Here are other directory sites of note for this region:

- **123India.com**
  http://www.123india.com

- **Asian Connection**
  http://www.asianconnect.com/home.shtml

- **Asian Studies WWW Virtual Library**
  http://coombs.anu.edu.au/WWWVL-AsianStudies.html

- **AsiaProfile.com**
  http://www.asiaprofile.com
  Offers a "directory of directories" for China, Hong Kong, India, Indonesia, Japan, Korea, Malaysia, Pakistan, Philippines, Singapore, Sri Lanka, Taiwan, Thailand, and Vietnam.

- **East & Southeast Asia—An Annotated Directory of Internet Resources**
  http://newton.uor.edu/Departments&Programs/
  AsianStudiesDept/index.html
  From the University of Redlands in Redlands, CA, this directory's sites are sorted by country.

- **EuroSeek Asia**
  http://webdir.euroseek.com/?ilang=en&catid=262
  This site sorts by country and by topic. Unfortunately, some Middle Eastern and Eastern European countries are also thrown in, which can cause some confusion.

- **EuroSeek Oceania**
  http://webdir.euroseek.com/?ilang=en&catid=269
  This EuroSeek site is similar to the previous one, except that it covers the Pacific/Oceania countries.

- **The Nanyang Technological University Library WWW Sites and Information Gateways in Asia**
  http://www.ntu.edu.sg/library/asia/www.htm

- **SearchDragon**
  http://www.searchdragon.com
  SearchDragon covers Hong Kong, Indonesia, Macau, Malaysia, Philippines, Singapore, Taiwan, and Thailand. Choosing any of the subject categories such as Banking and Finance, Business Centres, Government, Telecommunications, Trade Information, returns a linked list of Web sites, with a short description of each.

• **Sri Lanka Explorer Search Engine**
http://www.infolanka.com/org/srilanka/business.html
This URL links directly to the Business and Finance directory
section.

Search Engines

Locate India [http://locateindia.com] refers to itself as "The best
search engine for information on Indian subjects." I was skeptical at
first, as it looked very much like all of the company directory sites (see
Figure 9.1). But if you keep following links for a search, the results you
receive are much like what you'd receive from a search engine. They are
links to other sites, rather than to company descriptions. Personally, due
to the relatively small number of "hits," I feel the site is more of a hybrid
"search engine/directory," in that it appears to be searching an internal
database, rather than a large portion of the Web.

For example, starting with Business & Economy and then
Business Information, fifty-seven Web sites relating to business
information in India appeared, along with brief site descriptions.

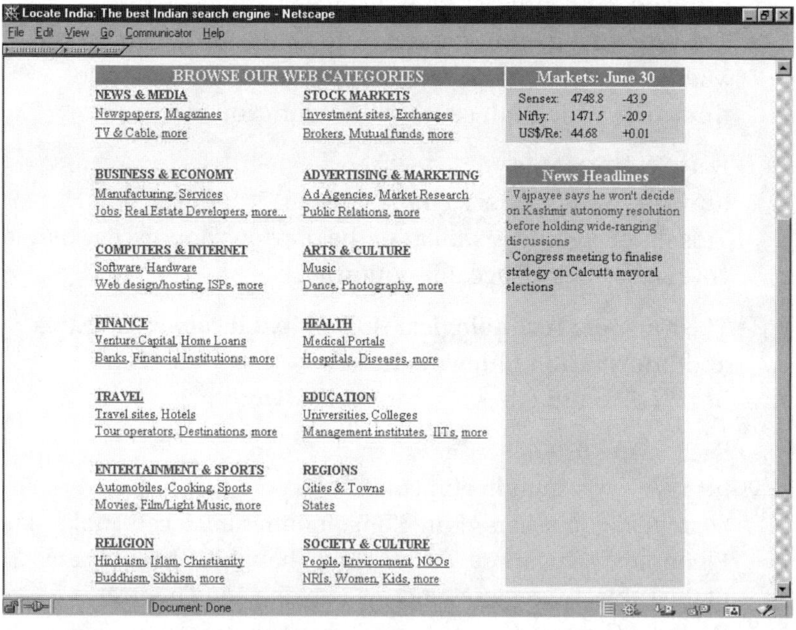

Figure 9.1   Locate India's Categories

Sites included the Centre for Monitoring Indian Economy, Economic Times: Guide to Doing Business in India, Indian Investment Centre, and Reuters India.

Here are some other specialized search engines for this region:

- **AAA Matilda**
  http://www.aaa.com.au
  There are actually two search engines at this site: Boomerang, covering just Australia, and Matilda, which provides international coverage.

- **Access New Zealand**
  http://accessnz.co.nz
  You can limit your search to the .nz (New Zealand) domain.

- **Cari Malaysia Search**
  http://www.cari.com.my

- **NZExplorer**
  http://nzexplorer.co.nz
  Here is another search engine that limits to the .nz (New Zealand) domain.

- **PNG Net Search**
  http://www.pngnetsearch.com
  This site is the search engine for Papua New Guinea.

- **Sofcom Internet Directory**
  http://www2.sofcom.com.au/Directories
  Searches in this directory cover over 40,000 pre-determined Australian sites.

News Resources

The Asia Society is a nonprofit educational organization focused on building awareness of more than thirty Asian/Pacific countries. Its Web site, AsiaSource [http://www.asiasource.org], has vastly improved and expanded its content recently. In the left column, click on Asia Today for links to the day's top news stories from a wide variety of publications and sources (BBC, *Christian Science Monitor*, *Financial Times*, Reuters, *Business Times*, CNN, etc.). The stories are arranged by category and geography:

- Arts & Culture
- AustralAsia

- Business & Economics
- Central Asia
- Commentary
- East Asia
- Magazine Articles
- Social Issues
- South Asia
- Southeast Asia
- Technology
- Top News Stories

For further news, the left side of the page lists Asia News Links and includes wire services, weekly publications, newspapers, networks, and more (see Figure 9.2).

Back on the main page, choose Policy & Government from the top of the page. Scroll a bit more than halfway down the page and on the right you will see a box called Resources. Choosing Government Directory, you will find biographical and contact information for the

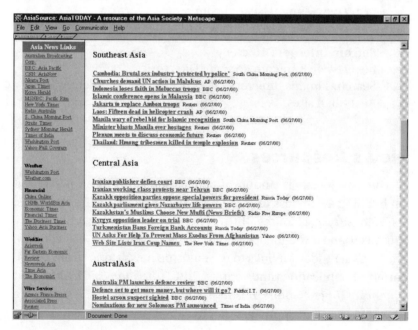

Figure 9.2   AsiaSource News

leaders of more than forty countries, as well as an extensive listing of other high-ranking government officials.

Asia Links brings you to a page that looks like a directory site; the categories Business Sectors and Business & Economics are the two most useful.

An interesting topic often overlooked, but very important in this multicultural region, is Business Protocol. AsiaSource has primers for the following countries:

• China	• Malaysia
• Hong Kong	• Philippines
• India	• Singapore
• Indonesia	• Taiwan
• Japan	• Thailand
• Korea	• Vietnam

Subjects covered include Meeting and Greeting, Names and Titles, Business Cards, Body Language, Clothing (business and casual dress are discussed), and Gifts. One should know about all these subjects when conducting business in this region. I will admit, though, it can become quite confusing. For example, in India, one greets Hindus with "namaste" (na-mass-TAY); except in the South, where Hindus are greeted by saying "namaskaram" (nah-mahss-CAR-am). However, to greet Muslims, one says "salam alaikum"(sah-LAAM a-LEH-come) and Sikhs with "sat sri akal" (sut shree ah-kaal). It's even more confusing when you add in the different gestures. But how can you get to know someone's religious convictions before you've even introduced yourself? Well, you could guess, but that's not a particularly effective method. Do a little research before you meet the person. Are they located in a part of their country that is predominantly one religion? Does one religion dominate business and industry in the country? Are there any visual clues (clothing, religious artifacts) that you might notice when entering someone's home or office? Of course, in the end, there aren't any foolproof methods to ascertain someone's religion prior to meeting them. Perhaps you could find someone who knows.

Before leaving AsiaSource, check the offerings in Links, Experts, Profiles, Dictionary Tool, and Language Resources.

AccessAsia [http://www.accessasia.com] has some sections only accessible by subscription ($95/year). However, without subscribing, you can still use the site to reach a nice list of links to English-language newspapers and magazines (see Figure 9.3).

Figure 9.3   AccessAsia's News Links

Other news sources you'll want to investigate:

• **Asia Pacific Management Forum**
http://www.apmforum.com
Scroll to the middle of the page and follow the Asia Business News link.

• **The China Business Review**
http://www.chinabusinessreview.com/back.html
This is the official magazine of the U.S.-China Business Council. Its goal is to help U.S. companies conduct business successfully in China. While you must have a subscription to read the current issue, selected articles from the archives are available online for free.

• **NikkeiNet Interactive**
http://www.nni.nikkei.co.jp
Great coverage of Japanese business news is provided here. Unfortunately, only a small portion of the site is available without a subscription.

- **Taiwan Headlines**
  http://www.taiwanheadlines.gov.tw
  Updated daily Monday through Friday, the site is searchable and has archives and a separate category for business news. Free daily summaries are available for transmission via e-mail.

Yellow Pages

Let's check out the Singapore Yellow Pages [http://www.yellowpages.com.sg/cgi-bin/syphome/syphome.pl]. The ads on the main page are a bit overwhelming (oh, the price we pay for free information), so look toward the left portion of the page for the Yellow Pages information. Here you can search by company name, classification (sector), product or service, or brand name. If you have some contact information for a company but need more, you can also search by e-mail address, building name, phone or fax number, or street.

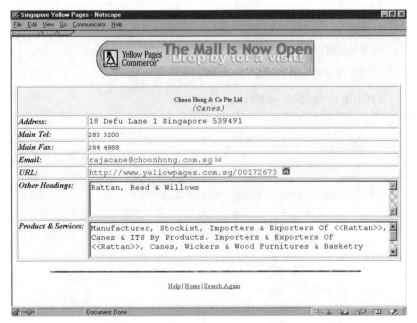

Figure 9.4   Sample Entry from Singapore Yellow Pages

I know that parts of Asia are known for making rattan furniture, so let's look to see if we can find any rattan manufacturers in Singapore. Searching on the word "rattan" under the Products/Services listings, we get three records. Looking at the record for the first entry, we see that Choon Hong & Co. Pte. Ltd. manufactures, imports, and exports rattan canes and furniture. Address, telephone and fax numbers, and e-mail addresses appear in the listing. The little house on the right lets us know that we can link to the company's Web site directly from here (see Figure 9.4).

There are several other Asian Yellow Pages directories on the Internet; some are obviously better than others. The following list should get you started:

- **Australia Yellow Pages Online**
  http://www.yellowpages.com.au

- **Bangladesh Yellow Pages Online**
  http://www.tripleyes.com/bypo/iphone.html

- **China**
  http://www.chinatone.com/category/yellowpage/frame_e.html

- **ChinaBIG Yellow Pages**
  http://www.chinabig.com/en/srch

- **Hong Kong Yellow Pages**
  http://www.yp.com.hk/eng/index.html

- **India Yellow Pages**
  http://www.indiayellowpages.com

- **Indonesian Yellow Pages on the Internet**
  http://www.yellowpages.co.id

- **Korea Yellow Pages**
  http://www.ypkorea.com

- **Macau Yellow Pages**
  http://www.yellowpages.com.mo/eng

- **Malaysia Yellow Pages**
  http://www.malaysiayellowpages.com

- **New Zealand Yellow Pages**
  http://www.yellowpages.co.nz

- **Yellow Pages of Pakistan**
  http://www.jamal.com

- **Vietnam Internet Yellow Pages**
  http://www.vietnamonline.com/vnypg

Banking, Finance, and Stock Exchanges

ASIC, the Australian Securities and Investments Commission [http://www.asic.gov.au] is similar to the Securities and Exchange Commission (SEC) in the U.S. For the life of me, I couldn't figure out the Searching and Lodging category; I couldn't understand what looking for hotels would have to do with Australian securities. Then, I noticed the phrase "our FREE Company Alert service to find out which documents are being lodged by companies you're monitoring." "Lodging" is the Australian equivalent of "filing."

ASIC has several databases that you may search for free:

- National Names Index—Here you'll find an index of Australian corporate and registered business names. Listings contain the company's registration number, current status, a complete list of documents filed by the company since January 1991, and more.

- OFFERlist—This section provides a database of all disclosure documents for fundraising offers filed with ASIC.

- Professional Registers—This area lists the people or organizations which ASIC registers or licenses and includes investment advisers, registered liquidators, securities dealers, official liquidators, futures advisers, general insurance brokers, futures brokers, life insurance brokers, registered auditors, and foreign insurance brokers.

- Banned and Disqualified Registers—Here it lists people disqualified from involvement in the management of a corporation or banned from practicing as investment advisers in the securities or futures industries.

- Identical Names Check—This functions as a facility for those intending to register a new company name. It allows one to check whether the proposed company name matches any already registered on the ASIC database.

Irasia.com [http://www.irasia.com], established in 1996, provides investor relations information on Asian listed companies. Over 2,000 companies are profiled by Irasia.com from the following countries:

- Australia
- Hong Kong
- Indonesia
- Korea
- Malaysia
- Philippines
- Singapore
- Thailand

More countries are being added. The Listed Companies link allows you to search for companies on the various stock exchanges in Asia. You can search by stock code, company name, country of listing, or industry sector. Company entries generally include a profile (as short as one sentence or as long as a full page), the annual reports from the previous year or two, interim reports, and extremely detailed contact information that may include the Board of Directors, Principal Bankers, Auditors and Accountants, Legal Advisors, and more.

The Nanyang Technological University Library Financial Data and Resource Locators—Singapore [http://www.ntu.edu.sg/library/biz/finsg.htm#topmenu] is a directory covering three financial topics: Stock Market and Financial Reports, Banks and Financial Institutions, and Unit Trusts and Fund Management.

Other useful sites in the financial arena are listed here:

- **Arab—Malaysian Banking Group**
  http://ambg.com.my/html/finance_info_fr.html

- **Bangkok Bank**
  http://www.bbl.co.th

- **Bank of Japan**
  http://www.boj.or.jp/en/index2.htm

- **Bank of Thailand**
  http://www.bot.or.th/govnr/public/BOT_Homepage/EnglishVersion/index_e.htm

- **Central Bank of Malaysia**
  http://www.bnm.gov.my

- **Central Bank of Sri Lanka**
  http://www.oub.com.sg/financial_review/index.html

- **Export—Import Bank of Korea**
  http://www.koreaexim.go.kr/english/engindex.html

- **National Bank of New Zealand**
  http://www.nationalbank.co.nz

- **Office of the Securities and Exchange Commission—
  Thailand**
  http://secwww.sec.or.th/indexe.html

- **Overseas Union Bank—Singapore**
  http://www.oub.com/sg/am/myoub/pages/welcome.jsp

- **Reserve Bank of India**
  http://www.rbi.org.in

- **Reserve Bank of New Zealand**
  http://www.rbnz.govt.nz

- **Siam Commercial Bank**
  http://www.scb.co.th

These Asia/Pacific Stock Exchanges have Internet sites:

- **Australia—Australian Stock Exchange**
  http://www.asx.com.au

- **China—Shanghai Stock Exchange (not the actual exchange)**
  http://www.comnex.com/stocks/stocks.htm

- **Hong Kong—Hong Kong Stock Exchange**
  http://www.sehk.com.hk

- **India—National Stock Exchange of India**
  http://www.nse-india.com

- **India—Stock Exchange of Mumbai**
  http://www.bseindia.com

- **Indonesia Stock Closings**
  http://www.indoexchange.com

- **Indonesia—Surabaya Stock Exchange**
  http://www.bes.co.id

- **Indonesia—Jakarta Stock Exchange**
  http://www.jsx.co.id

- **Japan—Tokyo Stock Exchange**
  http://www.tse.or.jp/eindex.html

- **Korea Stock Exchange**
  http://www.kse.or.kr/e_index.html

- **Malaysia Stock Exchange (not the actual exchange)**
  http://biz.thestar.com.my/business/bizwatch.asp

- **New Zealand Stock Exchange**
  http://www.nzse.co.nz

- **Pakistan—Karachi Stock Exchange**
  http://www.kse.com.pk

- **Singapore—Stock Exchange of Singapore**
  http://www.ses.com.sg

- **Sri Lanka—Colombo Stock Exchange**
  http://www.lanka.net/stocks

- **Taiwan Stock Exchange**
  http://www.tse.com.tw/docs1/index.html

- **Thailand—Stock Exchange of Thailand**
  http://www.set.or.th

- **Turkey—Istanbul Stock Exchange**
  http://www.ise.org

Chambers of Commerce and Industry

As usual, some Chamber sites in the region are filled with useful data, some provide direction to print resources, and some merely provide you with contact information, which isn't necessarily a bad thing, either. Here are some of the American Chambers of Commerce for this region along with the highlights of what you will find at the sites:

American Chambers of Commerce (AmChams)

- **American Chamber of Commerce in Australia**
  http://www.amcham.com.au
  Descriptions and a means for ordering two print publications: USA/Australia Trade Directory and More Business Down Under; check both the About Australia and the Resources sections for links.

- **American Chamber of Commerce in Bangladesh**
  http://www.amchambd.org
  Not too much information is presented here, but it does have contact information and information about its annual Trade Show.

- **Guam Chamber of Commerce**
  http://www.guamchamber.com.gu
  This searchable site offers publications for sale and has a Business Relocation section.

- **American Chamber of Commerce in Hong Kong**
  http://www.amcham.org.hk
  An article archive, economic indicators, business outlook survey, trade and investment resources, and useful links can be found here.

- **American Chamber of Commerce in Indonesia**
  http://www.amcham.or.id
  Offers publications for sale.

- **American Chamber of Commerce in Japan**
  http://www.accj.or.jp/default.asp
  Users must register at the site to use most of the functions (free). There is a cursory search function for news articles.

- **The American Chamber of Commerce in Korea**
  http://www.amchamkorea.org
  A list of Marketing Insight Reports is available from the U.S. Embassy. Selected articles from the AMCHAM Journal, publications for purchase, information on trade policy changes, new laws, and business-related press releases are also provided.

- **American Malaysian Chamber of Commerce**
  http://www.jaring.my/amcham
  Offers publications for purchase.

- **American Chamber of Commerce—People's Republic of China**
  http://www.amcham-china.org.cn
  Position papers and a white paper on American business in China are presented along with useful links.

- **American Chamber of Commerce in Guangdong, PRC**
  http://www.amcham-guangdong.org

- **The American Chamber of Commerce of the Philippines**
  http://www.amchamphil.com.ph
  This site contains a directory of member companies with contact information and offers publications for sale.

- **American Chamber of Commerce in Singapore**
  http://www.amcham.org.sg
  Provides useful links and offers publications for purchase.

- **American Chamber of Commerce in Sri Lanka**
  http://www.amchamsl.org

- **American Chamber of Commerce in Taipei**
  http://www.amcham.com.tw
  R.O.C. government updates, excerpts from Guide for Doing Business in Taiwan, Taiwan at a Glance (annual white paper) are available here, along with a company search function.

- **American Chamber of Commerce in Vietnam**
  http://www.amchamvn.com
  Information includes Doing Business in Vietnam, general export and import issues, overviews of several industries.

Other Chambers (not AmChams)

- **U.S.-India Business Council**
  http://www.usibc.com
  News, useful links are presented here.

Business Directories

As in all the other regions, there is a plethora of company directory sites on Asia and the Pacific. Try these when looking for a particular company and haven't found it anywhere or if you're looking for a manufacturer, importer, exporter, or supplier of a specific good or service.

- **Asiaco**

  http://search.asiaco.com

  Asiaco covers most Asian countries, each country has its own section; a bit cumbersome to get through and a lot of non-business information, but if you follow the right links (which should be evident) you will eventually find companies in different sectors.

- **Asia-Pacific.com Data Links**

  http://www.asia-pacific.com/links.htm

  Contains links to numerous Asia/Pacific business information sites.

- **Beijing Business Directory**

  http://chinavista.com/beijing/business/directory.html

- **EDSA—The Philippine Search Engine**

  http://www.edsa.com.ph

  Although called a search engine, it is most useful for finding companies and connecting to their Web sites.

- **Government Information Office—Republic of China**

  http://th.gio.gov.tw/search

  Follow the Economy link and choose from about twenty different industry sectors. The company names take you directly to the company's Web site.

- **Guanghou Business Directory**

  http://chinavista.com/guanghou/business/directory.html

- **MeetChina.com**

  http://www.meetchina.com

- **MOFTEC—Ministry of Foreign Trade and Economic Cooperation—PRC**

  http://www.moftec.gov.cn

  Use the China Companies link to reach the directory, which offers numerous categories and subcategories.

- **Shanghai Business Directory**

  http://chinavista.com/shanghai/business/directory.html

- **WebSite URLs of Japanese Companies**

  http://www.toyokeizai.co.jp/english/e_link/index.html

  As the name implies, this is an alphabetical listing of over 800 Web sites of Japanese companies, all in English.

- **World Trade Data Base (WTDB)**

  http://www.wtdb.com

  Use the Companies On Line section to locate companies in China in several categories. No need to search, as the companies are listed and are linked to either their own Web site or an expanded directory-type listing (see Figure 9.5).

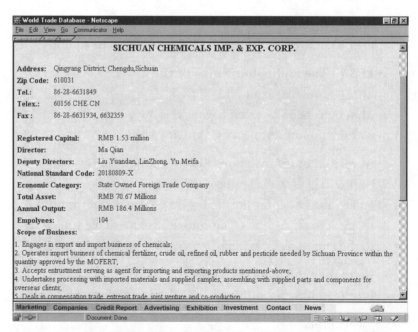

Figure 9.5 Partial Company Listing from World Trade Data Base

Regional Resources

Skali.com [http://www.skali.com] is a great portal for just about anything pertaining to Asia, including business information. Out of its ten channels, the following should be most useful to the business searcher:

- Today—Links to current articles in the areas of World News, Economy, Markets, Information Technology, Joint Ventures, Asian Business, Aviation, Banking, Energy, Infrastructure, Telecommunications, and Automotive. While some of the articles are brief, they are in full text and display the date and source.

- Technology—Links to articles covering various aspects of technology including Technews, Science, Legal, Space, Telecommunications, and Internet.

- Business—Categories of articles include Markets, Transportation, Automotive, Environment, Tenders/Projects, Economy/Politics, Education, and Retail. Note that even though this channel and the Today channel have some of the same categories, different articles appear in each, as the articles are geared to the topic of the channel.

In the center of the main page there is an area called Quick Guide. Selecting Today, Business, or Technology allows you to focus the articles on a particular country. The main page also has links for Malaysian and Chinese Web sites.

The site also has industry profiles; however, they are very well hidden. Every time you follow a link from the main page, check to see if the right hand column has the category Related Content. This is where the profiles are kept (some are actually company profiles). Most of the reports are prepared by Asia Pulse analysts. When I last visited, there were close to thirty profiles, none of them over three months old. These sample titles were among them:

- Australia's Housing Industry

- China's Petroleum Industry

- Indonesia's Motorcycle Industry

- Japan's Electric Power Industry

- Japan's Retail Industry

- Philippine's Tourism Industry

I'm certain that if you continued to poke around the Skali.com site, you would find even more valuable information tucked away somewhere. And yes, the site is searchable.

Asia BIG [http://www.asiabig.com] is produced jointly by InfoAd Publishing Consultants and Sing Tel Yellow Pages, both of Singapore, and covers Hong Kong, Jakarta, Klang Valley (Malaysia), Philippines, Singapore, and Taiwan. BIG refers to the Business and Industrial Guides produced for each of these countries. Unfortunately, on my last visit to the site, I could no longer find the Business and Industrial Guides, somewhat invalidating the site's name. Now the only useful feature of the site is the ability to search for companies by either name or products/services. The information returned is the usual cursory contact information. I'd hope that this site is a "work in progress" and the great information there previously will return.

Singapore

An interesting site with a variety of business (and nonbusiness) information is AsiaOne [http://www.asiaone.com]. Launched in June 1995 by Singapore Press Holdings, the site contains a mix of Singapore-specific and general Asian information. In January 2000, AsiaOne announced plans to develop the most comprehensive portals in Asia for e-commerce, news, and information in both English and Chinese. The main page has headlines to current news articles that link not just to the text of the article, but to the entire current issue of the publication. If you don't have time to do in-depth reading and just need a quick overview of the day's news, try Quick Read, a summary of the day's top stories. Unfortunately, the site has undergone a redesign and Quick Read is no longer easy to find. To do so, on the main page, scroll down to AsiaOne Sites (left column). From there, click on New Paper and you will go to a page called The Electronic New Paper. Right at the top, you will see the link for Quick Read.

Interested in the Information Technology (IT) sector in Asia? Follow the IT link for IT news, product, and corporate announcements (Just In).

On the main AsiaOne page, choose Site Map (see Figure 9.6). The News column provides links to many publications specializing in Asian news. Business & Finance is probably the most useful for our

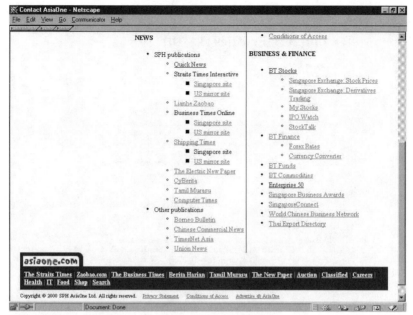

Figure 9.6 Portion of AsiaOne Site Map

purposes. Here you will find stock market information for Singapore, as well as for other markets in the region including Kuala Lumpur, Bangkok, Jakarta, Manila, Sydney, Wellington, Hong Kong, China, Taipei, Seoul, and Tokyo. IPO Watch contains articles on upcoming and recently listed IPOs and other IPO news.

The Enterprise 50 link takes you to a section with an annual list of the fifty most enterprising, privately held companies in Singapore. This list, started in 1995, is compiled jointly by Andersen Consulting, *Business Times*, and the Economic Development Board of Singapore. The most recent list I found was dated 1998 and included links to articles about some of the companies as well as short profiles of each company. Rankings and profiles are included for 1997, 1996, and 1995 winners too (see Figure 9.7).

The Singapore Business Awards include the Businessman of the Year (1985-1998), Outstanding Chief Executive (1990-1997), and the Enterprise Award presented to small or medium-sized companies (1986-1997). (Note: This is not the same as the previously mentioned Enterprise 50.) This is a great place to find background information on influential business people in Singapore.

Singapore Connect can help locate companies by name, sector, or product through its basic directory information. You can also find

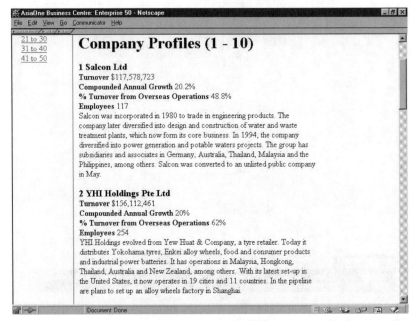

Figure 9.7   Enterprise 50 Company Profiles

companies specifically looking for partners as well as companies belonging to particular trade associations.

The Thailand Export Directory is produced by Business Day, a Thai international business daily. You can search by product or supplier (company) name and receive a range of information. For some companies, only contact details appear; for others, a Show Room with pictures and specifications of products, a Company Profile, and a link to the company's home page.

I warn you that the AsiaOne site has ads sprinkled all over the pages. However, none of them are pop-up ads, so after awhile, one learns to ignore them.

Those interested in Singapore should also look at Singapore Inc. [http://www.singapore-inc.com/home.html]. In the Business Info section, you will find the requisite Doing Business In … guide, a rather thorough one that hits most of the points.

In the Import and Export Information section, you will find explanations of the documentation needed, how to file it, etc. Basically this is the "nuts and bolts" of the operation. You will also find links to several banks and the government Web site.

One such link leads to Statistics Singapore [http://www. singstat.gov.sg], the government statistical agency. One never knows what one might find here. On my last visit, the Do You Know section contained the following tidbits of information and more:

- Baby boomers make up almost one-third of Singapore's population.

- There is an increasing demand for health food in Singapore. In 1987, there were only eleven health food retailers with sales of $2.1 million; ten years later, there were 155 health food retailers and sales of $68.8 million.

- On the average, the Singaporean household earned lower income in 1999 than in 1998; average household income declined by 2.7 percent.

Now, these might seem like interesting bits of trivia, but they each could have far-reaching implications on a company planning to do business in Singapore.

Taiwan

As I thought about writing the Asia/Pacific chapter for this book, I knew that there would be a great deal of interest in business information about the Republic of China (Taiwan). I spent a lot of time Web-site hopping, but initially found nothing useful. Some sites only carried Chinese language information. Others seemed to be composed entirely of dead links—sites virtually content-free. Even the site for the Information Division of the Taipei Economic and Cultural Office [http://www.roc-taiwan.org] proved disappointing. Some topics on the main page looked promising, but most had dead links. Don't cross this one off of the list yet, however, as it still may develop into a useful site.

Finally, I hit pay dirt and discovered CETRA, the China External Trade Development Council [http://mart.cetra.org.tw/home/default.asp]. CETRA, a nonprofit trade promotion organization, was founded in 1970 as a joint effort between the government and industrial and commercial associations. It has more than forty branch offices worldwide, including four in the U.S. (New York, Chicago, Miami, and San Francisco). Start exploring the site by choosing Trade Kit from the top of the page; this section has more to offer than one would expect from a free site. The Trade with Taiwan section (found by following the Doing Business with Taiwan link) presents an overall picture of trading with Taiwan with topics such as major imports, exports, trading partners, and basic trade information. What to Sell and Buy is a must-read section. The Taiwan Industry Reports provide specifics on the following industries (see Figure 9.8):

- Auto Parts
- Bicycles
- Consumer Electronics
- Giftware and Housewares
- Hardware
- Sporting Goods
- Stationery
- Timepieces
- Toys

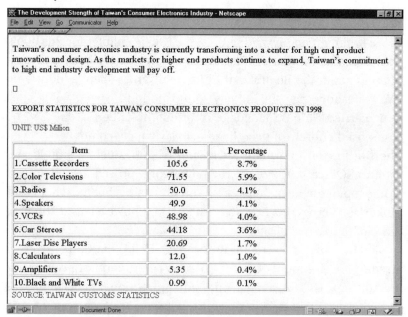

Figure 9.8   Excerpt from CETRA Industry Reports

The rest of the Trade Kit includes hints and tips for those working in Taiwan. Areas covered include business cards, visas, transportation, language, currency, accommodations, electric supply, business hours, etc.

A great portion of the site is taken up by the Taiwan Products Magazine, though a recent redesign has made finding it a little tricky. Choose the Site Map tab at the top of the main page, look at About CETRA on the left, and you will see a link to Taiwan Products Magazine. Nine broad industry categories (plus a miscellaneous category) are covered:

- Auto Parts and Motorcycles
- Computers and Peripherals
- Electronics and Communications
- Giftware, Stationery, and Housewares
- Hardware and Furniture
- Machinery
- Medical Equipment
- Sporting Goods and Bicycles
- Textiles and Textile Machinery

Each industry category is broken into segments with lengthy overviews for each category. Descriptions of some of the leading companies, interviews with industry experts, and trade show reports are also included. As examples of the information in this section, I quickly learned the following:

- Taiwan is the world's third largest supplier of information technology products; only the U.S. and Japan supply more.
- The U.S. is the largest importer of medical equipment from Taiwan.
- Taiwan ranks third in the world's production of man-made fibers, behind the U.S. and mainland China.

For those needing more detailed information on the computer, electronics, hardware, bicycle, gift and stationery, sporting goods, or machinery industries, the main page of the site offers the Showcases section. These Showcases contain more in-depth industry information and can be searched for companies within a specific industry.

If you're looking for a product or a company, you can search the site by product, company name, brand, and category, though the site does not support Boolean searching. The FAQ section will explain both the most efficient way to search the site and how to interpret the search results.

If all else fails and you have still not satisfied your information needs, CETRA can provide customized market research services, including local market surveys, trade and marketing strategy consulting, seminars, and more. With four offices in the U.S., contact them and discuss your requirements.

Japan

When I first started my own business, the second project that came my way involved identifying various consulting firms in Japan and the sectors (agriculture, environment, etc.) with which the firms were involved. I fumbled around a bit on the Internet and made a few phone calls. Along the way, someone suggested that I contact JETRO. I had never heard of JETRO and didn't have a clue as to what it was.

Too afraid of showing ignorance, I thanked the person for the suggestion and quickly started searching for JETRO on the Internet. I soon found out that JETRO was the Japan External Trade Organization [http://www.jetro.go.jp/top/index.html] and a literal gold mine of information. Unfortunately, at that time, I don't believe they had a Web site yet, so I had to do my research using the good old-fashioned telephone. Today, thankfully, JETRO has a wonderful Web site that can answer an array of questions. Frankly, this site has so much information, it's difficult to know where to begin.

Focus Japan is one of JETRO's print publications. It publishes ten times a year with selected articles from each issue available online going back to May 1998. (The cost for a print subscription is $40/year.) Here are a few examples of articles at the site:

- JETRO Report—Asian Economies—Investing in ASEAN and South Korea

- Market Trend—Berries—Blueberries and Cranberries are Drawing Attention

- Regulation—Labor Market Flexibility—Restrictions Lifted for Temporary Staffing

- Trade Statistics—Japan's Surplus on a Clear Downtrend

The Japanese Market Report Series consists of almost fifty extensive market studies. The one I reviewed, Jam and Canned Fruit, ran about twenty-five pages. All of the reports are relatively current; none more than three years old. The range of industries is very broad and includes nonprescription drugs, jewelry, franchise business, electric commerce, automotive parts aftermarket, medical equipment, and personal computer software. In the Research section, you can find a searchable Market Report Database that contains more than 350 Market Reports. As well as searching, you can browse the reports by product category. The reports are quite lengthy and contain an amazing amount of information. They definitely rival the reports for which we pay top dollar from the well known market research firms, yet these reports are free. The only downside is that some of the reports are a bit dated, but certainly look here.

Japan has twenty-one Foreign Access Zones (FAZs) and the JETRO site provides very complete details on all of them. It explains the applicable laws and outlines each of the twenty-one FAZs. Topics covered are as follows:

- Characteristics of Airport/Port

- Foreign Trade at FAZ Area

- Outline of FAZ Facilities

- Projects Around FAZ Area

- Transportation Access to FAZ Area

Several databases appear on the site:

- Cyber Showcase—Here is a way for Japanese importers to connect with foreign exporters. The two segments covered are Building Materials and Home Care and Rehabilitation.

- Database of Research-Based Industries in Japan—Searchable by company or region, this database also includes a related links section.

- Japan Trade Directory 2000-2001—A searchable directory covers almost 24,000 products and 2,250 companies seeking international business opportunities.

- Japanese Government Procurement—An explanation of government procurement procedures and a searchable database of government projects can be found here.

- Potential Importers—This searchable database is designed to be used by foreign exporters. Criteria can be very specific, including location, activity, annual sales, capital, and more.

- Technology Tie-Up Promotion Program (TTPP)—Foreign companies looking for high-tech business partners in Japan for joint ventures, product licensing, OEM production, joint R&D, and technology import and export should look here.

The section Trade Entering Japan has some interesting documents. The Survey on Actual Conditions Regarding Access to Japan is actually a series of reports covering housing, medical equipment, chemical products, cosmetics, processed foods, construction materials, pharmaceuticals, and telecommunications equipment industries. Depending upon the industry, some or all of the following points are discussed:

- Cost comparisons with other countries

- Distribution and business practices

- Official regulations for the industry

- Product categories surveyed

- Reasons for the industry's inclusion in the study

This section also carries reports from the Japan Automobile Importers Association. These reports, Number of Newly Registered Imported Cars, publish monthly and go back to January 1998 online.

The Publications and Video section contains items available for purchase, as well as those you may download for free. Free publications include Doing Business in Japan, Industrial Property Rights in Japan, Changing Face of Japanese Retail, and more (see Figure 9.9).

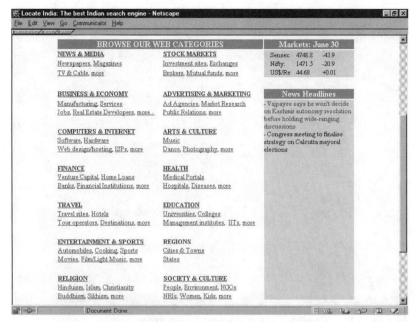

Figure 9.9   Free Publications Available from JETRO

One last word about the JETRO site. It can be extremely fickle. There were days that I used the site without a problem. Pages would load like a dream over my 56K modem. Other times, the pages were so slow to load that I'd leave to go make coffee and when I came back, the page still hadn't finished loading. When that happened, I'd leave the site, wait a few hours, and then try again. Generally, when I returned to the site, things would run smoothly. So, rather than screaming at the computer when the site is slow, take a deep breath, do something else for a while, and try it again later.

The Japan Information Network (JIN) [http://www.jinjapan.org] can help the business searcher in two ways. First, it can provide up-to-date statistics about every aspect of Japan imaginable. The Industry section has six broad categories of statistics with the type of data gathered very similar to that in the U.S. Census of Manufacturers.

The second area of interest is the contact information provided. Here you will find links to and directory information about government offices and agencies, business organizations, labor unions, consumer groups, newspapers, and more. If you haven't yet found the information you seek on the Internet, you will probably find new directions to follow here (see Figure 9.10).

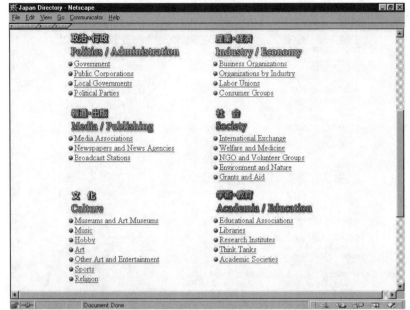

Figure 9.10   Contact Information Links from the Japan Information Network

Australia

Austrade, the Australian Government's international trade and investment agency, has a useful site for Australian business information, Austrade Online [http://www.austrade.gov.au/International]. The various sections of the site list in a column on the left. The first section, Australia on Display, allows you to search for companies, products, or services in twenty-two categories:

- Agriculture, Forestry & Fishing

- Construction

- Cultural & Recreational Services

- Defense

- Education

- Finance & Insurance

- Food & Beverage

- Footwear & Leather

- Health & Community Services

- IT (information technology)

- Manufacturing

- Marine

- Mining & Energy

- Multimedia

- Printing, Publishing & Recorded Media

- Property & Business Services

- Retail Trade

- Telecommunications

- Textiles & Clothing

- Tourism

- Transport & Storage

- Water & Environment

Each category in turn has multiple subcategories to help focus the search. There are three sections to the company listings: Products and Services, Company Message, and Contact Details.

Next in line is the Capability Showcase that profiles several Australian industries. Topics covered vary by industry but usually include an overview; leading manufacturers and market share; the products, services, and capabilities of the industry; key contacts; and industry links.

Investing in Australia answers the question, "Why do businesses choose to invest in Australia?" and outlines the government incentives for doing so. Discussion of Australia's tax reform and its implications for exporters and importers appears in the section Importing from Australia. Links connect you to various government offices for further information.

For questions not answered at the Austrade Online site, you can contact Austrade offices all over the world—six in the U.S. alone: Atlanta, Detroit, Los Angeles, New York, San Francisco, and Washington, DC.

The Australian government appears to be on the ball when it comes to providing information and organizing it in a way that makes it easy to find. The Australian Commonwealth Government Entry Point has a page at its site [http://fed.gov.au/sitelists/web_port.htm] where various government offices list by portfolio (subject area). You can either click on a subject to link directly to the specific government agency or you can use the Complete List of Portfolio Sites to find all agencies that might assist you.

The site for Australian Business [http://www.australianbusiness. com.au] has a couple of useful sections. The company has relationships with industry associations in the following areas:

- Building and Construction
- Chemicals, Flavors, and Fragrances
- Food and Beverage
- Glass
- Intellectual Property
- Wheat

Associations for those industries list at the site, along with links directly to the associations. In addition, Australian Business has a good set of useful business links.

BRW [http://www.brw.com.au] is an Australian weekly business magazine that annually publishes several very useful lists regarding Australian companies:

- The BRW Rich 200—the 200 wealthiest families and individuals in Australia
- The BRW Top 500 Public Companies
- The BRW 100 Fastest Growing Private Companies
- The 2000 Power Pack—the fifty most powerful people in Australian business
- The 1999 BRW Top 1000—a ranking, by revenue, of the largest listed, private, government, and foreign enterprises operating in Australia
- The BRW Top 500 Private Companies

On a bit of a less serious note, there is also a list of the Top 50 Entertainers.

New Zealand

Most people, outside of those in Australia and New Zealand, think that Australia and New Zealand are practically the same country—after all, two English-speaking countries so geographi-cally close to each other. Not true! The two countries are nearly 2,000 miles apart. And, when it comes to looking for business information on the Internet, Australia is a piece of cake compared to New Zealand. However, I have found a couple of New Zealand sources that can help.

The New Zealand Herald Online [http://www.nzherald.co.nz] is the online version of New Zealand's largest newspaper. Having separate sections for business news and technology news with full-text articles makes the online newspaper even more useful for the business searcher. The site updates every morning, Monday through Saturday, and has searchable archives extending back to December 1998.

The UBD E-Directory [http://www.ubd.co.nz] covers more than 140,000 New Zealand businesses. This directory allows you to search for businesses in New Zealand in numerous fashions. You can search by keyword, business name, suburb, town, business category, or prod-uct. You can also use the Industry Search to choose from twenty-four different industries or the Local Search, where you can choose the region of the country from a map (see Figure 9.11).

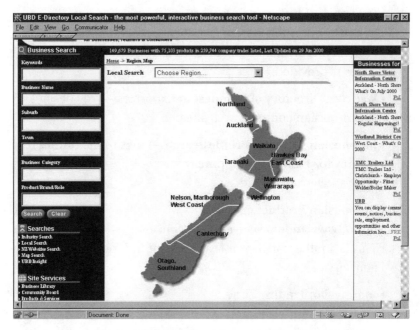

**Figure 9.11   Map of New Zealand from Regional Search—
UBD E-Directory**

In addition to contact information, directory listings also include products, brand names, trade categories, and SIC descriptions. UBD E-Directory also has a link to a subscription directory, UBD Insight, that provides more detailed company information including company directors, associated companies, number of employees, topline financials, major shareholders, and recent news articles.

The commercial law firm Russell McVeagh has developed a useful guide called Investment in New Zealand [http://www.rmmb. co.nz/investnz/Welcome.html]. This guide covers topics such as business structure, government policy on foreign investment, banking and finance, and employment issues.

Indonesia

The Industry and Trade Division of the Embassy of Indonesia in Canada has put together a wonderful online guide, Doing Business with Indonesia [http://www.prica.org/commerce/index2a.html]. While the site itself doesn't provide any value-added content, it carries a Buyer's Guide loaded with links, including the following:

- **Directory of Indonesian Exporters**—Search for companies by the harmonized system classification or company name; directory information provided. (A link for looking up the HS codes is provided.)

- **Web Site Directory of Indonesian Exporters**—Provides links to Indonesian company Web sites.

- **Indonesian Exporter Profile Search**—Links to the **National Agency for Export Development**
  http://www.nafed.go.id

- **Indonesian Product.com**
  http://www.Indonesian-Product.com
  This is another facility for searching for Indonesian goods and services.

- **Indonesian Trading Zone**
  http://www.indotradezone.com
  Trade data, economic statistics and trends, market research reports, and tax laws are provided.

- **APEC Tariff Database**
  http://www.apectariff.org/tdb.cgi/ff3237/apeccgi.cgi?ID
  Includes a tariff schedule available for downloading.

- **Indonesian Commodity Association**
  http://www.nafed.go.id/menu2/asosiasi.htm
  Extensive listing of industry associations also provides contact information.

- **IndoExchange**
  http://www.indoexchange.com
  You'll find market studies, economic trends, capital market data.

- **Indonesian Central Bureau of Statistics**
  http://www.bps.go.id
  This site provides economic statistics, census information, and regional statistical profiles.

Hong Kong

The Hong Kong Trade Development Council [http://www.tdctrade.com] has a site worth checking out. On the left side of the page you will see links to Business News and Stock Quotes/Exchange Rates. Scrolling a bit more than halfway down the page, you find a heading HK Economy, Trade and Business; this is where the going gets good. The Manufacturing link takes you to close to thirty industry profiles including these:

- Auto Parts & Accessories
- Building Materials & Hardware
- Furniture & Furnishings
- Jewelry
- Telecommunications Equipment

There are similar profiles for four major categories (and several subcategories) of service industries (see Figure 9.12):

- Communications & Media Services
- Financial Services
- Professional Services
- Trade-Related Services

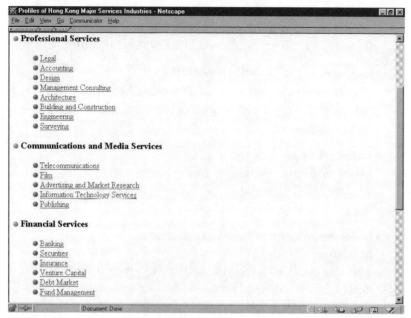

Figure 9.12   Partial Listing of Service Industries Profiled by the Hong Kong Trade & Development Council

Various trade statistics such as exports and imports by country and region are also available in the HK Economy, Trade and Business area.

Thailand

Business Gate [http://www.okeydonkey.com/donkey1] does have a strange URL and I must admit, I was a bit skeptical at first. But then, it turned out to have useful information on Thailand and was very easy to navigate. The Business Directory has many of the usual categories found in such directories: Agriculture, Jewelry, Metal & Supplies, and so on. Just follow the appropriate link and you will receive the name and linked URL to companies in that category. (Note: In some cases, the company name didn't appear. But, the URL still took you to the requested site.) Try two other sections of the site—Thai Government, which brings up an extensive, linked list of government offices, and News, which links to Thai news in English.

India

IndiaOneStop [http://www.indiaonestop.com] is a strange look-ing site. If it didn't say that it was an affiliate of The Wall Street

Journal Interactive Edition, I probably wouldn't have given it a second thought. The main page is extremely colorful, to say the least, with flashing ads everywhere. Though hardly one of the greatest sites of all time, it did have a couple of redeeming features.

The General Info section has some interesting portions, particularly for those unfamiliar with the culture and practices of India. There is also a listing of the top thirty Indian markets along with some discussion of the markets, links to trade and industry associations, a Macro Economy portion that includes risks to foreign investors, and overviews of the consumer market and the agricultural, service, and industry sectors. Other useful features include links to various government agencies, found in several locations at the site, and current business news.

Nepal

NepalPages.com [http://www.nepalpages.com] has a good, although a bit dated, Doing Business section (see Figure 9.13). Most of the usual business topics are covered here. In one interesting note, while the U.S. doesn't even make it into the top fourteen countries from which Nepal imports, the U.S. ranks second on the list of countries receiving Nepalese exports.

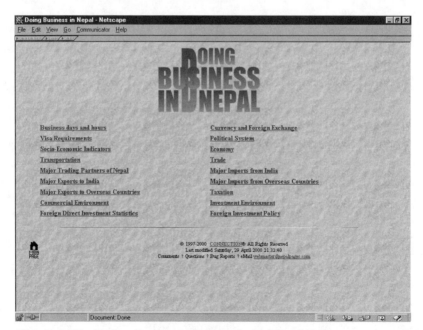

Figure 9.13   Doing Business in Nepal—Table of Contents

Regional Wrap-Up

That finishes our jaunt through the region of Asia and the Pacific. As in much of the rest of the world, each country is unique. Again, we had to overcome the roadblocks of numerous languages, religions, and cultures; a vast geographical area; finding information on small, developing countries; and more. With many of the countries in this region, keep your expectations low but aim high. With luck, you won't be disappointed in what you find.

CONCLUSION

It has taken us many pages, but we've finally completed our trip around the international business world. While we didn't visit every country along the way, we certainly did hit a lot of them. You should now feel a bit more comfortable about searching for international business information on the Internet. As with most types of research, a little creativity goes a long way in finding what we need. A "cookie-cutter" approach just won't work.

Whatever your international business information needs, we hope some of the tools we've covered help make your international searching a bit easier. One problem many readers may run into is finding the information you need, but not in English. Then what do you do?

There are some Internet translation options. Some will translate the entire Web page; others will translate a word or a phrase. Here are a few to look at:

- **AltaVista Translations—Babel Fish**
  http://babelfish.altavista.com/translate.dyn
  You can enter text for translation or enter a URL to translate a Web site. It translates between English and French, German, Portuguese, Spanish, and Italian; also German to French, French to German, and Russian to English.

- **Go Translator—Walt Disney Internet Group**
  http://translator.go.com
  As with Babel Fish, enter text for translation or a URL to

translate a Web site. This site translates between English and Spanish, French, German, Italian, and Portuguese.

- **Free Translation.com—Transparent Language Inc.**
http://www.freetranslation.com
This site also translates text or a Web site and translates between English and Spanish, French, German, Italian, Norwegian, and Portuguese.

- **InterTran—Translation Experts Ltd.**
http://www.tranexp.com:2000/InterTran?
You'll find the same capabilities as the above sites, but with many more languages offered. In addition to the usual languages, it also includes Greek, Hungarian, Icelandic, Japanese, Polish, Romanian, Russian, Serbian, Slovenian, and Welsh and distinguishes between European Spanish and Latin American Spanish.

- **WorldLingo.com**
http://www.worldlingo.com
Translates text or Web sites involving the following languages: French, German, Italian, Spanish, Portuguese, Chinese, Japanese, and Russian.

- **AlphaWorks—IBM and alphaWorks**
http://www.alphaworks.ibm.com/aw.nsf/html/mt
Functions the same as the other sites; offers German, Japanese, Italian, Spanish, Chinese Simplified, Chinese Traditional, and French.

- **Travlang's Translating Dictionaries—Travlang.com (subsidiary of iiGroup Inc.)**
http://dictionaries.travlang.com
This site only translates one word at a time, not phrases or Web sites. Its extensive list of language pairs includes German, Dutch, French, Spanish, Portuguese, Italian, Danish, Swedish, Finnish, Norwegian, Frisian, Afrikaans, Hungarian, Czech, Esperanto, and Latin.

- **Gist-in-Time—Alis Technologies**
http://www.alis.com
Translates text, but not Web sites; offers French, German, Spanish, Italian, Portuguese, Japanese, Simplified Chinese, and Traditional Chinese.

Now, I can't vouch for the translation abilities of any of these sites, as I've not used many of them. Keep in mind, that with any machine translation, the results will be less (far less) than perfect. Hopefully they will work well enough to let you know whether or not you're on the right track.

There are also software packages that can translate Web pages. One that I have used, although not recently and I know it's been redesigned, is Web Translator, a component of Power Translator from Lernout & Hauspie [http://www.lhsl.com/powertranslator]. There are many other translation software packages available, including Universal Translator (Language Force) [http://www.eurohost. com/matchfon/pages/translation.html], Simply Translating Deluxe (Lernout & Hauspie) [http://www.translation.net/simply.html], and several products from Systran [http://www. systransoft.com]. Some of these only translate text and others handle both text and Web pages. I would suggest that if you have an ongoing need for translating Web pages, you might want to consider a software package rather than relying on the free Internet translations. I admit I haven't tested them, but I would bet that you may get better results with the purchased software.

Even so, take any machine translation results "with a grain of salt," as they are definitely not flawless translations. But, if they help you to get the gist of what you're reading, that certainly is a help.

Looking for international business information, particularly on the Internet, will never become a rote activity, but we've learned enough to make the search easier. Some of the sources mentioned may have already been familiar to you; some may have been completely new; others you may have used in the past but forgotten about. Hopefully we have sparked your interest and encouraged you to follow different avenues in your international searching. As with any research, have a fair amount of skepticism until you've ascertained a site's origin. Always look for a Chamber of Commerce, resources from the U.S. Department of Commerce, a Yellow Pages directory, an official government site and, when you find a good international directory site or search engine—bookmark it!

I hope you have found our journey around the world both interesting and informative. For me it's been quite an adventure. To paraphrase the Rolling Stones, you can't always get what you want, but if you try enough sources, you'll get what you need.

APPENDIX A

URLs OF WEB SITES MENTIONED IN THE BOOK

(Note: The complete list of URLs in this book is also available online at http://www.infotoday.com/ibidirectory.htm.)

Chapter 1—International Business Research

EDGAR—The Electronic Data Gathering, Analysis, and Retrieval System
http://www.sec.gov/edgarhp.htm

FreeEDGAR
http://www.FreeEDGAR.com

LIVEDGAR
http://www.gsionline.com

Report Gallery
http://www.reportgallery.com

The Public Register's Annual Report Service
http://www.annualreportservice.com

SEDAR—System for Electronic Document Analysis and Retrieval
http://www.sedar.com

Hoover's Online
http://www.hoovers.com

U.S. Industry & Trade Outlook 2000
http://www.ita.doc.gov/td/industry/otea/outlook/index.html

**U.S. Census Bureau—American FactFinder—
Industry Quick Reports**
http://factfinder.census.gov/java_prod/dads.ui.iqr.IndProfPage

U.S. Census Bureau—Current Industrial Reports
http://www.census.gov/ftp/pub/cir/www

U.S. Census Bureau—Statistical Abstract of the United States
http://www.census.gov/statab/www

Chapter 2—The World

U.S. Government Sources

World Factbook—Central Intelligence Agency
http://www.odci.gov/cia/publications/factbook/index.html

U.S. State Department Background Notes
http://www.state.gov/www/background_notes

**International Trade Administration (ITA)—
Department of Commerce**
http://www.ita.doc.gov

ITA Trade Compliance Center
http://www.mac.doc.gov/tcc/index.html

U.S. Department of Commerce—USATrade.gov
http://www.usatrade.gov/Website/ccg.nsf

STAT-USA Internet
http://www.stat-usa.gov

U.S. Commercial Service
http://www.usatrade.gov/website

Worldwide Directory Sites

Statistical Data Locators
http://www.ntu.edu.sg/library/stat/statdata.htm

University of Strathclyde Department of Information Science—Glasgow, Scotland

- **Directories: Worldwide and Other Countries**
  http://www.dis.strath.ac.uk/business/directories.html
- **Company Profiles and Financial Information**
  http://www.dis.strath.ac.uk/business/financials.html
- **Trade Directories**
  http://www.dis.strath.ac.uk/business/trade.html
- **Statistical, Economic, and Market Information**
  http://www.dis.strath.ac.uk/business/market.html
- **Country Information**
  http://www.dis.strath.ac.uk/business/countries.html
- **Commercial Market Research Companies**
  http://www.dis.strath.ac.uk/business/marketres.html

BUBL 5:15

- **BUBL World Area Studies**
  http://bubl.ac.uk/link/five/wor.html
- **BUBL Updates**
  http://bubl.ac.uk/link/updates/current.html
- **BUBL Countries and Continents**
  http://bubl.ac.uk/link/countries.html

Michigan State University Center for International Business Education and Research (MSU-CIBER)—International Business Resources on the WWW
http://ciber.bus.msu.edu/busres.htm

Philadelphia University—Everything International
http://faculty.philau.edu/russowl/russow.html

Global Reach—Global Business Center
http://www.glreach.com/gbc/index.php3

Marketing and International Business Links
http://wtfaculty.wtamu.edu/~sanwar.bus/otherlinks.htm

VIBES—Virtual International Business & Economic Sources
http://libweb.uncc.edu/ref-bus/vibehome.htm

Nanyang Technological University Library
http://www.ntu.edu.sg/library/biz/inttrade.htm

Rutgers University Libraries (RUL)
Resources for International Business
http://www.libraries.rutgers.edu/rul/rr_gateway/research_
guides/busi/intbus.shtml

- **Banks and Financial Services**
  http://www.libraries.rutgers.edu/rul/rr_gateway/research_
  guides/busi/banks.shtml
- **Company Research**
  http://www.libraries.rutgers.edu/rul/rr_gateway/research_
  guides/busi/company.shtml

Global Business Web
http://www.globalbusinessweb.com

Pepperdine University Libraries
International Business Web Sites
http://rigel.pepperdine.edu/resources/Guides/Bibintl.htm

Worldclass Supersite
http://web.idirect.com/~tiger/supersit.htm

International Search Engines

Arnold IT International Search Engines
http://www.arnoldit.com/lists/intlsearch.asp

Search Engine Colossus
http://www.searchenginecolossus.com

Search Engines Worldwide
http://www.twics.com/~takakuwa/search/search.html

Global International Business Information

Tradeport
http://www.tradeport.org

Financial Times—FT.com
http://news.ft.com

World Bank Competitiveness Indicators
http://wbln0018.worldbank.org/psd/compete.nsf

Ernst & Young International Doing Business In ...
http://www.doingbusinessin.com

Pricewaterhouse Coopers International Briefings
http://www.pwcglobal.com/extweb/frmclp11.nsf/
ViewAgentByCurrMonth?OpenAgent

Data Downlink's .xls
http://www.xls.com

Dun & Bradstreet Internet Access for Credit Card Customers
https://www.dnb.com/product/retail/menu.htm

Economic and Financial Information

Worldclass Stocks by Country
http://web.idirect.com/~tiger/stockcou.htm

**Institute of Finance and Banking at the University of
Göttingen—Market Places and Quotations**
http://www.gwdg.de/~ifbg/stock1.htm

**Institute of Finance and Banking at the University of
Göttingen—Banks of the World**
http://www.gwdg.de/~ifbg/bank_2.html

The Internationalist—Stock Markets of the World
http://www.internationalist.com/business/Stocks.html

The Bank for International Settlements
http://www.bis.org/cbanks.htm

IndustryWeek's Ranking of the World's Top 50 Banks
http://www.industryweek.com/iwinprint/data/chart2-4.html

IndustryWeek's Ranking of the World's Top Securities Dealers
http://www.industryweek.com/iwinprint/data/chart2-7.html

Euromoney.com
http://www.euromoney.com/index.html

BankInfo.com
http://www.bankinfo.com/intereye/international.html

Ohio State University—Virtual Finance Library
http://fisher.osu.edu/fin/overview.html

BankSITE Global Directory
http://www.banksite.com/cmapitl.htm

Qualisteam
http://www.qualisteam.com

The Dismal Scientist
http://www.dismal.com

**OECD—Organisation for Economic
Co-operation and Development**
http://www.oecd.org/

OECD—Frequently Requested Statistics
http://www.oecd.org/std/fas.htm

Embassies and Links to Governments

The Embassy Web
http://www.embpage.org

The Electronic Embassy
http://www.embassy.org

Algeria
http://www.algeria-un.org/nspage.html

Antigua & Barbuda
http://www.undp.org/missions/antigua_barbuda

Argentina
http://www.embassyofargentina-usa.org

Armenia
http://www.armeniaemb.org

Australia
http://www.austemb.org

Austria
http://www.austria.org

Azerbaijan
http://www.azembassy.com

Bahrain
http://www.bahrainembassy.org

Bangladesh
http://un.int/bangladesh

Belarus
http://www.undp.org/missions/belarus/index.html

Belgium
http://www.belgium-emb.org/Atlas/atlas.asp?lng=EN

Bosnia and Herzegovina
http://www.bosnianembassy.org

Brazil
http://www.brasilemb.org

Bulgaria
http://www.bulgaria-embassy.org

Burkina Faso
http://www.burkinaembassy-usa.org

Cambodia
http://www.embassy.org/cambodia

Chad
http://www.chadembassy.org

China—People's Republic of
http://www.china-embassy.org

China—Republic of
http://www.taipei.org

Colombia
http://www.colombiaemb.org

Costa Rica
http://www.costarica.com/embassy

Croatia
http://www.croatiaemb.org

Czech Republic
http://www.czech.cz/washington

Denmark
http://www.denmarkemb.org

Dominican Republic
http://www.domrep.org

Ecuador
http://www.ecuador.org

Estonia
http://www.estemb.org

Finland
http://www.finland.org/index.html

France
http://www.info-france-usa.org

Georgia
http://www.georgiaemb.org

Germany
http://www.germany-info.org/f_index.html

Ghana
http://www.undp.org/missions/ghana

Greece
http://www.greekembassy.org

Guatemala
http://www.guatemala-embassy.org

Haiti
http://www.haiti.org

Hungary
http://www.hungaryemb.org

Iceland
http://www.iceland.org/index.html

India
http://www.indianembassy.org/

Indonesia
http://www.kbri.org

Iran
http://www.daftar.org/default_eng.htm

Ireland
http://www.irelandemb.org

Israel
http://www.israelemb.org

Italy
http://www.italyemb.org

Jamaica
http://www.emjam-usa.org

Japan
http://www.embjapan.org

Jordan
http://www.jordanembassyus.org

Kenya
http://www.kenyaembassy.com

Korea
http://www.mofat.go.kr/en_usa.htm

Kuwait
http://www.undp.org/missions/kuwait

Laos
http://www.laoembassy.com/

Latvia
http://www.latvia-usa.org

Lebanon
http://www.lebanonembassy.org

Liberia
http://www.liberiaemb.org/

Lithuania
http://www.ltembassyus.org

Madagascar
http://www.embassy.org/madagascar

Malaysia
http://www.undp.org/missions/malaysia

Mali
http://www.maliembassy-usa.org

Marshall Islands
http://www.rmiembassyus.org/usemb.html

Mauritius
http://www.idsonline.com/usa/embasydc.html

Mexico
http://www.embassyofmexico.org/english/main2.htm

Micronesia
http://www.fsmgov.org/fsmun

Moldova
http://www.rol.org/moldova

Mongolia
http://members.aol.com/monemb

Nepal
http://www.undp.org/missions/nepal

Netherlands
http://www.netherlands-embassy.org/f_netscape.html

New Zealand
http://www.nzemb.org

Norway
http://www.norway.org/index.html

Pakistan
http://www.pakistan-embassy.com

Papua New Guinea
http://www.pngembassy.org

Peru
http://www.peruemb.org/intro.html

Philippines
http://www.embassyonline.com

Poland
http://www.polishworld.com/polemb

Portugal
http://www.portugalemb.org

Romania
http://www.roembus.org

Russian Federation
http://www.russianembassy.org

St. Kitts and Nevis
http://www.stkittsnevis.org

Saudi Arabia
http://www.saudiembassy.net

Singapore
http://www.gov.sg/mfa/washington

Slovak Republic
http://www.slovakemb.com

Slovenia
http://www.embassy.org/slovenia/

South Africa
http://usaembassy.southafrica.net

Spain
http://www.spainemb.org/ingles/indexing.htm

Sudan
http://www.sudanembassyus.org

Sweden
http://www.swedenemb.org

Switzerland
http://www.swissemb.org

Thailand
http://www.thaiembdc.org

Turkey
http://www.turkey.org/start.html

Turkmenistan
http://www.turkmenistanembassy.org

Uganda
http://www.ugandaweb.com/ugaembassy

Ukraine
http://www.ukremb.com

United Kingdom
http://www.britain-info.org/

Uruguay
http://www.embassy.org/uruguay

Uzbekistan
http://www.uzbekistan.org

Venezuela
http://www.embavenez-us.org

Vietnam
http://www.vietnamembassy-usa.org

Yemen
http://www.yemenembassy.org

Purdue University Libraries: THOR—The Online Resource
http://thorplus.lib.purdue.edu/vlibrary/reading/govdocs/
foreign.html

Chambers of Commerce

U.S. Chamber of Commerce International Division
http://www.uschamber.org/intl/index.html

American Chambers of Commerce Abroad (AmChams)
http://www.uschamber.org/intl/amcham.htm

World Chambers Network
http://www.worldchambers.com

International Lists

The 2000 Forbes International 800
http://www.forbes.com/international800

The 2000 Fortune Global 500
http://www.fortune.com/fortune/global500/index.html

The BusinessWeek Global 1000
http://www.businessweek.com/1999/99_28/g1000.htm
http://www.businessweek.com/2000/00_28/b3689009.htm

IndustryWeek
http://www.industryweek.com

Stock Markets of the World by Market Capitalization
http://www.industryweek.com/iwinprint/data/chart2-1.html
Largest Advertising Agencies by Billings
http://www.industryweek.com/iwinprint/data/chart2-3.html
Largest International Law Firms
http://www.industryweek.com/iwinprint/data/chart2-5.html
Top 25 International Accounting Networks
http://www.industryweek.com/iwinprint/data/chart2-6.html
World's Top 50 Transnational Corporations
http://www.industryweek.com/iwinprint/data/chart8.html
Largest Executive Search Firms
http://www.industryweek.com/iwinprint/data/chart2-2.html
Top 1000 Global Manufacturers
http://www.industryweek.com/iwinprint/data/chart3-1.html
Industry Financial Performance Benchmarks
http://www.industryweek.com/iwinprint/data/chart3-2.html
World's Best-Managed Companies
http://www.industryweek.com/iwinprint/data/chart3-4.html
World's Largest Steel Producers
http://www.industryweek.com/iwinprint/data/chart4-3.html
International Electricity Costs
http://www.industryweek.com/iwinprint/data/chart4-5.html
100 Largest IT Companies
http://www.industryweek.com/iwinprint/data/chart4-7B.html
World's Top Airlines
http://www.industryweek.com/iwinprint/data/chart4-8.html
World's Best Hotels
http://www.industryweek.com/iwinprint/data/chart4-9.html
International Freight and Passenger Transport by Country
http://www.industryweek.com/iwinprint/data/chart4-13.html

World Trade Centers
http://www.industryweek.com/iwinprint/data/chart5-4.html

Top Consulting Firms
http://www.industryweek.com/iwinprint/data/chart6-2.html

Commercial Online Services

The Dialog Corporation
http://www.dialog.com

The Dialog Corporation—Subject Content Page
http://www.dialog.com/info/content/subject

Factiva
http://www.factiva.com

Lexis-Nexis
http://lexis-nexis.com/lncc

Lexis-Nexis Source Locator
http://lexis-nexis.com/lncc/sources

Chapter 3—Western Europe

The European Union

The European Union in the U.S.
http://www.eurunion.org

The European Union Business Resources
http://www.eurunion.org/infores/index.htm

Western European Search Engines and Directories

EuroFerret
http://www.euroferret.com/old_version.html

WebTop.com
http://www.webtop.com/search/topferret?PAGE=search&
LOOK=euroferret

Europages
http://www.europages.com

Thomas Register of European Manufacturers (TREM)
http://www.tremnet.com

About.com—European Search Engines & Directories
http://websearch.about.com/internet/websearch/
msub12-m13.htm

EuroSeek—European Directory
http://webdir.euroseek.com/?ilang=en&catid=260

**VIBES—Virtual International Business & Economic
Sources—Western Europe**
http://libweb.uncc.edu/ref-bus/reg.htm#eurw

Search Europe
http://www.searcheurope.com

Belgian Search and Navigation Matrix
http://mailserv.cc.kuleuven.ac.be/belgiansearch.html

AltaVista United Kingdom
http://uk.altavista.com

DENet
http://info.denet.dk

Sear.ch
http://search.bluewindow.ch/search?pg=home&lang=en

Voila
http://www.voila.com/Network

The Web Collection
http://www.hugmot.is/ssafn/english

UK Plus http://www.ukplus.co.uk/ukplus/SilverStream/Pages/
pgUKPlusHome.html

Western European Yellow Pages

Yell Business—UK
http://www.yellowpagesbusiness.co.uk

Austrian Yellow Pages

http://www.gelbeseiten.at

Belgium Yellow Pages

http://www.infobel.com/belgium/yp/search/default.asp

Danish Yellow Pages

http://www.degulesider.dk (not in English)
http://www.yellowpages.dk (English)

French Yellow Pages

http://wf.pagesjaunes.fr/pj.cgi?lang=en

German Yellow Pages

http://www.teleauskunft.de/NSAPI/Anfrage?AKTION=
zeSuchseiteGelbeSeiten&SPRACHE=EN&SESSIONID=
0380b1902938aa7a210007a40b&VERZEICHNIS=3&BUAB=
BUNDESWEIT&H_NUTZUNGSBEDINGUNGEN=TRUE

Irish Yellow Pages

http://www.goldenpages.ie

Italian Yellow Pages

http://multilingua.seat.it/cgi-bin/webdriver?MIval=mdrindex&
lingua=INGL

Luxembourg Yellow Pages

http://www.directory.lu/ap/default.asp?lang=3

Netherlands Yellow Pages (not in English)

http://www.detelefoongids.nl

Norwegian Yellow Pages

http://www.gulesider.no/index.jsp?spraak=3

Portuguese Yellow Pages

http://www.paginasamarelas.pt/home_e.html

Spanish Yellow Pages (not in English)

http://www.paginas-amarillas.es/buscador/home_f.html

Swedish Yellow Pages

http://www.foretagstele.se/home-en.html

Swiss Yellow Pages

http://www.directories.ch/index-en.html

Western European Stock Markets

Austria—Vienna Stock Exchange
http://www.wbag.at/index_english.html

Belgium—Brussels Exchange
http://www.stockexchange.be

Denmark—Copenhagen Stock Exchange
http://www.xcse.dk/uk/index.asp

Europe—Pan European Exchange
http://www.easdaq.be/easdaq.htm

Finland—Helsinki Stock Exchange
http://www.hex.fi/eng/index.html

France—Paris Stock Exchange
http://www.bourse-de-paris.fr

Germany—Frankfurt Stock Exchange
http://www.exchange.de/INTERNET/EXCHANGE/index_e.htm

**Germany—Baden-Württembergische Wertpapierbörse
zu Stuttgart**
http://www.boerse-stuttgart.de

Germany—Bayerische Börse—Munich Stock Exchange
http://www.bayerischeboerse.de/start.html

Italy—Italian Stock Exchange
http://www.borsaitalia.it/29/129.html

Italy—Milan Stock Exchange—Stock Quotes
http://robot1.texnet.it/finanza

Luxembourg—Luxembourg Stock Exchange
http://www.bourse.lu/english/index.shtml

Netherlands—Amsterdam Exchange
http://www.aex.nl/aex.asp?taal=en

Norway—Oslo Stock Exchange
http://www.ose.no/english

Portugal—Lisbon Stock Exchange
http://www.bvl.pt

Spain—Barcelona Stock Exchange
http://www.borsabcn.es

Spain—Bolsa de Madrid
http://www.bolsamadrid.es/homei.htm

Sweden—Stockholm Stock Exchange
http://www.omgroup.com/transaction

Switzerland—Swiss Exchange
http://www.swx.com/top/index_en.html

United Kingdom—London Stock Exchange
http://www.londonstockexchange.com

Western European Chambers of Commerce

Eurochambres—Association of European Chambers of Commerce and Industry
http://www.eurochambres.be

American Chamber of Commerce in Austria
http://www.amcham.or.at

American Chamber of Commerce in Belgium
http://www.amcham.be

American Chamber of Commerce in Denmark
http://www.amcham.dk

American Chamber of Commerce in France
http://www.amchamfrance.org

American Chamber of Commerce in Germany
http://www.amcham.de

American Chamber of Commerce in Italy
http://www.amcham.it

American Chamber of Commerce in Luxembourg
http://www.amcham.lu

American Chamber of Commerce in the Netherlands
http://home.planet.nl/~amchamnl

U.S. Chamber of Commerce in Norway
http://www.am-cham.com

American Chamber of Commerce in Sweden
http://www.amchamswe.se

Swiss-American Chamber of Commerce
http://www.amcham.ch

Miscellaneous

Bureau van Dijk
http://www.bvdsuite.com

Belgium

Belgian Foreign Trade Board (BFTB)
http://www.obcebdbh.be/en/obce/index.html

The Federation of Belgian Companies (VBO/FEB)
http://www.vbo-feb.be/ukindex.htm

Denmark

Invest in Denmark
http://www.investindk.com

Danish Electronics Industry Association
http://www.ei.dk/default.asp

Danish IT Industry Association
http://www.itb.dk

France

Invest in France Agency—North America
http://www.investinfrancena.org

Germany

Commerzbank
http://www.commerzbank.com

Federal Commissioner for Foreign Investment in Germany
http://www.foreign-direct-investment.de

Federal Statistical Office—Germany
http://www.statistik-bund.de/e_home.htm

Institute for Economic Research
http://www.ifo.de/orcl/dbssi/main_e.htm

Hamburg Institute for Economic Research
http://www.hwwa.de/hwwa_engl.html

Confederation of German Employers' Associations
http://www.bda-online.de/www/bdaonline.nsf/EnglishFrameSet

Invest in Germany
http://www.invest-in-germany.de/Engl/index1.htm

Seibt Directories
http://industrie.seibt.com/e_index.htm

Hoppenstedt Company Database
http://www.Firmendatenbank.de/endex.html

Italy

Italian Trade Commission in Canada (ITC)
http://www.italcomm.com/e/index.html

National Institute of Statistics (Italy)
http://www.istat.it/homeing.html

Italian Ministry of Foreign Affairs
http://www.esteri.it/eng/index.htm

Netherlands

Netherlands Foreign Investment Agency (NFIA)
http://www.nfia.com/

Spain

Spain–U.S. Chamber of Commerce
http://www.spainuscc.org/index.html

Typically Spanish
http://www.typicallyspanish.com/

Invest in Spain
http://www.investinspain.org/

Instituto Nacional de Estadística (National Statistics Institute)
http://www.ine.es/

Portugal

Welcome to Portugal
http://www.portugal.org

PortugalOffer
http://www.portugaloffer.com

Sweden

BolagsFakta
http://www.bolagsfakta.se/bolagsfakta/index_eng_start.html

United Kingdom

Company Annual Reports On Line (CAROL)
http://www.carol.co.uk

Corporate Reports
http://www.corpreports.co.uk

The Trade Association Network Challenge
http://www.brainstorm.co.uk/TANC/Welcome.html

Companies House
http://www.companies-house.gov.uk

Companies House—Free Information
http://www.companies-house.gov.uk/frame.cgi?OPT=free

AppleGate Directories
http://www.apgate.com

The Enterprise Zone
http://www.enterprisezone.org.uk

British Trade International
http://www.brittrade.com

TradeUK
http://www.tradeuk.com

Search Engine.com
http://uk.searchengine.com/english

Yahoo! Finance—UK & Ireland
http://uk.biz.yahoo.com/p/ukie/a

HM Customs and Excise Information Service
http://www.hmce.gov.uk

The Charity Commission for England and Wales
http://www.charity-commission.gov.uk

Chapter 4—Central and Eastern Europe

Central & Eastern European Search Engines & Directories

Orientation
http://www.orientation.com

Orientation—Central & Eastern Europe
http://eeu.orientation.com

Central and Eastern European Business Directory
http://www.ceebd.co.uk/ceebd/business.htm

VIBES—Virtual International Business & Economic Sources—Eastern Europe
http://libweb.uncc.edu/ref-bus/reg.htm#eure

DIR.bg—The Bulgarian Directory
http://www.dirbg.com

CARNet—Croatian Academic and Research Network Directory
http://www.hr/wwwhr

East European Search Engine—Sherlock
http://www.sherlock.cz

RoBBy—The Hellenic Search Engine
http://www.robby.gr

Internet Resources in Kyrgyzstan
http://www.kg

LATNET—Welcome to Latvia
http://www.latnet.lv

List of Home Pages in Lithuania
http://neris.mii.lt/serveriai/bendra/servers.html

Russia on the Net
http://www.ru

YuSearch.com (Yugoslavia)
http://www.yusearch.com/start.html

REESWeb—University of Pittsburgh
http://www.ucis.pitt.edu/reesweb/Econ/econind.html

REENIC—Russian and East European Network Information Center
http://reenic.utexas.edu/reenic.html

SEEBN.net—Southeastern Europe Business Network
http://www.seebn.net/search.cfm

Kyrgyzstan On-line
http://www.online.kg

Moldova Internet Resources
http://www.ournet.md

Central & Eastern European Yellow Pages

YelloWeb Hungary
http://www.yelloweb.hu/index.asp?lang=1

Romanian Yellow Pages
http://www.yellowpages.ro

Romanian Yellow Pages
http://www.romanianyellowpages.com

Romanian Yellow Pages Online
http://www.imago.ro

Moscow Business Telephone Guide
http://www.mbtg.net

Business Belarus
http://www.telemedia.by

Czech Republic Golden Pages
http://www.zlatestranky.cz/enindex.html

Czech Yellow Pages
http://www.infobank.sk/cz/indexe.htm

Croatian Telecommunications Telephone Directory
http://imenik.hinet.hr/imenik-asp/index.asp?lang=us

Hellas Yellow Pages—Greece
http://www.hellasyellow.gr

Latvia Yellow Pages
http://www.telemedia.lv/en

Lithuanian Internet Yellow Pages
http://www.visalietuva.lt/starten.htm

Moldova Yellow Pages
http://www.moldova.net/english

Slovakia Yellow Pages
http://www.yellowpages.sk

Poland Yellow Pages
http://www.yellowpages.pl

Hungarian Internet Yellow Pages
http://www.yellowpages.hu/default.asp

Central & Eastern European Chambers of Commerce—AmChams

American Chamber of Commerce in Bulgaria
http://www.amcham.bg

American Chamber of Commerce in Estonia
http://www.acce.ee

American Chamber of Commerce in Hungary
http://www.amcham.hu

American Chamber of Commerce in Latvia
http://www.amchamlatvia.lv

American Chamber of Commerce in Lithuania
http://www.acc.lt

American Chamber of Commerce in Poland
http://www.amcham.com.pl

American Chamber of Commerce in Romania
http://www.amcham.ro

American Chamber of Commerce in Russia
http://www.amcham.ru

American Chamber of Commerce in Ukraine
http://www.amcham.kiev.ua

American Chamber of Commerce in Azerbaijan
http://www.amchamaz.org

American Chamber of Commerce in the Czech Republic
http://www.amcham.cz

Central & Eastern European Chambers of Commerce—Not AmChams

Athens Chamber of Commerce and Industry
http://www.acci.gr

Association of Balkan Chambers
http://www.abcinfos.com

Russian Federation Chamber of Commerce and Industry
http://www.rbcnet.ru/eng_home.htm

Chamber of Economy of Bosnia and Herzegovina
http://www.komorabih.com/eindex.html

Croatian Chamber of Economy
http://www.hgk.hr

Bulgarian Chamber of Commerce and Industry
http://www.bcci.bg

Chamber of Commerce and Industry of Romania and Bucharest
http://www.ccir.ro

Yugoslav Chamber of Commerce and Industry
http://www.pkj.co.yu/YCCI.htm

Economic Chamber of Macedonia
http://info.mchamber.org.mk

Latvian Chamber of Commerce and Industry
http://sun.lcc.org.lv

Russian American Chamber of Commerce
http://www.rmi.net/racc

Banking and Finance

European Bank for Reconstruction and Development (EBRD)
http://www.ebrd.org

EBRD Country Investment Profiles
http://www.ebrd.org/english/opera/Country/index.htm

The Federal Commission for the Securities Market (FCSM)
http://www.fedcom.ru/ewelcome.html

Skate Financial Network
http://www.skatefn.com

The Central Bank of the Russian Federation
http://www.cbr.ru/eng

Croatian National Bank
http://www.hnb.hr

The National Bank of the Czech Republic
http://voskovec.radio.cz/gov-cr/bank.html

Bank of Estonia
http://www.ee/epbe/en

The National Bank of Hungary
http://www.mnb.hu/index-a.htm

The National Bank of Moldova
http://www.bnm.org/english/index.htm

The National Bank of Slovakia
http://www.nbs.sk/INDEXA.HTM

The Bank of Slovenia
http://www.bsi.si/html/eng/index.html

The Bank of Lithuania
http://www.lbank.lt/Eng/DEFAULT.HTM

Central & Eastern European Stock Exchanges

Bulgaria—Bulgarian Stock Exchange
http://www.onlinebg.com

Croatia—Zagreb Stock Exchange
http://www.zse.hr

Cyprus—Cyprus Stock Exchange
http://www.cse.com.cy

Czech Republic—Prague Stock Exchange
http://stock.eunet.cz/bcpp_e.html

Estonia—Tallinn Stock Exchange
http://www.tse.ee/english/index.html

Greece—Athens Stock Exchange
http://www.ase.gr

Hungary—Budapest Stock Exchange
http://www.fornax.hu/fmon/stock/data/bethath.html

Latvia—Riga Stock Exchange
http://www.rfb.lv

Lithuania—National Stock Exchange of Lithuania
http://www.nse.lt

Macedonia—Macedonian Stock Exchange
http://www.mse.org.mk

Romania—Bucharest Stock Exchange
http://www.bse.ro

Russia—Federal Commission for the Securities Market
http://www.fedcom.ru/ewelcome.html

Slovakia—Bratislava Stock Exchange
http://www.bsse.sk/bsseApp/index.asp?LANG=EN&ITM=HOME

Slovenia—Ljubljana Stock Exchange
http://www.ljse.si/StrAng/PrvaStr/PrvaStr.asp

Central & Eastern European U.S. Government Sources

Business Information Service for the Newly Independent States (BISNIS)
http://www.bisnis.doc.gov

CEEBICnet—Central and Eastern Europe Business
Information Center
http://www.mac.doc.gov/eebic/ceebic.html

Central & Eastern European Newspapers, Magazines, & More

Business Europa
http://www.business-europa.co.uk/bemag.html

Central Europe Review
http://www.ce-review.org/index.html

The Prague Post Online
http://www.praguepost.cz

CEEBIZ.com
http://www.ceebiz.com

Czech the News
http://www.czech.cz/washington/newslet/newslet.htm

The Warsaw Voice
http://www.warsawvoice.com.pl

The Slovak Spectator
http://www.slovakspectator.sk

Central Europe Online
http://www.centraleurope.com

The Moscow Times
http://www.themoscowtimes.com

The St. Petersburg Times
http://www.sptimes.ru/cgi-bin/home.cgi

Interfax
http://www.interfax-news.com

Newspapers of the Czech Republic
http://www.columbia.edu/~js322/czech.html

Azerbaijan

State Statistical Committee of Azerbaijan Republic
http://www.statcom.baku-az.com

US-Azerbaijan Council
http://ourworld.compuserve.com/homepages/usazerb

Azerbaijan Internet Links
http://resources.net.az

Czech Republic

Prague Business Journal Lists
http://www.pbj.cz/common/bol/default.asp?site=1

Czech Republic
http://www.czech.cz

Czech Info Center
http://www.muselik.com/czech/frame.html

Estonia

Estonian Trade Council
http://www.ee/ETC

Ekspress Hotline
http://www.1182.ee/eng

Hungary

Budapest Business Journal Lists
http://www.bbj.hu/common/bol/default.asp?site=3

Latvia

Latvian Business Pages
http://www.expo.lv

Latvian Business Directory
http://www.zl.lv/new1/region-eng.htm

Lithuania

Advantage Lithuania
http://www.lda.lt

Greece

Invest in Greece (INVgr)
http://www.invgr.com/

Poland

Business Polska
http://www.polska.net/

Hotels Poland: Castles and Palaces
http://www.HotelsPoland.com/castle_palace

Inside Poland
http://www.insidepoland.com.pl

The Warsaw Business Journal Lists
http://www.wbj.pl/common/bol/default.asp?site=2

Russia

Russia Today
http://www.russiatoday.com

Russia at Your Fingertips
http://www.publications-etc.com/russia/index2.html

Bucknell University—US Firms in Russia
http://web3.departments.bucknell.edu/scripts/russian/usfirms

Chapter 5—Latin America and the Caribbean

Latin American and Caribbean Search Engines and Directories

Latin American Network Information Center (LANIC)
http://lanic.utexas.edu

CaribSeek
http://www.caribseek.com

International Studies—Americas (Rhodes College)
http://blair.library.rhodes.edu/ishtmls/americas.html

International Studies—South America (Rhodes College)
http://www.rhodes.edu/ishtmls/SAmerica.html

VIBES—Virtual International Business and Economic Sources—Latin America
http://libweb.uncc.edu/ref-bus/reg.htm#latin

@BRINT—Americas: Business & Technology
http://www.brint.com/Country.htm#IntAmerica

Caribbean Cyberspace
http://www.CaribbeanCyberspace.com

Caribe Search
http://www.caribesearch.com

Costa Rica Internet Directory
http://www.arweb.com/cr

Yaguá Business
http://www.yagua.com/cgi-local/categorias.cgi?categoria=
Comercio_y_Empresas

Centramerica.com
http://directory.centramerica.com

Central America on the Net
http://www.latinworld.com/centro

The Caribbean on the Net
http://www.latinworld.com/caribe/index.html

South America on the Net
http://www.latinworld.com/sur/index.html

EuroSeek Caribbean
http://webdir.euroseek.com/?ilang=en&catid=271

EuroSeek Central America
http://webdir.euroseek.com/?ilang=en&catid=266

EuroSeek South America
http://webdir.euroseek.com/?ilang=en&catid=265

**Latin American/South American Search Engines
and Directories**
http://websearch.about.com/internet/websearch/
msub12-m14.htm

Latin American & Caribbean Chambers of Commerce

**Association of American Chambers of Commerce in Latin
America (AACCLA)**
http://www.aaccla.org

American Chamber of Commerce in Argentina
http://www.amchamar.com.ar

American Chamber of Commerce of Bolivia
http://www.bolivianet.com/amcham

**American Chamber of Commerce for Brazil, Rio de Janeiro
(Portuguese only)**
http://www.amchamrio.com.br

American Chamber of Commerce for Brazil, São Paulo
http://www.amcham.com.br/english

Chilean-American Chamber of Commerce
http://www.amchamchile.cl

Colombian-American Chamber of Commerce
http://www.amchamcolombia.com.co

Costa Rican-American Chamber of Commerce
http://www.amcham.co.cr

American Chamber of Commerce of the Dominican Republic
http://www.amcham.org.do

Ecuadorian-American Chamber of Commerce, Guayaquil
http://www.caecam.org/amcham.html

American Chamber of Commerce of El Salvador
http://www.amchamsal.com

American Chamber of Commerce in Guatemala
http://www8.bcity.com/amcham2

American Chamber of Commerce in Jamaica
http://www.amchamjamaica.org

American Chamber of Commerce of Nicaragua
http://amchamnic.com/index1.htm

American Chamber of Commerce and Industry of Panama
http://www.panamcham.com

American Chamber of Commerce of Trinidad & Tobago
http://www.amchamtt.com

Chamber of Commerce Uruguay-U.S.A.
http://www.zfm.com/amchamuru

Venezuelan-American Chamber of Commerce & Industry
http://www.venamcham.org/ingles/welcoeng.htm

Latin American & Caribbean Stock Exchanges

Center for Latin American Capital Markets
http://www.netrus.net/users/gmorles

Argentina—Bolsa de Comercio de Buenos Aires
http://www.bcba.sba.com.ar/sib_i.htm

Barbados—Security Exchange of Barbados
http://www.cweek.com/sebact.html

Bermuda—Bermuda Stock Exchange
http://bsx.com/cgi-win/bsx.exe/bsxindex

Bolivia—Bolsa Boliviana de Valores
http://bolsa-valores-bolivia.com

Brazil—Rio de Janeiro Stock Exchange
http://www.bvrj.com.br

Brazil—São Paulo Stock Exchange
http://www.bovespa.com.br/indexi.htm

Cayman Islands —Cayman Islands Stock Exchange
http://www.csx.com.ky

Chile—Bolsa de Comercio de Santiago
http://www.bolsadesantiago.com/english/index.asp

Colombia—Bolsa de Occidente
http://www.bolsadeoccidente.com.co/0index_en.html

Colombia—Bolsa de Bogotá
http://www.bolsabogota.com.co

Ecuador—Bolsa de Valores de Guayaquil
http://www4.bvg.fin.ec/eng/default

Ecuador—Bolsa de Valores de Quito
http://www.ccbvq.com/bolsa/html/home.html

Honduras—Bolsa Centroamericana de Valores
http://www.bcv.hn

Jamaica—Jamaica Stock Exchange
http://www.jamstockex.com

Nicaragua—Bolsa de Valores de Nicaragua
http://www.bolsanic.com/engl.html

Paraguay—Bolsa de Valores de Asuncion
http://www.pdv.com.py/bolsa/index.html

Peru—Lima Stock Exchange
http://www.bvl.com.pe/homepage2.html

Tinidad and Tobago—Tinidad and Tobago Stock Exchange
http://stockex.co.tt

Venezuela—Caracas Stock Exchange
http://www.caracasstock.com/newpage/english/english.htm

Latin American & Caribbean Banking & Finance

Banco Central de la República de Argentina
http://www.bcra.gov.ar/english/e_english.htm

Central Bank of Barbados
http://www.centralbank.org.bb

Banco Central de Bolivia
http://www.bcb.gov.bo

Banco Central do Brasil
http://www.bcb.gov.br/defaulti.htm

Banco Central de Chile
http://www.bcentral.cl

Banco Central de la República—Colombia
http://www.banrep.gov.co/home4.htm

Banco Central de Costa Rica
http://www.bccr.fi.cr

Banco Central de la República Dominicana
http://www.bancentral.gov.do

Banco Central del Ecuador
http://www.bce.fin.ec

Banco Central de Reserva de El Salvador
http://www.bcr.gob.sv/ebcr000.htm

Banco de Guatemala
http://www.banguat.gob.gt/menugen.asp?kmenu=INDICE

Banco Central de Honduras
http://www.bch.hn

Bank of Jamaica
http://www.boj.org.jm/home30.html

Central Bank of the Netherlands Antilles
http://www.centralbank.an

Banco Central de Nicaragua
http://www.bcn.gob.ni

Central Reserve Bank of Peru
http://www.bcrp.gob.pe/english/e-Default.htm

Banco Central del Uruguay
http://www.bcu.gub.uy

Banco Central de Venezuela
http://www.bcv.org.ve

Latin American & Caribbean Exporters' and Business Directories

DdeX Venezuela
http://www.ddex.com/index-e.html

Bolivia Business Online
http://www.boliviabiz.com/business/company.htm

BrazilBiz
http://www.brazilbiz.com.br/english

Trade Venezuela Trade Directory
http://www.trade-venezuela.com/DIRENG.HTM

El Salvador Directory of Importers and Exporters
http://www.elsalvadortrade.com.sv/i_html/directorio.html

Haiti Business Directory
http://www.haiti-business.com/INDEX.CFM?ACTION_
RECHERCHE=RECHERCHE_ANGLAIS

Latinvestor—Chilean Listed Companies
http://www.latinvestor.com/listed%20companies/listed-ch.htm

Latinvestor—Colombian Listed Companies
http://www.latinvestor.com/listed%20companies/listed-co.htm

Peruvian Business Directory
http://www.denperu.com/denexe/home-e.asp

Uruguay.com
http://www.uruguay.com/enlaces/yellow.html

Latin Export
http://www.latinexport.com

Latin American & Caribbean Yellow Pages

Argentina—Páginas Amarillas
http://www.paginasamarillas.com.ar

Argentina—Páginas Doradas
http://www.paginas-doradas.com.ar/PDPortal/guia_
clasificada/guia_clasificada.asp

Bermuda Yellow Pages
http://www.bermudayp.com

Brazil Biz
http://www.brazilbiz.com.br/english

Chile—Las Amarillas de Internet
http://www.amarillas.cl

Chile Business Directory
http://www.chilnet.cl/consultas/abajoesp.asp

Colombian Yellow Pages
http://www.quehubo.com

Costa Rica Páginas Amarillas
http://www.costaricapages.com/local/localhome.htm

Páginas Amarillas de El Salvador
http://www.paginasamarillas.com/paginasamarillas/Salvador/
Salvador.asp?NuevaB=2

Páginas Amarillas de Guatemala
http://www.paginasamarillas.com/paginasamarillas/guatemala/
guatemala.asp

Páginas Amarillas de Panama
http://www.paginasamarillas.com/paginasamarillas/Panama/
Panama.asp?NuevaB=4

Paraguay Páginas Amarillas
http://www.uninet.com.py/GUITEL/paginas_amarillas.html

Páginas Amarillas de Peru
http://www.paginasamarillas.telefonica.com.pe

Páginas Amarillas de Uruguay
http://www.guiatelefonica.com.uy/principal/index.htm

Venezuela—La Guia
http://www.caveguias.com.ve

Latin American & Caribbean Local Government Information

American Governments on the WWW
http://www.gksoft.com/govt/en/america.html

Organization of American States (OAS) Trade Unit—Foreign Trade Information System (SICE)
http://www.sice.oas.org

Argentina

Fundación Invertir
http://www.invertir.com

Brazil

Brazil InfoNet (Business section)
http://www.brazilinfo.net/sky3/usbrazil2/public_html/
business.html

Brazil TradeNet
http://www.braziltradenet.gov.br/e/usrenglish.htm

The Brazilianist
http://www.brazilianist.com

Caribbean

Caribbean News Agency (CANA)
http://www.cananews.com

Eastern Caribbean Investment Promotion Service (ECIPS)
http://www.ecips.com

Tourism and Industrial Development Company of Trinidad and Tobago Limited (TIDCO)
http://www.tidco.co.tt

Investing in Trinidad and Tobago (TIDCO)
http://www.investtnt.com

Trinidad and Tobago Trade Information (TIDCO)
http://www.tradetnt.com

Trinidad and Tobago Manufacturers Association
http://www.ttma.com

Caribbean Week
http://www.cweek.com

Guatemala

Guatemala Online
http://www.quetzalnet.com

AGEXPRONT
http://www.agexpront.com

Chapter 6—The Middle East and North Africa

Middle East & North African Region

ArabNet
http://www.arab.net

Arab World Online
http://www.awo.net

Middle East & North African Directories

Al Mashriq—the Levant
http://almashriq.hiof.no

Al-Murshid
http://www.murshid.com

EuroSeek.com
http://webdir.euroseek.com/?ilang=en&catid=264

The Center for Middle Eastern Studies from the University of Texas at Austin
http://menic.utexas.edu/menic.html

Middle East Directory
http://www.middleeastdirectory.com

The Middle East Information Network
http://www.mideastinfo.com

iGuide
http://www.iguide.co.il

Lebanon Online
http://www.lol.com.lb/index.shtml

Libanis
http://libanis.com

1001 Sites.com
http://www.1001sites.com

Arabist
http://www.arabist.com

EgyptSearch.com
http://www.egyptsearch.com

ArabInfo.org
http://www.arab-trade.com

Middle East & North African Search Engines

Cyprus 2000
http://www.cyprus2000.com/search

Search Egypt Web
http://Search.EgyptWeb.com/#SearchTable

Robby—The Hellenic Search Engine
http://www.robby.gr/

Arab Sites.com
http://arabsites.com/index.html

Lebanese Sites Search Engine
http://www.netgate.com.lb/bigbang

Middle East & North African Banking and Finance

The Emirates Bank Group
http://emiratesbank.com/ebg

HSBC Bank Middle East—United Arab Emirates
http://www.hsbc.com

HSBC Bank Middle East—Bahrain
http://www.hsbc.com

HSBC Bank Middle East—Egypt
http://www.hsbc.com

HSBC Bank Middle East—Jordan
http://www.hsbc.com

HSBC Bank Middle East—Lebanon
http://www.hsbc.com

HSBC Bank Middle East—Oman
http://www.hsbc.com

HSBC Bank Middle East—Qatar
http://www.hsbc.com

The National Bank of Kuwait
http://www.nbk.com

Jordan Kuwait Bank
http://www.jordan-kuwait-bank.com

Mizrahi Bank
http://www.mizrahi.co.il

Bank Hapoalim
http://www2.bankhapoalim.co.il/national/index.html

Bank Hapoalim/Standard & Poor's
http://www.standardpoor.co.il/bankhapoalim

Middle East & North African Stock Exchanges

Bahrain—Bahrain Stock Exchange
http://www.bahrainstock.com

Egypt—Cairo & Alexandria Stock Exchanges
http://www.egyptse.com

Iran—Tehran Stock Exchange
http://www.neda.net/tse/

Kuwait—Kuwaiti Stock Prices (not the actual exchange)
http://www.alsadon.com/rates.html

Lebanon—Beirut Stock Exchange
http://www.bse.com.lb

Morocco—Casablanca Stock Exchange
http://www.casablanca-bourse.com/homeen.html

Palestine—Palestine Securities Exchange
http://www.p-s-e.com

Tel Aviv Stock Exchange (TASE)
http://www.tase.co.il/buildpage.cgi

Amman Financial Market (AFM)
http://www.access2arabia.com/afm

Tunisia—Tunis Stock Exchange
http://www.tunisie.com/BusinessInfo/stock.html

Turkey—Istanbul Stock Exchange
http://www.ise.org

Middle East & North African American Chambers of Commerce

American Chamber of Commerce of Egypt
http://www.amcham.org.eg

Israel-America Chamber of Commerce & Industry
http://www.amcham.co.il

The American Chamber of Commerce in Morocco
http://www.amcham-morocco.com

Middle East & North African Other Chambers— Not AmChams

Arab Chambers of Commerce Offices in the Arab World
http://www.awo.net/commerce/arabcoc/coc.asp

National U.S.-Arab Chamber of Commerce
http://www.nusacc.org

Bahrain Chamber of Commerce and Industry
http://www.bahchamber.com

**Chamber of Commerce and Industry—
Haifa and Northern Israel**
http://haifachamber.com

Federation of Israeli Chambers of Commerce
http://www.chamber.org.il

Federation of Jordanian Chambers of Commerce
http://www.fjcc.com

Amman Chamber of Industry (Jordan)
http://www.aci.org.jo

Chamber of Commerce and Industry—Beirut (Lebanon)
http://www.ccib.org.lb

Palestinian Chambers of Commerce, Industry, and Agriculture
http://www.pal-chambers.com

Palestine Chamber of Commerce
http://www.g77tin.org/pccghp.html

Council of Saudi Chambers of Commerce and Industry
http://www.awo.net/saudicouncil

Jeddah Chamber of Commerce and Industry (Saudi Arabia)
http://www.awo.net/commerce/arabcoc/home.asp

Riyadh Chamber of Commerce and Industry (Saudi Arabia)
http://www.riyadh-chamber.org

US-Saudi Arabian Business Council
http://www.us-saudi-business.org

Federation of Syrian Chambers of Commerce
http://www.fedcommsyr.org

Abu Dhabi Chamber of Commerce and Industry (United Arab Emirates)
http://www.adcci-uae.com

Ajman Chamber of Commerce and Industry (United Arab Emirates)
http://www.ajcci.co.ae/ajcci.htm

Sharjah Chamber of Commerce and Industry (United Arab Emirates)
http://www.sharjah.gov.ae/scci

Middle East & North African Yellow Pages

Bahrain Yellow Pages
http://www.bahrainyellowpages.com

Cyprus Yellow Pages
http://www.cyprusyellowpages.com

Iran Yellow Pages
http://www.iranyellowpages.net

Israel Golden Pages
http://www.yellowpages.co.il/yp/yp.cgi?lang=E&clear=1

Lebanon Internet Yellow Pages
http://www.yellowpages.com.lb

Morocco Yellow Pages
http://www.maroc.net/yp

Palestine Yellow Pages
http://www.palestine-yellowpages.com

Tunisia Yellow Pages (French only)
http://www.pagesjaunes.com.tn

United Arab Emirates
http://uae-ypages.com/html/1.htm

Middle East & North African News

Arabia.On.Line
http://www.arabia.com

Arabian Business.com
http://www.itp.net/corporate/current/97478350998941.htm

Middle East Economic Survey (MEES)
http://www.mees.com

MEES—Newspapers and News Agencies
http://www.mees.com/dotcom/newspapers/index.html

Israel's Business Arena
http://www.globes.co.il/serveen

Egypt

Egypt State Information Service (SIS)
http://www.uk.sis.gov.eg

Business Today Egypt Online
http://www.businesstoday-eg.com

Israel

Israel Association of Electronics Industries
http://www.iaei.org.il

US-IBEX—U.S. Israel Business Exchange
http://www.israelemb.org/economic/economic_frame.htm

Israel Foreign Ministry
http://www.israel-mfa.gov.il/mfa/go.asp?MFAH00kj0

Lebanon

Lebanon.com
http://www.lebanon.com

IDREL
http://www.idrel.com.lb

Palestine

Arab Supernet
http://www.a-supernet.net/default.asp

PALTRADE
http://www.paltrade.org

Other Countries

La Maison du Maroc—The House of Morocco
http://www.maroc.net

Sudan.Net
http://www.sudan.net

Bahrain Promotions and Marketing Board (BPMB)
http://www.bpmb.com

The U.S.-Saudi Arabian Business Council
http://www.us-saudi-business.org

Chapter 7—Sub-Saharan Africa

Sub-Saharan African Directories

Stanford University Libraries & Academic Information Resources—Africa South of the Sahara—Selected Internet Resources
http: //www-sul.stanford.edu/depts/ssrg/africa

The J. Murrey Atkins Library & Information Services of the University of North Carolina at Charlotte
http://libweb.uncc.edu/ref-bus/reg.htm

The Electronic African Bookworm
http://www.hanszell.co.uk/indexlink.htm

Columbia University Libraries—African Studies Internet Resources
http://www.cc.columbia.edu/cu/libraries/indiv/area/Africa

EuroSeek.com—Africa
http://webdir.euroseek.com/?ilang=en&catid=263

Harambee Africa Links
http://www.harambee.co.uk/links.htm

Index on Africa
http://www.africaindex.africainfo.no/pages

African Studies Center—University of Pennsylvania
http://www.sas.upenn.edu/African_Studies/Home_Page/Country.html

Jump Start
http://www.mg.co.za/mg/jump/j-africa.htm

NewAfrica.com
http://www.newafrica.com

Sub-Saharan African Search Engines

Ananzi
http://www.ananzi.co.za

WoYaa
http://www.woyaa.com

Aardvark
http://www.aardvark.co.za

AAA Matilda Angola
http://aaa.com.au/images/logos/searches/ao.shtml

Max
http://www01.max.co.za

Sub-Saharan African Chambers of Commerce

Cameroon Chamber of Commerce and Industry
http://www.g77tin.org/ccimhp.html

Addis Ababa (Ethiopia) Chamber of Commerce
http://www.addischamber.com/

Mauritius Chamber of Commerce and Industry
http://www.mcci.org

Uganda National Chamber of Commerce and Industry
http://www.uganda.co.ug/commerce.htm

Confederation of Zimbabwe Industries
http://www.czi.org.zw

South African Chamber of Business
http://www.sacob.co.za

**The Alberton (South Africa) Chamber of
Commerce and Industry**
http://www.alberton.com

Johannesburg Chamber of Commerce and Industry
http://www.jcci.co.za

**Bloemfontein (South Africa) Chamber of
Commerce and Industry**
http://www.bcci.co.za

Cape (South Africa) Chamber of Commerce and Industry
http://www.capechamber.co.za

Durban (South Africa) Chamber of Commerce and Industry
http://www.durbanchamber.co.za

Greater Germiston (South Africa) Chamber of Commerce and Industry
http://www.ggcci.co.za

Pietermaritzburg (South Africa) Chamber of Commerce and Industries
http://www.pcci.org.za

Port Elizabeth (South Africa) Regional Chamber of Commerce and Industry
http://www.pechamber.org.za

Eurochamber of Commerce in Southern Africa
http://www.eurochamber.co.za

Ghana National Chamber of Commerce
http://www.g77tin.org/gncchp.html

U.S.-Angola Chamber of Commerce
http://www.us-angola.org

Sub-Saharan African Yellow Pages

Ethiopia Yellow Pages
http://www.ethioyellowpages.com/pages/ethiopia.htm

Kenya Yellow Pages
http://www.postel.co.ke

South Africa—EasyInfo Internet Directory
http://www.easyinfo.co.za

Ghana Yellow Pages
http://www.ghanaforum.com/directory.htm

Nigeria Yellow Pages
http://www.yellowpages.com.ng

South Africa Internet Directory
http://iafrica.com/directories/business/index.htm

Sub-Saharan African News

Financial Mail
http://www.fm.co.za

AfricaNews Online
http://www.africanews.org

African Business Information Services (AfBIS)
http://www.afbis.com

Ghana Classifieds
http://www.ghanaclassifieds.com

NewsAfrica.com
http://www.africanews.com

Nigeria.com Daily News
http://www.nigeria.com

Ghana Review International
http://212.67.202.38/~gri

International Political Economy Network—News Links
http://csf.colorado.edu/ipe/africa.html

AfricaNet.com
http://www.africanet.com

E&P Media Links Online Directory—Africa
http://emedia1.mediainfo.com/emedia/africa.htm

Sub-Saharan African U.S. Government Sources

United States Agency for International Development (USAID)
http://www.info.usaid.gov

**U.S. Merchandise Trade with Developing Countries—
Sub-Saharan Africa**
http://www.info.usaid.gov/economic_growth/trdweb/africa.html

**USAID Africa Bureau Information Center—Internet Resource
Guide—Selected Sites with Special Reference to Africa**
http://www.info.usaid.gov/regions/afr/abic/guides/afrsites.htm

USAID Global Technology Network (GTN)
http://www.usgtn.org

GTN African Regional Information
http://www.usgtn.org/Africa%20FG/Africa%20Homepage.html

GTN Africa Overview
http://www.usgtn.org/Africa%20FG/Africa%20Overview%20(long).html

Sub-Saharan Africa—Searching for Companies

Braby's Red Index
http://www.redindex.com

Internext Gateway to South Africa
http://www.zaworm.co.za

Southern Africa Directory
http://www.sadirectory.co.za

South Africa Online Business Directory
http://www.southafrica.co.za/busfin

Buy SA.com
http://www.1023.co.za

East Africa Sources Trade Directory
[http://www.eastafrica-sources.com/cgi-bin/w3-msql/trading_directory/index.html?ID=GUEST]

KenyaWeb
http://www.kenyaweb.com

GhanaWeb Directory of Businesses
http://www.ghanaweb.com/main/overview.php3?CAT=B

Sub-Saharan African Regional

MBendi AfroPaedia
http://www.mbendi.co.za

The Africa Business Network—The International Finance Corporation/World Bank
http://www.ifc.org/abn

Africa Dot Com
http://africa.com

Corporate Council on Africa (CCA)
http://www.africacncl.org

The Common Market for Eastern and Southern Africa
(COMESA)
http://www.comesa.int

Sub-Saharan African Stock Exchanges

Botswana—Botswana Stock Exchange
http://mbendi.co.za/exbo.htm

Ghana—Ghana Stock Exchange
http://www.gse.com.gh

Mauritius—The Stock Exchange of Mauritius
http://www.semdex.com

Nigeria—Nigerian Stock Exchange
http://www.nse.com.ng

South Africa—The Johannesburg Stock Exchange
http://www.jse.co.za

Zambia—Lusaka Stock Exchange
http://www.pangaeapartners.com/luseinfo.htm

Zimbabwe—Zimbabwe Stock Exchange
http://www.zse.co.zw

Sub-Saharan African Central Banks

Central Bank of the West African States
http://www.bceao.int/internet/bcweb.nsf/pages/us

South African Reserve Bank
http://www.resbank.co.za

Central Bank of Swaziland
http://www.centralbank.sz/cbs.html

The Bank of Zambia
http://www.boz.zm.

The Central Bank of Kenya
http://www.africaonline.co.ke/cbk/index.html

Banco Nacional de Angola
http://www.ebonet.net/bna/bna.htm

Central Bank of Lesotho
http://www.centralbank.org.ls

Banco de Mozambique
http://www.bancomoc.mz

Angola

Embassy of the Republic of Angola
http://www.angola.org

Botswana

Government of Botswana
http://www.gov.bw/home.html

Ethiopia

Ethiopian Embassy in Washington, DC
http://www.ethiopianembassy.org

Swaziland

Swazi.com
http://www.swazi.com

Uganda

Uganda Home Page
http://www.uganda.co.ug

Zambia

ZamNet
http://www.zamnet.zm

ZamNet's Zambian Business WWW Pages
http://www.zamnet.zm/zamnet/zambus/zambushome.html

Export Board of Zambia
http://www.zamnet.zm/zamnet/ebz/ebz.htm

Zambia Investment Center
http://www.zic.org.zm

Zimbabwe

High Commission of the Republic of Zimbabwe—Ottawa, Canada
http://www.DocuWeb.ca/Zimbabwe/index.html

ZimTrade
http://www.zimtrade.co.zw

Chapter 8—Mexico and Canada

NAFTA

LANIC—University of Texas at Austin's Latin American Network Information Center—NAFTA Resources
http://www.lanic.utexas.edu/la/Mexico/nafta/index.html

VIBES—Virtual International Business & Economic Sources—University of North Carolina at Charlotte
http://libweb.uncc.edu/ref-bus/reg.htm#nafta

NAFTA Secretariat
http://www.nafta-sec-alena.org

NAFTA Customs
http://www.nafta-customs.org

SECOFI-NAFTA
http://www.naftaworks.org

Mexico

Mexican Directory Sites

Mexico Channel
http://www.trace-sc.com

EuroSeek—Mexico
http://webdir.euroseek.com/?ilang=en&catid=26584

Mexican Search Engines

Yahoo!—Mexico
http://dir.yahoo.com/regional/countries/mexico

Explore Mexico
http://www.explore-mex.com

Mexican Yellow Pages

MexSearch Yellow Pages
http://www.yellow.com.mx/indexs.html

Mexican Chambers of Commerce

American Chamber of Commerce of Mexico, A.C.
http://www.amcham.com.mx/amchamber/english/index21.html

**American Chamber of Commerce of Mexico—
Guadalajara Chapter**
http://www.amchamgdl.com.mx/english/framesidx.html

**American Chamber of Commerce of Mexico—
Monterrey Chapter**
http://www.usmcoc.org/monterrey.html

Mexican Company Directories

Mexico Web
http://mexico.web.com.mx/english

Mexico Online
http://www.mexonline.com/business.htm

The Mx International—Mexico
http://www.mxsearch.com/mexico

Information Mexico—Business
http://www.mexicosi.com

Infosel Cdmex
http://cdmex.infosel.com

Mexican Associations and Industry Sites

**ANIQ, Asociación Nacional de la Industria Química or the
National Association of the Chemical Industry**
http://www.aniq.org.mx/iindex.htm

Consejo Mexicano del Cafe—the Mexican Coffee Council
http://www.sagar.gob.mx/cmc/cafe01in.htm

Mexican Bank for Foreign Trade (BANCOMEXT)—Mexican Textile & Apparel Showroom
http://www.mexicanshowroom.com

Mexican Mining Information Centre
http://www.mexmin.com

Mexican Finance, Stock Market, Banking

Bolsa Mexicana de Valores
http://www.bmv.com.mx/bmving/index.html

Banco de México
http://www.banxico.org.mx/siteBanxicoINGLES/index.html

Mexico Online—Banking and Finance
http://www.mexonline.com/banks.htm

BankSITE Global Directory
http://www.banksite.com/intbanks/north_america_banks.htm

Investing in Mexico

Mexican Investment Board
http://www.mib.org.mx

BANCOMEXT, the Mexican Bank for Foreign Trade
http://www.mexico-trade.com

The Mexican Intelligence Report
http://www.mex-i-co.com

Canada

Canadian Directories

National Library of Canada
http://www.nlc-bnc.ca/caninfo/ecaninfo.htm

Internet Sources for Journalists and Broadcasters
http://www.synapse.net/~radio/welcome.html

**Internet Sources for Journalists and Broadcasters—
Business and Finance**
http://www.synapse.net/~radio/business.htm

Yahoo! Regional Canada
http://dir.yahoo.com/regional/countries/canada

Yahoo! Canada
http://ca.yahoo.com

Canadopedia
http://www.canadopedia.com

Canadian Links
http://www.canadian-links.com

Canadian Webs
http://www.canadianwebs.com

EuroSeek Canada
http://webdir.euroseek.com/top/catid=87439/ilang=en

GDSourcing—A Reference Point for Canadian Statistics
http://www.gdsourcing.com/about.htm

Sympatico.ca
http://www1.sympatico.ca

Price's List of Lists—Canadian Business
http://gwis2.circ.gwu.edu/~gprice/listof.htm#
CanadianBusiness

Canadian Search Engines

Canada.com
http://www.canada.com/home

Maple Square
http://www.maplesquare.com

AltaVista Canada
http://www.altavistacanada.com/cgi-bin/query

MyBC.com
http://www.mybc.com/

Alberta.com
http://www.alberta.com

Canadian Yellow Pages

Canada Yellow Pages
http://canadayellowpages.com

Canadian Yellow Business Directory
http://www.yellow.ca

Canada 411
http://canada411.sympatico.ca

Yellow Pages.ca
http://www.yellowpages.ca/bin/cgidir.dll?mem=800&MG=

WorldPages.com
http://www.worldpages.com/bus

QuebecTel's Yellow Pages
http://pagesjaunesqctel.com/eindex.html

Mysask.com
http://www.mysask.com

myWinnipeg.com
http://www.mywinnipeg.com

Canadian Chambers of Commerce

The Canadian Chamber of Commerce
http://www.chamber.ca/newpages/main.html

British Columbia Chamber of Commerce
http://www.bcchamber.org

Calgary Chamber of Commerce
http://www.calgarychamber.com

Niagara Falls Chamber of Commerce
http://www.nflschamber.com

Ottawa Board of Trade
http://www.board-of-trade.org

Ontario Chamber of Commerce
http://www.occ.on.ca

Canadian Associations

Aerospace Industries Association of Canada
http://www.aiac.ca

Canadian Chemical Producers' Association
http://www.ccpa.ca/english/index.html

Canadian Soft Drink Association
http://www.softdrink.ca

Canadian Steel Producers Association
http://www.canadiansteel.ca

Canadian Association of Petroleum Producers
http://www.capp.ca/capframe.html

Canadian Gas Association
http://www.cga.ca

Canadian Petroleum Perspective
http://www.mossr.com

Canadian Electricity Association
http://www.canelect.ca/connections_online/home.htm

Petroleum Services Association of Canada
http://www.psac.ca

Mining Association of Canada
http://www.mining.ca/english

Canadian Bankers Association
http://www.cba.ca

Canadian Lists

The Globe and National Report on Business Magazine
http://www.robmagazine.com

**The Globe and National Report on Business Magazine—
List Links**
http://www.robmagazine.com/top1000/index.html

**Deloitte & Touche Canada—
1999 Canadian Technology Fast 50 List**
http://www.deloitte.ca/en/industries/HiTech/Fast50_
99ranking.ASP

**Deloitte & Touche Canada—
1998 Canadian Technology Fast 50 List**
http://www.deloitte.ca/en/industries/HiTech/Fast55_
98ranking.ASP

Canadian Business Magazine
http://www.canbus.com/CB500/p500.htm

Profit, The Magazine for Canadian Entrepreneurs
http://www.profit100.com/1999/99home.htm

Canadian Business Directories

Canadian Exporters Catalogue
http://www.canadianexporterscatalogue.com

Ontario Online
http://www.OOL-inc.com

Alcanseek
http://www.alcanseek.com

CanadaOne
http://www.canadaone.com/business/index.html#businesses

Search BC.com
http://www.searchbc.com

VanLink
http://www.vanlink.com

The Montreal Page
http://www.pagemontreal.qc.ca/english

SurfOttowa.com
http://www.surfottawa.com

Canadian Business Directory
http://www.cdnbusinessdirectory.com

Marketplace.ca
http://www.marketplace.ca

Canadian Trade Index
http://www.ctidirectory.com

Strategis—Company Directories
http://strategis.ic.gc.ca/sc_coinf/engdoc/homepage.html

Strategis—Canadian Business Map
http://strategis.ic.gc.ca/scdt/bizmap/nav.html

Canadian Banking, Finance, and the Stock Market

Strategis—Regional Economic Overview
http://strategis.ic.gc.ca/sc_ecnmy/mera/engdoc/09.html

Canadian Department of Finance
http://www.fin.gc.ca/fin-eng.html

Advice for Investors
http://www.fin-info.com

About.com's Investing in Canada Links
http://investingcanada.about.com/money/investingcanada/
msub45.htm?once=true&

About.com's Canadian High Tech Investing Links
http://investingcanada.about.com/money/investingcanada/
msub28.htm?once=true&

Office of the Superintendent of Financial Institutions
http://www.osfi-bsif.gc.ca/eng/default.asp?ref=home

Canadian Bankers Association—Useful Financial, Economic and Banking Links
http://www.cba.ca/eng/links_index.htm

**Canadian Bankers Association—
Top 150 Banks Worldwide by Size of Assets**
http://www.cba.ca/eng/Statistics/Stats/bankrankings.htm

North America Bank Directory of Bank Web Sites
http://www.banksite.com/intbanks/north_america_banks.htm

The Bank of Canada
http://www.bank-banque-canada.ca/english

**SEDAR, the System for Electronic Document
Analysis and Retrieval**
http://www.sedar.com/homepage.htm

Winnipeg Commodity Exchange
http://www.wce.mb.ca/market/_activepages/market.htm

Winnipeg Stock Exchange
http://www.wse.ca/start.html

Alberta Stock Exchange Market Quotes
http://www.telenium.ca/ASE/index.html

Montreal Exchange
http://www.me.org

Toronto Stock Exchange Market Quotes
http://www.telenium.ca/TSE/index.html

Canadian Venture Exchange
http://www.cdnx.ca

Canadian News

Canadian Business Magazine
http://www.canadianbusiness.com/index.shtml

Canadian Corporate News (CCN)
http://www.cdn-news.com/company/index.html

The Financial Post—Canoe Money
http://www.canoe.ca/FP/home.html

Canada NewsWire
http://www.newswire.ca

The Globe and Mail
http://www.globeandmail.ca

Maclean's Online
http://www.macleans.ca/index.stm

Silicon Valley North
http://www.silvan.com

NewsCentral—Canadian Newspapers A-M
http://www.all-links.com/newscentral/northamerica/
canada.html

NewsCentral—Canadian Newspapers N-Z
http://www.all-links.com/newscentral/northamerica/
canada2.html

Canada's Information Resource Center
http://circ.micromedia.on.ca

Canadian Industry Information

Invest in Canada
http://napoleon.ic.gc.ca/scdt/bizinvst/interface2.nsf/
engdoc/0.html

**The Canadian Broadcasting Corporation—
Research Department**
http://www3.cbc.ca/research/hpenglish.html

Strategis
http://strategis.ic.gc.ca/engdoc/main.html

Strategis—Canadian Industry Statistics
http://strategis.ic.gc.ca/sc_ecnmy/sio/homepage.html

Chapter 9—Asia and the Pacific

Asia & Pacific Directories

Australian National University Library
http://anulib.anu.edu.au
- **Asia/Pacific Internet Resources**
  http://anulib.anu.edu.au/clusters/ap/subjects/
  subjects.html
- **Commerce Resources**
  http://anulib.anu.edu.au/clusters/ssh/subjects/
  commerce.html

- **Statistics Resources**
  http://anulib.anu.edu.au/clusters/ssh/subjects/statistics.html
- **Economics Resources**
  http://anulib.anu.edu.au/clusters/ssh/subjects/economics.html
- **Business Administration Resources**
  http://anulib.anu.edu.au/clusters/ssh/subjects/busadmin.html

Asian Studies WWW Virtual Library
http://coombs.anu.edu.au/WWWVL-AsianStudies.html

Asia-Pacific.com Data Links
http://www.asia-pacific.com/links.htm

123India.com
http://www.123india.com

Asian Connection
http://www.asianconnect.com/home.shtml

Sri Lanka Explorer Search Engine
http://www.infolanka.com/org/srilanka/business.html

SearchDragon
http://www.searchdragon.com

ASNIC—The Asian Studies Network Information Center—University of Texas at Austin
http://asnic.utexas.edu/asnic.html

- **The All Asia Links**
  http://asnic.utexas.edu/asnic/pages/allasia.html
- **East Asia Links**
  http://asnic.utexas.edu/asnic/pages/EAsia.html
- **South Asia Links**
  http://asnic.utexas.edu/asnic/pages/SAsia.html
- **Asia-Pacific Links**
  http://asnic.utexas.edu/asnic/pages/AsiaPac.html
- **Southeast Asia Links**
  http://asnic.utexas.edu/asnic/pages/SEAsia.html
- **Countries of Asia**
  http://asnic.utexas.edu/asnic/pages/countries.html

AsiaProfile.com
http://www.asiaprofile.com

EuroSeek Asia
http://webdir.euroseek.com/?ilang=en&catid=262

EuroSeek Oceania
http://webdir.euroseek.com/?ilang=en&catid=269

The Nanyang Technological University Library WWW Sites and Information Gateways in Asia
http://www.ntu.edu.sg/library/asia/www.htm

East & Southeast Asia—
An Annotated Directory of Internet Resources
http://newton.uor.edu/Departments&Programs/AsianStudies Dept/index.html

Asia & Pacific Search Engines

Locate India
http://locateindia.com

Cari Malaysia Search
http://www.cari.com.my

AAA Matilda
http://www.aaa.com.au

PNG Net Search
http://www.pngnetsearch.com

Access New Zealand
http://accessnz.co.nz

Sofcom Internet Directory
http://www2.sofcom.com.au/Directories

NZExplorer
http://nzexplorer.co.nz

Asian & Pacific Yellow Pages

Australia Yellow Pages Online
http://www.yellowpages.com.au

Bangladesh Yellow Pages Online
http://www.tripleyes.com/bypo/iphone.html

China
http://www.chinatone.com/category/yellowpage/frame_e.html

ChinaBIG Yellow Pages
http://www.chinabig.com/en/srch

Hong Kong Yellow Pages
http://www.yp.com.hk/eng/index.html

India Yellow Pages
http://www.indiayellowpages.com

Indonesian Yellow Pages on the Internet
http://www.yellowpages.co.id

Korea Yellow Pages
http://www.ypkorea.com

Macau Yellow Pages
http://www.yellowpages.com.mo/eng

Malaysia Yellow Pages
http://www.malaysiayellowpages.com

New Zealand Yellow Pages
http://www.yellowpages.co.nz

Yellow Pages of Pakistan
http://www.jamal.com

Singapore Yellow Pages
http://www.yellowpages.com.sg/cgi-bin/syphome/syphome.pl

Vietnam Internet Yellow Pages
http://www.vietnamonline.com/vnypg

Asia & Pacific Company Directories

World Trade Data Base (WTDB)
http://www.wtdb.com

MOFTEC—Ministry of Foreign Trade and Economic Cooperation—PRC
http://www.moftec.gov.cn

MeetChina.com
http://www.meetchina.com

WebSite URLs of Japanese Companies
http://www.toyokeizai.co.jp/english/e_link/index.html

Asiaco
http://search.asiaco.com

EDSA—The Philippine Search Engine
http://www.edsa.com.ph

Government Information Office—Republic of China
http://th.gio.gov.tw/search

Beijing Business Directory
http://chinavista.com/beijing/business/directory.html

Guanghou Business Directory
http://chinavista.com/guanghou/business/directory.html

Shanghai Business Directory
http://chinavista.com/shanghai/business/directory.html

Asia & Pacific Chambers of Commerce—AmChams

American Chamber of Commerce in Australia
http://www.amcham.com.au

American Chamber of Commerce in Bangladesh
http://www.amchambd.org

Guam Chamber of Commerce
http://www.guamchamber.com.gu

American Chamber of Commerce in Hong Kong
http://www.amcham.org.hk

American Chamber of Commerce in Indonesia
http://www.amcham.or.id

American Chamber of Commerce in Japan
http://www.accj.or.jp/default.asp

The American Chamber of Commerce in Korea
http://www.amchamkorea.org

American Malaysian Chamber of Commerce
http://www.jaring.my/amcham

American Chamber of Commerce—People's Republic of China
http://www.amcham-china.org.cn

American Chamber of Commerce in Guangdong, PRC
http://www.amcham-guangdong.org

The American Chamber of Commerce of the Philippines
http://www.amchamphil.com.ph

American Chamber of Commerce in Singapore
http://www.amcham.org.sg

American Chamber of Commerce in Sri Lanka
http://www.amchamsl.org

American Chamber of Commerce in Taipei
http://www.amcham.com.tw

American Chamber of Commerce in Vietnam
http://www.amchamvn.com

Asia & Pacific Other Chambers (Not AmChams)

U.S.-India Business Council
http://www.usibc.com

Asia & Pacific Banking & Finance

Irasia.com
http://www.irasia.com

The Nanyang Technological University Library Financial Data and Resource Locators—Singapore
http://www.ntu.edu.sg/library/biz/finsg.htm#topmenu

Reserve Bank of India
http://www.rbi.org.in

Bank of Japan
http://www.boj.or.jp/en/index2.htm

Export-Import Bank of Korea
http://www.koreaexim.go.kr/english.engindex.html

Central Bank of Malaysia
http://www.bnm.gov.my

Arab-Malaysian Banking Group
http://ambg.com.my/html/finance_info_fr.html

National Bank of New Zealand
http://www.nationalbank.co.nz

Reserve Bank of New Zealand
http://www.rbnz.govt.nz

Overseas Union Bank—Singapore
http://www1.oub.com.sg/am.myoub/pages/welcome.jsp

Central Bank of Sri Lanka
http://www.lanka.net/centralbank/

Bangkok Bank
http://www.bbl.co.th

Bank of Thailand
http://www.bot.or.th/govnr/public/BOT_Homepage/
EnglishVersion/index_e.htm

Siam Commercial Bank
http://www.scb.co.th

Office of the Securities and Exchange Commission—Thailand
http://secwww.sec.or.th/indexe.html

Asia & Pacific Stock Exchanges

ASIC, the Australian Securities and Investments Commission
http://www.asic.gov.au

Australia—Australian Stock Exchange
http://www.asx.com.au

China—Shanghai Stock Exchange (not the actual exchange)
http://www.comnex.com/stocks/stocks.htm

Hong Kong—Hong Kong Stock Exchange
http://www.sehk.com.hk

India—National Stock Exchange of India
http://www.nse-india.com

India—Stock Exchange of Mumbai
http://www.bseindia.com

Indonesia Stock Closings
http://www.indoexchange.com

Indonesia—Surabaya Stock Exchange
http://www.bes.co.id

Indonesia—Jakarta Stock Exchange
http://www.jsx.co.id

Japan—Tokyo Stock Exchange
http://www.tse.or.jp/eindex.html

Korea—Korea Stock Exchange
http://www.kse.or.kr/e_index.html

Malaysia—Malaysia Stock Exchange (not the actual exchange)
http://biz.thestar.com.my/business/bizwatch.asp

New Zealand—New Zealand Stock Exchange
http://www.nzse.co.nz

Pakistan—Karachi Stock Exchange
http://www.kse.com.pk

Singapore—Stock Exchange of Singapore
http://www.ses.com.sg

Sri Lanka—Colombo Stock Exchange
http://www.lanka.net/stocks

Taiwan—Taiwan Stock Exchange
http://www.tse.com.tw/docs1/index.html

Thailand—Stock Exchange of Thailand
http://www.set.or.th

Asia & Pacific News

AsiaSource
http://www.asiasource.org

AccessAsia
http://www.accessasia.com

Taiwan Headlines
http://www.taiwanheadlines.gov.tw

NikkeiNet Interactive
http://www.nni.nikkei.co.jp

The China Business Review
http://www.chinabusinessreview.com/back.html

Asia Pacific Management Forum
http://www.apmforum.com

Asia & Pacific Regional Information

Skali.com
http://www.skali.com

Asia BIG
http://www.asiabig.com

Australia

Austrade Online
http://www.austrade.gov.au/International

Australian Commonwealth Government Entry Point
http://fed.gov.au/sitelists/web_port.htm

Australian Business
http://www.australianbusiness.com.au

BRW
http://www.brw.com.au

China

CETRA, the China External Trade Development Council
http://mart.cetra.org.tw/home/default.asp

Hong Kong

Hong Kong Trade Development Council
http://www.tdctrade.com

Indonesia

Industry and Trade Division of the Embassy of Indonesia
http://www.prica.org/commerce/index2a.html

Indonesian Commodity Association
http://www.nafed.go.id/menu2/asosiasi.htm

National Agency for Export Development
http://www.nafed.go.id

Indonesian Product.com
http://www.Indonesian-Product.com

Indonesian Trading Zone
http://www.indotradezone.com

APEC Tariff Database
http://www.apectariff.org/tdb.cgi/ff3237/apeccgi.cgi?ID

IndoExchange
http://www.indoexchange.com

Indonesian Central Bureau of Statistics
http://www.bps.go.id

Japan

Japan External Trade Organization (JETRO)
http://www.jetro.go.jp/top/index.html

Japan Information Network (JIN)
http://www.jinjapan.org

New Zealand

The New Zealand Herald Online
http://www.nzherald.co.nz

The UBD E-Directory
http://www.ubd.co.nz

Investment in New Zealand
http://www.rmmb.co.nz/investnz/Welcome.html

Singapore

Singapore Inc.
http://www.singapore-inc.com/home.html

Statistics Singapore
http://www.singstat.gov.sg

AsiaOne
http://www.asiaone.com

Various Countries

Business Gate—Thailand
http://www.okeydonkey.com/donkey1

IndiaOneStop
http://www.indiaonestop.com

NepalPages.com
http://www.nepalpages.com

Taiwan—Information of the Taipei Economic and Cultural Office
http://www.roc-taiwan.org

Conclusion

Translation Tools

AltaVista Translations—Babel Fish
http://babelfish.altavista.com/translate.dyn

Go Translator
http://translator.go.com

Travlang's Translating Dictionaries
http://dictionaries.travlang.com

Free Translation.com

http://www.freetranslation.com

InterTran

http://www.tranexp.com:2000/InterTran?

Gist-in-Time

http://www.alis.com

WorldLingo.com

http://www.worldlingo.com

alphaWorks

http://www.alphaworks.ibm.com/aw.nsf/html/mt

Power Translator

http://www.lhsl.com/powertranslator

Universal Translator

http://www.eurohost.com/matchfon/pages/translation.html

Simply Translating Deluxe

http://www.translation.net/simply.html

Systran

http://www.systransoft.com

APPENDIX B

COUNTRY CODE TOP-LEVEL DOMAINS

The Internet Assigned Numbers Authority (IANA) is the overall authority for day-to-day administration of the Internet Domain Name System (DNS). IANA's responsibilities include the assignment of IP Addresses, Autonomous System Numbers, Top Level Domains (TLDs), and country-code Top Level Domains (ccTLDs). Two types of top-level domains exist: generic and country code. Generic domains were created for use by the general Internet public (.com, .org, .edu, .gov, etc.). Country code domains were established for use by individual countries (.uk, .jp, .au, .br, etc.) and represent the country or region of a site's publication, though registrants do not have to use the country code.

Sometimes a site or a search engine will allow you to search or limit by domain. When working with such a search engine, you might, for example, limit the search to only sites with the Brazilian domain, .br. Bear in mind, however, that this only guarantees that the sites retrieved will have a Brazilian domain; there very well may be other sites originating from Brazil that have a generic domain.

Below is a listing of the most recent Country Code Top-Level Domains. To check for additions or deletions to this list, please visit Internet Assigned Numbers Authority [http://www.iana.org/cctld/cctld.htm].

.ac	Ascension Island
.ad	Andorra
.ae	United Arab Emirates
.af	Afghanistan
.ag	Antigua and Barbuda
.ai	Anguilla
.al	Albania
.am	Armenia
.an	Netherlands Antilles
.ao	Angola
.aq	Antarctica
.ar	Argentina
.as	American Samoa
.at	Austria
.au	Australia
.aw	Aruba
.az	Azerbaijan
.ba	Bosnia and Herzegovina
.bb	Barbados
.bd	Bangladesh
.be	Belgium
.bf	Burkina Faso
.bg	Bulgaria
.bh	Bahrain
.bi	Burundi
.bj	Benin
.bm	Bermuda
.bn	Brunei Darussalam
.bo	Bolivia
.br	Brazil
.bs	Bahamas
.bt	Bhutan
.bv	Bouvet Island
.bw	Botswana
.by	Belarus
.bz	Belize
.ca	Canada
.cc	Cocos (Keeling) Islands
.cd	Congo, Democratic People's Republic
.cf	Central African Republic

.cg	Congo, Republic of
.ch	Switzerland
.ci	Cote d'Ivoire
.ck	Cook Islands
.cl	Chile
.cm	Cameroon
.cn	China
.co	Colombia
.cr	Costa Rica
.cu	Cuba
.cv	Cape Verde
.cx	Christmas Island
.cy	Cyprus
.cz	Czech Republic
.de	Germany
.dj	Djibouti
.dk	Denmark
.dm	Dominica
.do	Dominican Republic
.dz	Algeria
.ec	Ecuador
.ee	Estonia
.eg	Egypt
.eh	Western Sahara
.er	Eritrea
.es	Spain
.et	Ethiopia
.fi	Finland
.fj	Fiji
.fk	Falkland Islands (Malvina)
.fm	Micronesia, Federal State of
.fo	Faroe Islands
.fr	France
.ga	Gabon
.gd	Grenada
.ge	Georgia
.gf	French Guiana
.gg	Guernsey
.gh	Ghana
.gi	Gibraltar

.gl	Greenland
.gm	Gambia
.gn	Guinea
.gp	Guadeloupe
.gq	Equatorial Guinea
.gr	Greece
.gs	South Georgia and the South Sandwich Islands
.gt	Guatemala
.gu	Guam
.gw	Guinea-Bissau
.gy	Guyana
.hk	Hong Kong
.hm	Heard and McDonald Islands
.hn	Honduras
.hr	Croatia/Hrvatska
.ht	Haiti
.hu	Hungary
.id	Indonesia
.ie	Ireland
.il	Israel
.im	Isle of Man
.in	India
.io	British Indian Ocean Territory
.iq	Iraq
.ir	Iran (Islamic Republic of)
.is	Iceland
.it	Italy
.je	Jersey
.jm	Jamaica
.jo	Jordan
.jp	Japan
.ke	Kenya
.kg	Kyrgyzstan
.kh	Cambodia
.ki	Kiribati
.km	Comoros
.kn	Saint Kitts and Nevis
.kp	Korea, Democratic People's Republic
.kr	Korea, Republic of
.kw	Kuwait

.ky	Cayman Islands
.kz	Kazakhstan
.la	Lao People's Democratic Republic
.lb	Lebanon
.lc	Saint Lucia
.li	Liechtenstein
.lk	Sri Lanka
.lr	Liberia
.ls	Lesotho
.lt	Lithuania
.lu	Luxembourg
.lv	Latvia
.ly	Libyan Arab Jamahiriya
.ma	Morocco
.mc	Monaco
.md	Moldova, Republic of
.mg	Madagascar
.mh	Marshall Islands
.mk	Macedonia, Former Yugoslav Republic
.ml	Mali
.mm	Myanmar
.mn	Mongolia
.mo	Macau
.mp	Northern Mariana Islands
.mq	Martinique
.mr	Mauritania
.ms	Montserrat
.mt	Malta
.mu	Mauritius
.mv	Maldives
.mw	Malawi
.mx	Mexico
.my	Malaysia
.mz	Mozambique
.na	Namibia
.nc	New Caledonia
.ne	Niger
.nf	Norfolk Island
.ng	Nigeria
.ni	Nicaragua

.nl	Netherlands
.no	Norway
.np	Nepal
.nr	Nauru
.nu	Niue
.nz	New Zealand
.om	Oman
.pa	Panama
.pe	Peru
.pf	French Polynesia
.pg	Papua New Guinea
.ph	Philippines
.pk	Pakistan
.pl	Poland
.pm	St. Pierre and Miquelon
.pn	Pitcairn Island
.pr	Puerto Rico
.ps	Palestinian Territories
.pt	Portugal
.pw	Palau
.py	Paraguay
.qa	Qatar
.re	Reunion Island
.ro	Romania
.ru	Russian Federation
.rw	Rwanda
.sa	Saudi Arabia
.sb	Solomon Islands
.sc	Seychelles
.sd	Sudan
.se	Sweden
.sg	Singapore
.sh	St. Helena
.si	Slovenia
.sj	Svalbard and Jan Mayen Islands
.sk	Slovak Republic
.sl	Sierra Leone
.sm	San Marino
.sn	Senegal
.so	Somalia

.sr	Suriname
.st	Sao Tome and Principe
.sv	El Salvador
.sy	Syrian Arab Republic
.sz	Swaziland
.tc	Turks and Ciacos Islands
.td	Chad
.tf	French Southern Territories
.tg	Togo
.th	Thailand
.tj	Tajikistan
.tk	Tokelau
.tm	Turkmenistan
.tn	Tunisia
.to	Tonga
.tp	East Timor
.tr	Turkey
.tt	Trinidad and Tobago
.tv	Tuvalu
.tw	Taiwan
.tz	Tanzania
.ua	Ukraine
.ug	Uganda
.uk	United Kingdom
.um	U.S. Minor Outlying Islands
.us	United States
.uy	Uruguay
.uz	Uzbekistan
.va	Holy See (City Vatican State)
.vc	Saint Vincent and the Grenadines
.ve	Venezuela
.vg	Virgin Islands (British)
.vi	Virgin Islands (USA)
.vn	Vietnam
.vu	Vanuatu
.wf	Wallis and Futuna Islands
.ws	Western Samoa
.ye	Yemen
.yt	Mayotte
.yu	Yugoslavia

.za	South Africa
.zm	Zambia
.zr	Zaire
.zw	Zimbabwe

APPENDIX C

ACCEPTED COUNTRY ABBREVIATIONS

Occasionally when doing research, you might come across an article, table, or graph that refers to countries using a two-digit abbreviation. Generally such abbreviations will follow the ISO 3166: Codes for the Representation of Names of Countries (ISO 3166), prepared by the International Organization for Standardization. For easy reference, the ISO 3166 list follows:

Afghanistan	AF
Albania	AL
Algeria	AG
American Samoa	AS
Andorra	AD
Angola	AO
Anguilla	AI
Antarctica	AQ
Antigua and Barbuda	AG
Argentina	AR
Armenia	AM
Aruba	AW
Australia	AU
Austria	AT
Azerbaijan	AZ
The Bahamas	BS
Bahrain	BH
Bangladesh	BD

Barbados	BB
Belarus	BY
Belgium	BE
Belize	BZ
Benin	BJ
Bermud	BM
Bhutan	BT
Bolivia	BO
Bosnia and Herzegovina	BA
Botswana	BW
Bouvet Island	BV
Brazil	BR
British Indian Ocean	IO
British Virgin Islands	VG
Brunei	BN
Bulgaria	BG
Burkina Faso	BF
Burma	MM
Burundi	BI
Cambodia	KH
Cameroon	CM
Canada	CA
Cape Verde	CV
Cayman Islands	KY
Central African Republic	CF
Chad	TD
Chile	CL
China	CN
Christmas Island	CX
Cocos (Keeling) Islands	CC
Colombia	CO
Comoros	KM
Congo, Democratic Republic of the	ZR
Congo, Republic of the	CG
Cook Islands	CK
Costa Rica	CR
Cote d'Ivoire	CI
Croatia	HR
Cuba	CU
Cyprus	CY

Czech Republic	CZ
Denmark	DK
Djibouti	DJ
Dominica	DM
Dominican Republic	DO
East Timor	TP
Egypt	EG
El Salvador	SV
Equatorial Guinea	GQ
Eritrea	ER
Estonia	EE
Ethiopia	ET
Falkland Islands	FK
Faroe Islands	FO
Fiji	FJ
Finland	FI
France	FR
France, Metropolitan	FX
French Guiana	GF
French Polynesia	PF
French Southern and Antarctic Lands	TF
Gabon	GA
The Gambia	GM
Georgia	GE
Germany	DE
Ghana	GH
Gibraltar	GI
Greece	GR
Greenland	GL
Grenada	GD
Guadeloupe	GP
Guam	GU
Guatemala	GT
Guinea	GN
Guinea-Bissau	GW
Guyana	GY
Haiti	HT
Heard Island and McDonald Islands	HM
Holy See (Vatican City)	VA
Honduras	HN

Hong Kong	HK
Hungary	HU
Iceland	IS
India	IN
Indonesia	ID
Iran	IR
Iraq	IQ
Ireland	IE
Israel	IL
Italy	IT
Jamaica	JM
Japan	JP
Jordan	JO
Kazakhstan	KZ
Kenya	KE
Kiribati	KI
Korea, North	KP
Korea, South	KR
Kuwait	KW
Laos	LA
Latvia	LV
Lebanon	LB
Lesotho	LS
Liberia	LR
Libya	LY
Liechtenstein	LI
Lithuania	LT
Luxembourg	LU
Macau	MO
Macedonia, The Former Yugoslav Republic of	MK
Madagascar	MG
Malawi	MW
Malaysia	MY
Maldives	MV
Mali	ML
Malta	MT
Marshall Islands	MH
Martinique	MQ
Mauritania	MR
Mauritius	MU

Mayotte	YT
Mexico	MX
Micronesia, Federated States of	FM
Moldova	MD
Monaco	MC
Mongolia	MN
Montserrat	MS
Morocco	MA
Mozambique	MZ
Namibia	NA
Nauru	NR
Netherlands	NL
Netherlands Antilles	AN
New Caledonia	NC
New Zealand	NZ
Nicaragua	NI
Niger	NE
Nigeria	NG
Niue	NU
Norfolk Island	NF
Northern Mariana Islands	MP
Norway	NO
Oman	OM
Pakistan	PK
Palau	PW
Panama	PA
Papua New Guinea	PG
Paraguay	PY
Peru	PE
Philippines	PH
Pitcairn Islands	PN
Poland	PL
Portugal	PT
Puerto Rico	PR
Qatar	QA
Reunion	RE
Romania	RO
Russia	RU
Rwanda	RW
Saint Helena	SH

Saint Kitts and Nevis	KN
Saint Lucia	LC
Saint Pierre and Miquelon	PM
Saint Vincent and the Grenadines	VC
Samoa	WS
San Marino	SM
Sao Tome and Principe	ST
Saudi Arabia	SA
Senegal	SN
Sierra Leone	SL
Singapore	SG
Slovenia	SI
Solomon Islands	SB
Somalia	SO
South Africa	ZA
South Georgia and the South Sandwich Islands	GS
Spain	ES
Sri Lanka	LK
Sudan	SD
Suriname	SR
Svalbard	SJ
Swaziland	SZ
Sweden	SE
Switzerland	CH
Syria	SY
Taiwan	TW
Tajikistan	TJ
Tanzania	TZ
Thailand	TH
Togo	TG
Tokelau	TK
Tonga	TO
Trinidad and Tobago	TT
Tunisia	TN
Turkey	TR
Turkmenistan	TM
Turks and Caicos Islands	TC
Tuvalu	TV
Uganda	UG
Ukraine	UA

United Arab Emirates	AE
United Kingdom	GB
United States	US
United States Minor Outlying Islands	UM
Uruguay	UY
Uzbekistan	UZ
Venezuela	VE
Vietnam	VN
Virgin Islands	VI
Wallis and Futuna	WF
Western Sahara	EH
Yemen	YE
Yugoslavia	YU
Zambia	ZM
Zimbabwe	ZW

About the Author

Sheri R. Lanza is the president and owner of Global InfoResources, Inc., which provides business research services to a domestic and global clientele in the fields of international development, defense, healthcare, construction, and business consulting. Prior to starting her own company, Sheri worked for over 15 years in market research and analysis, financial analysis, and international trade. She was a Market Research Analyst for a large medical supply company, Director of Market Research and New Product Development for a cruise line, a financial analyst and software troubleshooter for a pension valuation company, the Commercial Attaché at the U.S. Embassy in Costa Rica, and a research consultant for a firm specializing in mergers and acquisitions. She began working with computers in the early 1970s, in the days of keypunch cards, and swore she'd never work with computers again. Now, nearly 30 years later, her days are spent with eyes glued to a computer screen.

She has written for various information industry publications including *Searcher*, *Database*, and *The Information Advisor*. She is the International Specialty Scan editor for The CyberSkeptic's Guide to Internet Research. She speaks frequently at conferences such as the annual conference for the Association of Independent Information Professionals (AIIP), Special Libraries Association (SLA), Open Source Solutions, and Internet Librarian. Topics range from the use of non-Internet sources for research to different aspects of international research, including Latin American telecommunications resources, international information on the Internet, and international business research.

Sheri holds a Master's of Business Administration degree in Marketing and Finance, and a Bachelor's degree in Mathematics. She lives in Vienna, Virginia (near Washington, DC) with her husband and two daughters.

About the Editor

After graduating library school in 1966, Barbara Quint went to work at the RAND Corporation, where she spent close to twenty years, almost all of it as head of Reference Services. In the course of that employment, she began her career as an online searcher. Her experience in founding the Southern California Online Users Group (SCOUG) led to her role as a "consumer advocate" for online searchers everywhere, a role that led her to leave familiar library work and become a leading writer and editor in the online trade press. In 1985, she began editing *Database Searcher* for the Meckler Corporation, which led in 1993 to her current position as Editor-in-Chief of *Searcher* magazine for Information Today, Inc. She has also spoken often at national and international meetings, writes the "Quint's Online" column for *Information Today,* and operates her own information broker service, Quint and Associates.

INDEX

More Great Books
from Information Today, Inc.

The Invisible Web
Uncovering Information Sources Search Engines Can't See

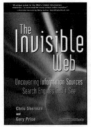

By Chris Sherman and Gary Price
Foreword by Danny Sullivan

Most people are unaware that most of the authoritative information accessible over the Internet is invisible to search engines like AltaVista, HotBot, and Google. This invaluable material resides on the "Invisible Web," which is largely comprised of content-rich databases from universities, libraries, associations, businesses, and government agencies around the world.

CyberAge Books • July 2001/softbound/ISBN 0-910965-51-X • $29.95

The Extreme Searcher's Guide to
Web Search Engines, 2nd Edition
A Handbook for the Serious Searcher

By Randolph Hock
Foreword by Reva Basch

In this completely revised and expanded version of his award-winning book, the "extreme searcher," Randolph (Ran) Hock, digs even deeper, covering all the most popular Web search tools, plus a half-dozen of the newest and most exciting search engines to come down the pike. This is a practical, user-friendly guide supported by a regularly updated Web site.

CyberAge Books • 2001/250 pp/softbound/ISBN 0-910965-47-1 • $24.95

Super Searchers Go to the Source
The Interviewing and Hands-On Information Strategies of Top
Primary Researchers—Online, on the Phone, and in Person

By Risa Sacks • Edited by Reva Basch

For the most focused, current, in-depth information on any subject, nothing beats going directly to the source—to the experts. This is "Primary Research," and it's the focus of the seventh title in the "Super Searchers" series. From the boardrooms of America's top corporations, to the halls of academia, to the pressroom of the *New York Times*, Risa Sacks interviews 12 of the best primary researchers in the business.

CyberAge Books • September 2001/320 pp/softbound ISBN 0-910965-53-6 • $24.95

Super Searchers on Mergers & Acquisitions

The Online Research Secrets of Top Corporate Researchers and M&A Pros

By Jan Davis Tudor • Edited by Reva Basch

The sixth title in the "Super Searchers" series is a unique resource for business owners, brokers, appraisers, entrepreneurs, and investors who use the Internet and online services to research Mergers & Acquisitions (M&A) opportunities. Leading business valuation researcher Jan Davis Tudor interviews 13 top M&A researchers, who share their secrets for finding, evaluating, and delivering critical deal-making data on companies and industries. As a reader bonus, "The Super Searchers Web Page" features links to the most important online information sources for M&A research.

CyberAge Books • 2001/208 pp/softbound/ISBN 0-910965-48-X • $24.95

The Quintessential Searcher

The Wit & Wisdom of Barbara Quint

Edited by Marylaine Block

Searcher Magazine editor Barbara Quint (bq) is not only one of the world's most famous online searchers, but the most creative and controversial writer, editor, and speaker to emerge from the information industry in the last two decades. Whether she's chastising database providers about unacceptable fees, interfaces, and updates; recounting the ills visited on the world by computer makers; or inspiring her readers to achieve greatness; her voice is consistently original and compelling. In this book, for the first time anywhere, hundreds of bq's most memorable, insightful, and politically incorrect quotations have been gathered for the enjoyment of her many fans.

Available: August 2001/220 pp/softbound/ISBN 1-57387-114-1 • $19.95

net.people

The Personalities and Passions Behind the Web Sites

By Eric C. Steinert and Thomas E. Bleier

With the explosive growth of the Internet, people everywhere are bringing their dreams and schemes to life as Web sites. In *net.people*, get up close and personal with the creators of 36 of the world's most intriguing online ventures. For the first time, these entrepreneurs and visionaries share their personal stories and hard-won secrets of Webmastering. You'll learn how all of them launched a home page, increased site traffic, geared up for e-commerce, found financing, dealt with failure and success, built new relationships—and discovered that a Web site had changed their lives forever.

CyberAge Books • 2000/317 pp/softbound/ISBN 0-910965-37-4 • $19.95

The Modem Reference, 4th Edition
The Complete Guide to PC Communications

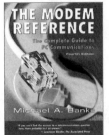

By Michael A. Banks

Now in its 4th edition, this popular handbook explains the concepts behind computer data, data encoding, and transmission, providing practical advice for PC users who want to get the most from their online operations. In his uniquely readable style, author and techno-guru Michael A. Banks (*The Internet Unplugged*) takes readers on a tour of PC data communications technology, explaining how modems, fax machines, computer networks, and the Internet work. He provides an in-depth look at how data is communicated between computers all around the world, demystifying the terminology, hardware, and software. *The Modem Reference* is a must-read for students, professional online users, and all computer users who want to maximize their PC fax and data communications capabilities.

CyberAge Books • 2000/306 pp/softbound/ISBN 0-910965-36-6 • $29.95

Internet Business Intelligence
How to Build a Big Company System on a Small Company Budget

By David Vine

According to author David Vine, business success in the competitive, global marketplace of the 21st century will depend on a firm's ability to use information effectively—and the most successful firms will be those that harness the Internet to create and maintain a powerful information edge. In *Internet Business Intelligence*, Vine explains how any company—large or small—can build a complete, low-cost, Internet-based business intelligence system that really works. If you're fed up with Internet hype and wondering, "Where's the beef?," you'll appreciate this savvy, no-nonsense approach to using the Internet to solve everyday business problems and stay one step ahead of the competition.

CyberAge Books • 2000/448 pp/softbound/ISBN 0-910965-35-8 • $29.95

Millennium Intelligence
Understanding and Conducting Competitive Intelligence in the Digital Age

Edited by Jerry P. Miller

With contributions from the world's leading business intelligence practitioners, here is a tremendously informative and practical look at the CI process, how it is changing, and how it can be managed effectively in the Digital Age. Loaded with case studies, tips, and techniques.

CyberAge Books • 2000/276 pp/softbound/ISBN 0-910965-28-5 $29.95